Mingong

Wolfgang Müller

Mingong

Die Suche nach dem Glück
The Pursuit of Happiness

Vice Versa Verlag

Für Arno Fischer

Baustellen, Verschiedene Orte	Construction Sites, Various Places
Textilfabrik, Nanjing	Textile Factory, Nanjing
Zhang Wei, Fensterputzer, Peking	Zhang Wei, Window Cleaner, Beijing
Xu Fang, Müllrecyclerin, Peking	Xu Fang, Garbage Recycler, Beijing
Spielzeugfabrik, Shenzhen	Toy Factory, Shenzhen
Wang Xiuxiu, Hostess, Dongguan	Wang Xiuxiu, Hostess, Dongguan
Li Bo, Zhou Dong, Müllsammler, Peking	Li Bo, Zhou Dong, Garbage Collectors, Beijing
Su Feng, Bettler, Guangzhou	Su Feng, Beggar, Guangzhou
Backsteinfabrik, Ordos	Brick factory, Ordos
Han Chun, Wang Li, SchmucksteinschleiferIn, Haifeng	Han Chun, Wang Li, Gemstone Cutters, Haifeng
He Juan, Wen Feng, KohlewäscherIn, Fushun	He Juan, Wen Feng, Coal Washers, Fushun

1

Baustellen, Verschiedene Orte
Construction Sites, Various Places

»Niemand hat doch hier einen Arbeitsvertrag. Und was machst du, wenn du am Ende des Jahres deinen Lohn nicht ausgezahlt bekommst? Dann hast du überhaupt nichts in der Hand.«

»No one here has an employment contract. And what can you do when you don't get your pay at the end of the year? You have nothing on them, nothing whatsoever.«

Wang Du, 42

»Eigentlich wollte ich was sehen von der Großstadt, in die ich gehe. Aber ich habe es vor lauter Arbeit noch nicht einmal geschafft, das Baustellengelände zu verlassen.«

»Actually, I wanted to see some of the big city that I went to. But with the work that's cut out for me here, I haven't even managed to leave the construction site premises yet.«

Xu Lin, 20

2

Textilfabrik, Nanjing
Textile Factory, Nanjing

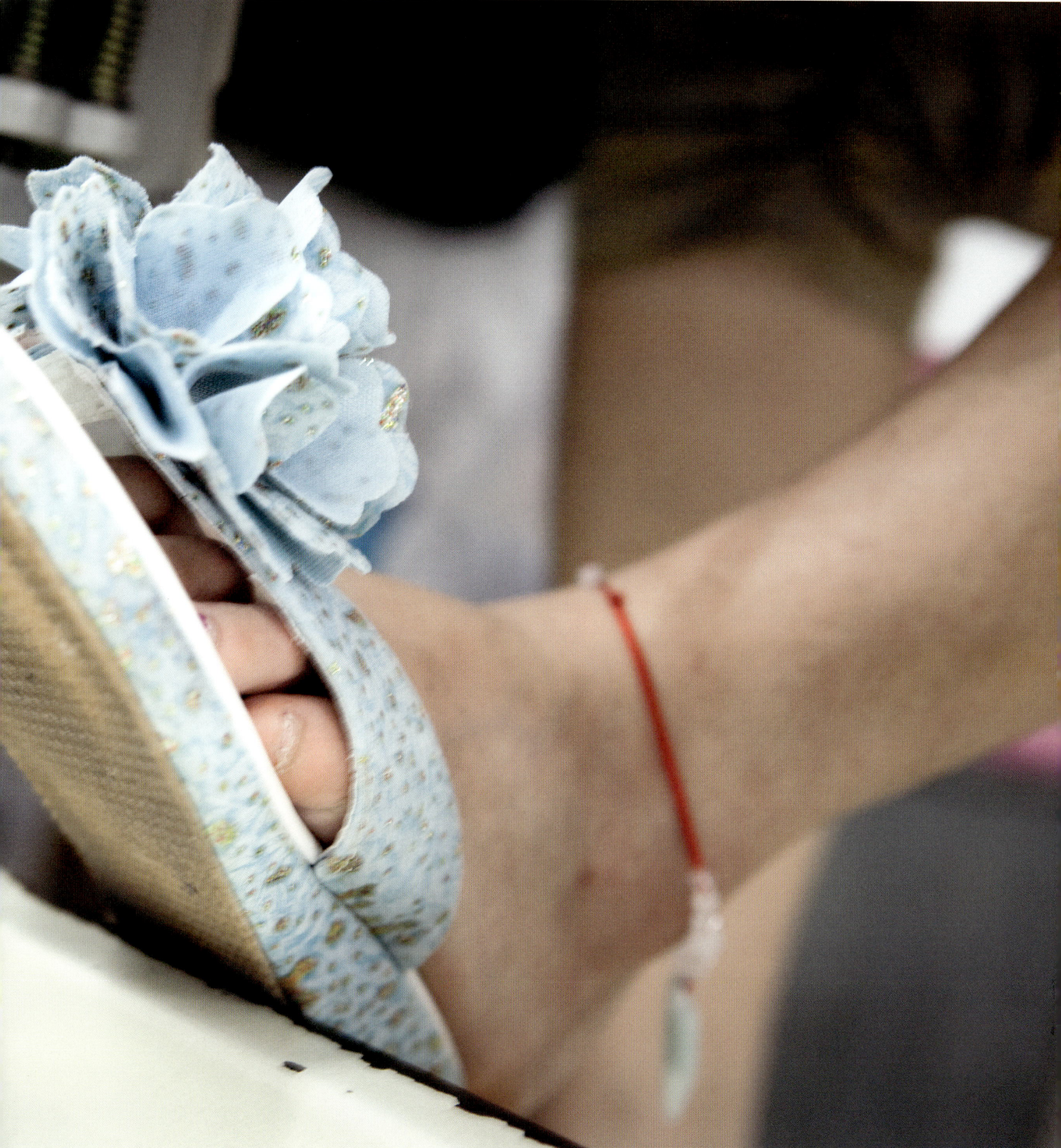

»Ich hätte gerne studiert. Aber mein Vater hat sich immer nur für meinen Bruder interessiert. Jetzt verlangt er von mir, dass ich das Geld für das Studium meines Bruders nach Hause schicke.«

»I would have loved to go to college. But my father was always only interested in my brother. Now he demands that I send home the money for my brother's college education.«

He Qing, 19

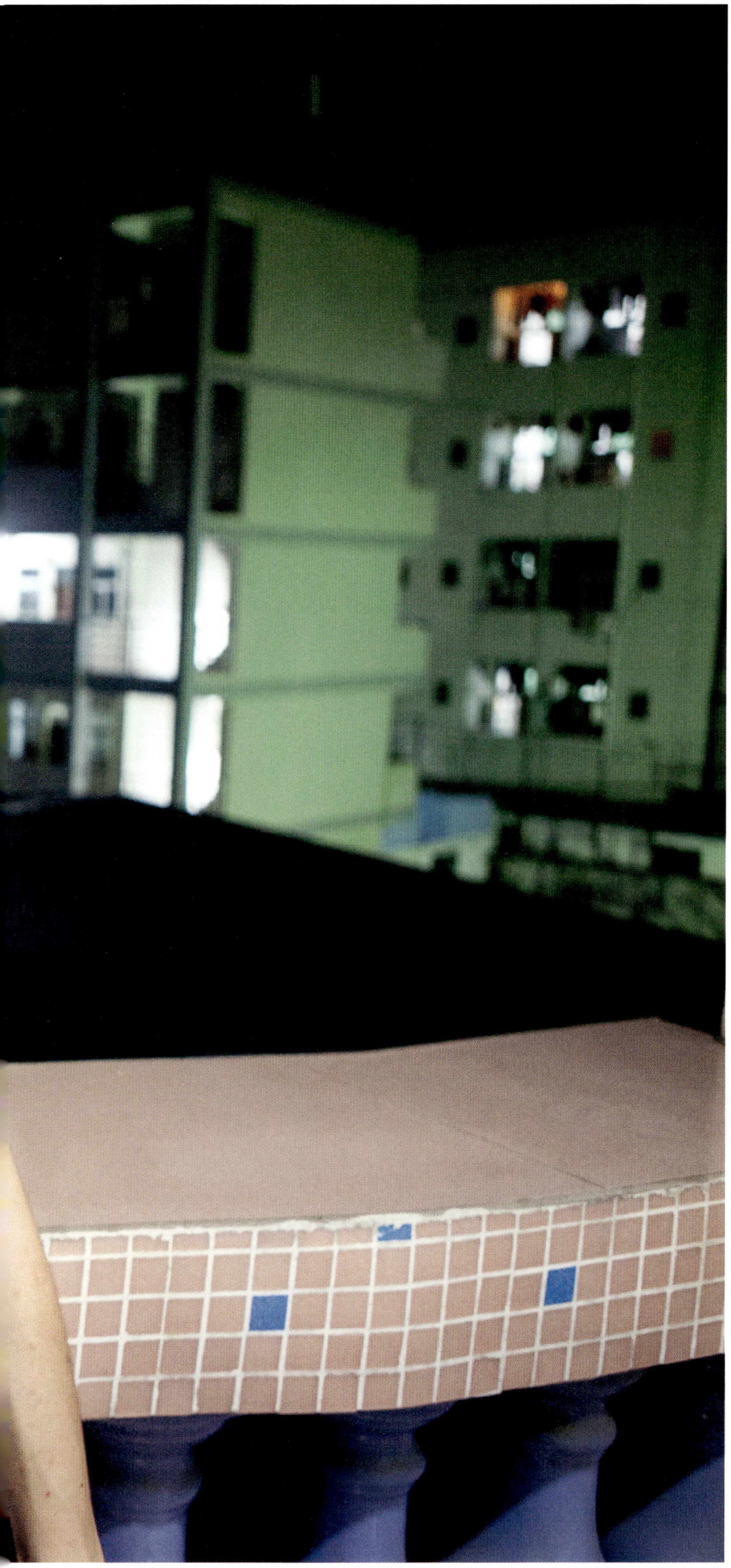

3

Zhang Wei

Fensterputzer, Peking
Window Cleaner, Beijing

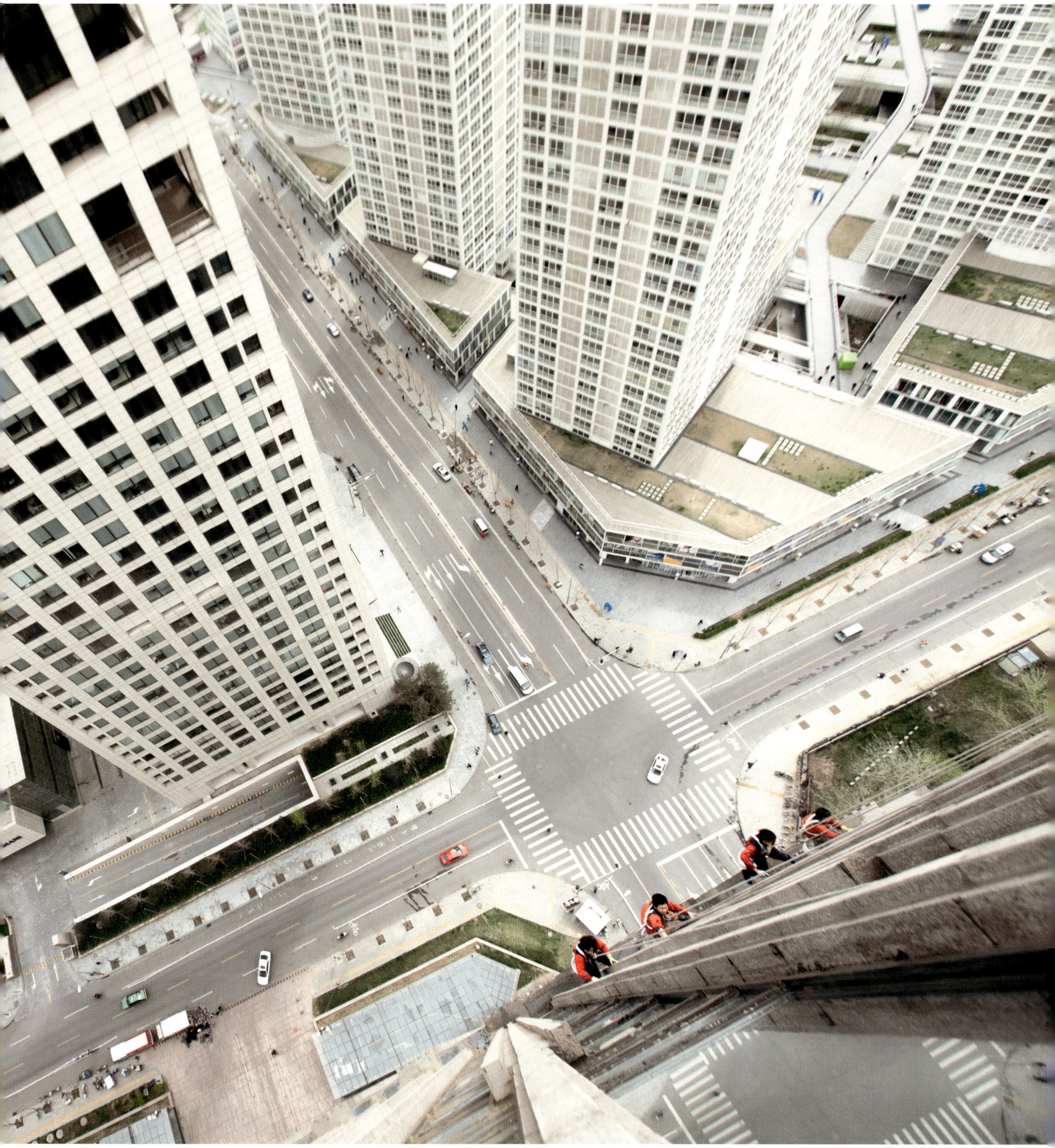

»Ich wollte was sehen von der Welt. Es war schon auch Abenteuerlust dabei, als ich mit 20 mein Heimatdorf verließ.«

»I wanted to see a bit of the world. I was keen for some adventure when I left my home village at twenty.«

Zhang Wei, 39

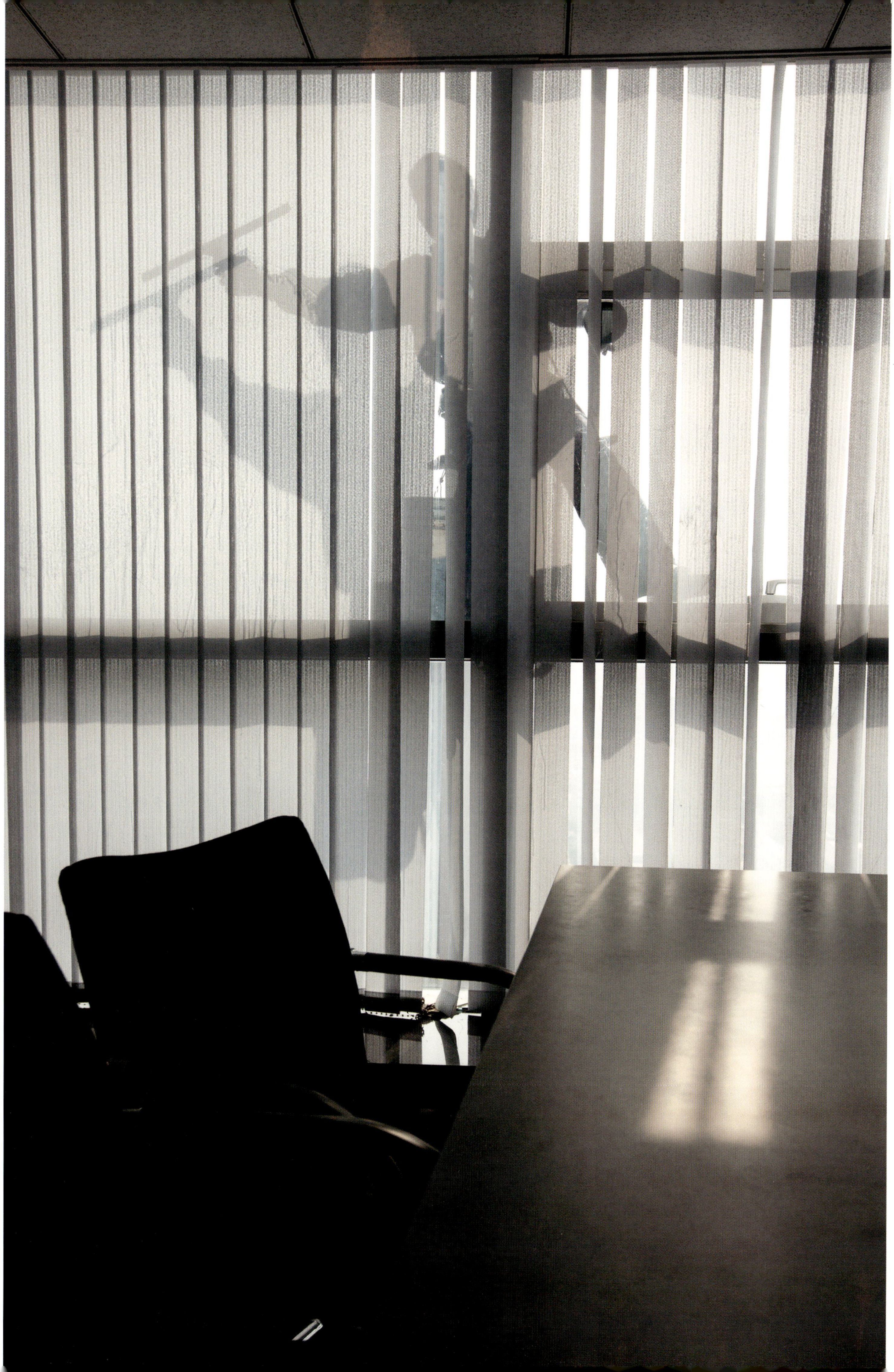

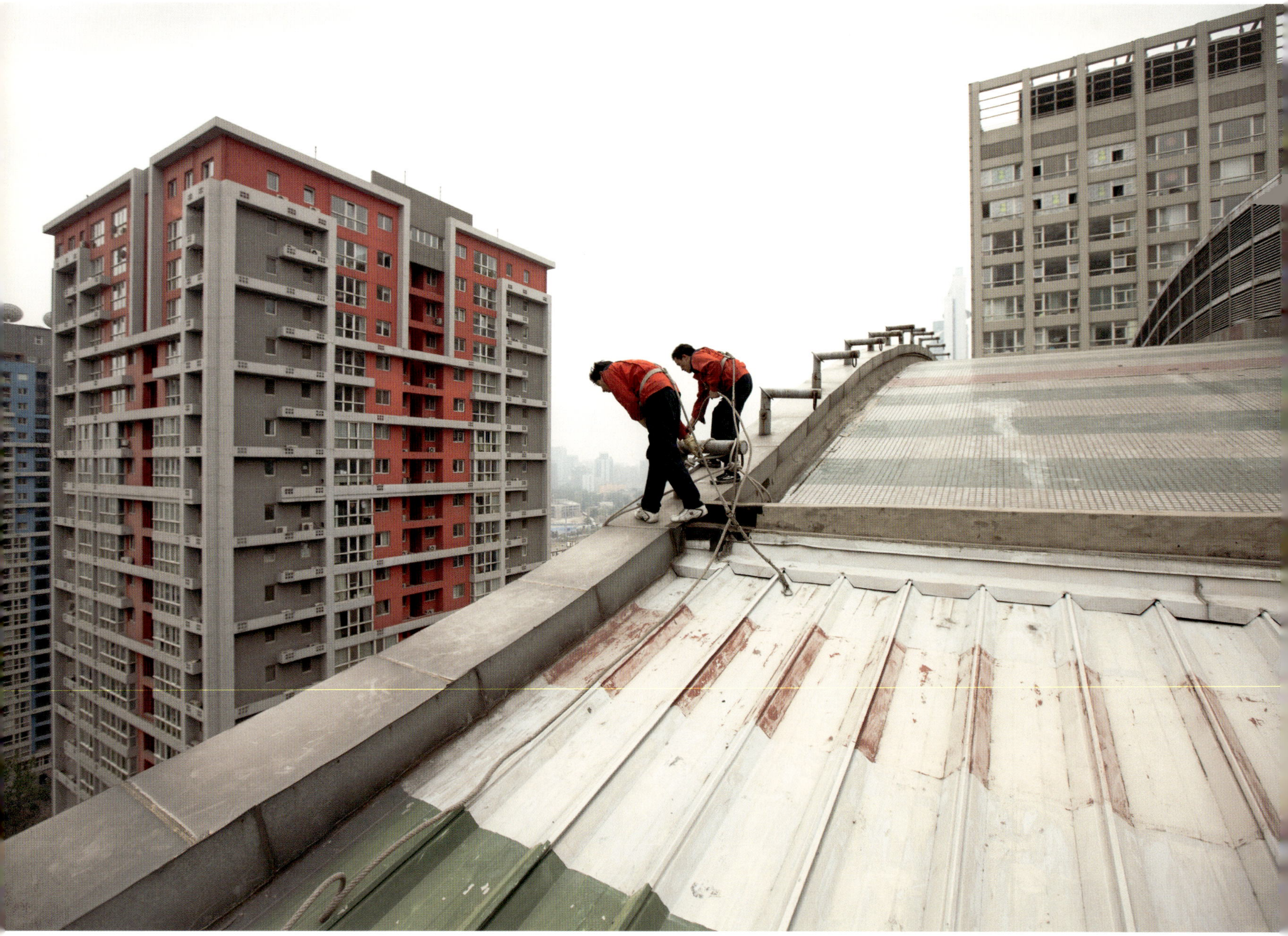

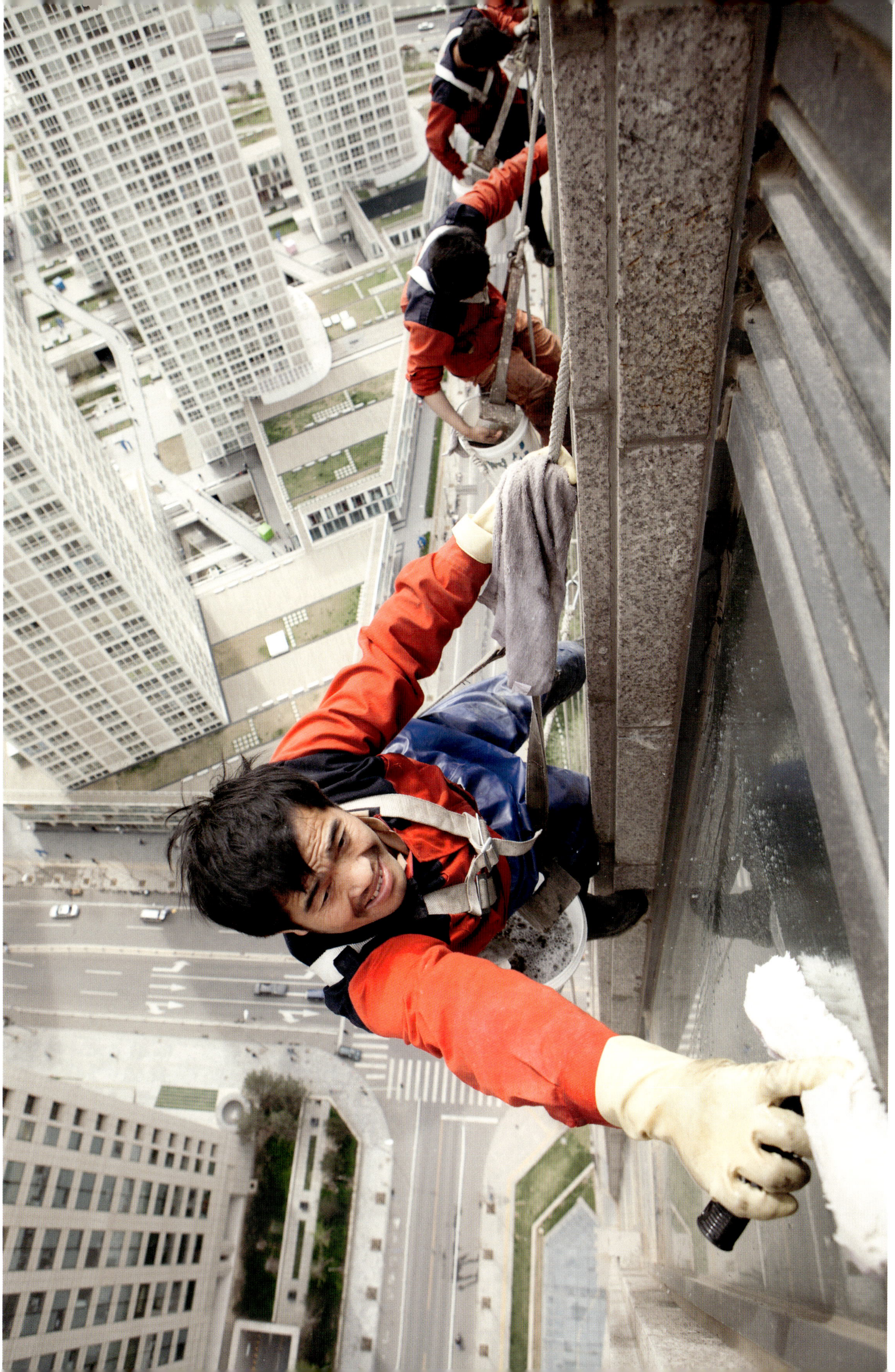

»Früher war ich immer gleich auf 180. Ich bin meinem Boss einmal mit 2 Messern an den Hals. Dafür habe ich aber auch mein Geld bekommen, während andere Kollegen leer ausgegangen sind.«

»I used to be rather hotheaded. I once threatened my boss with two knives. That, however, did get me my pay, while other colleagues went away empty handed.«

Zhang Wei, 39

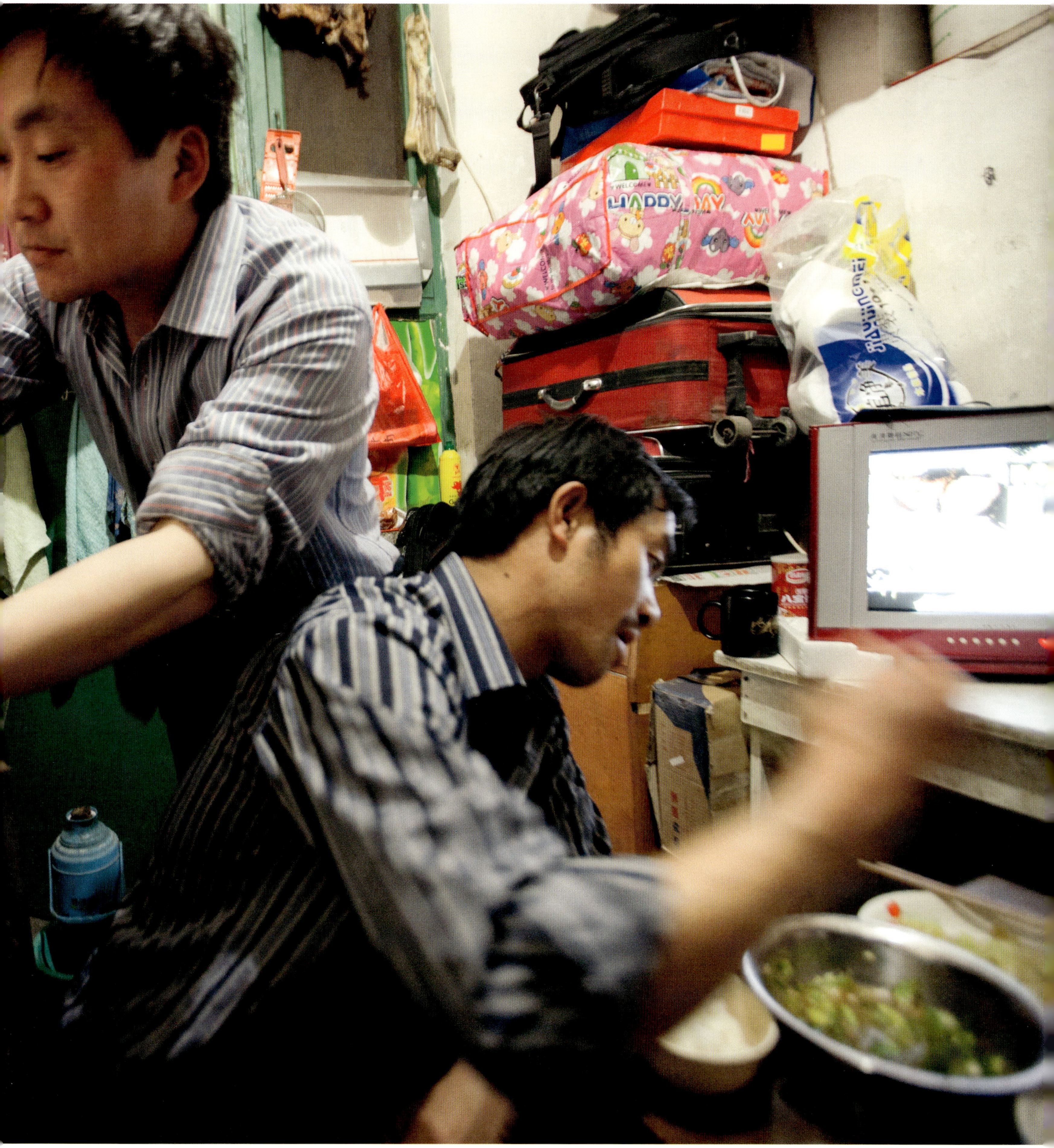

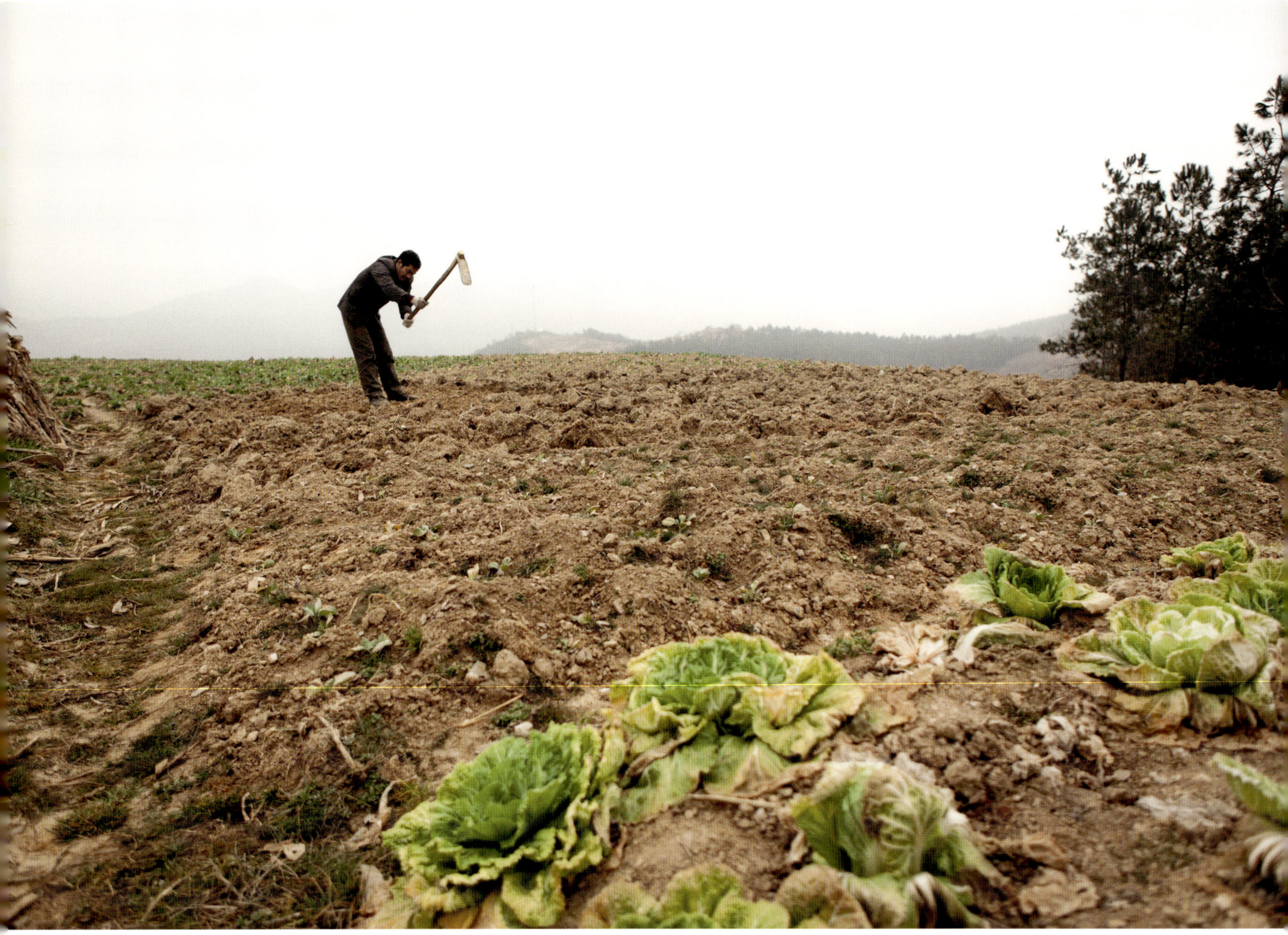

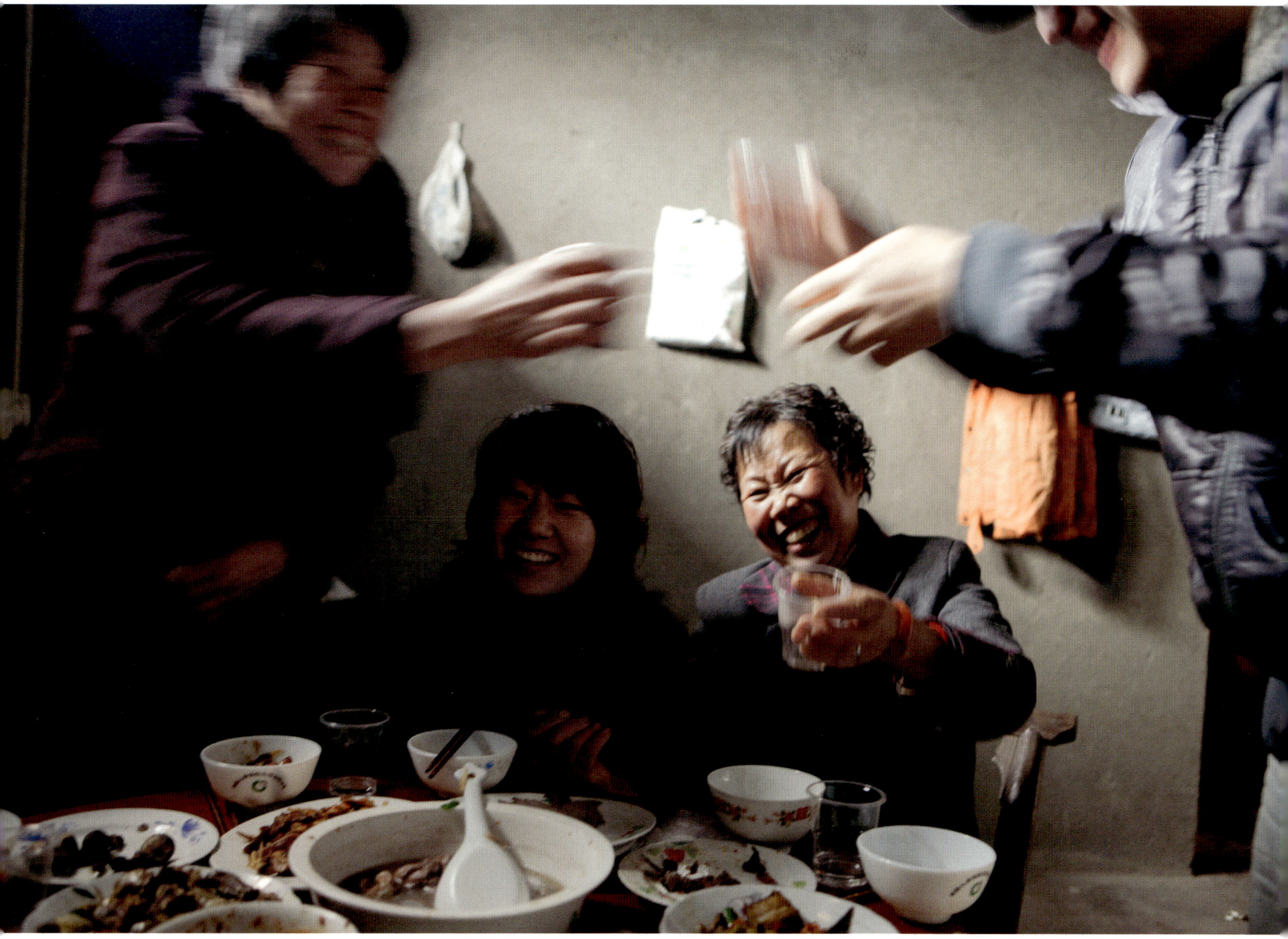

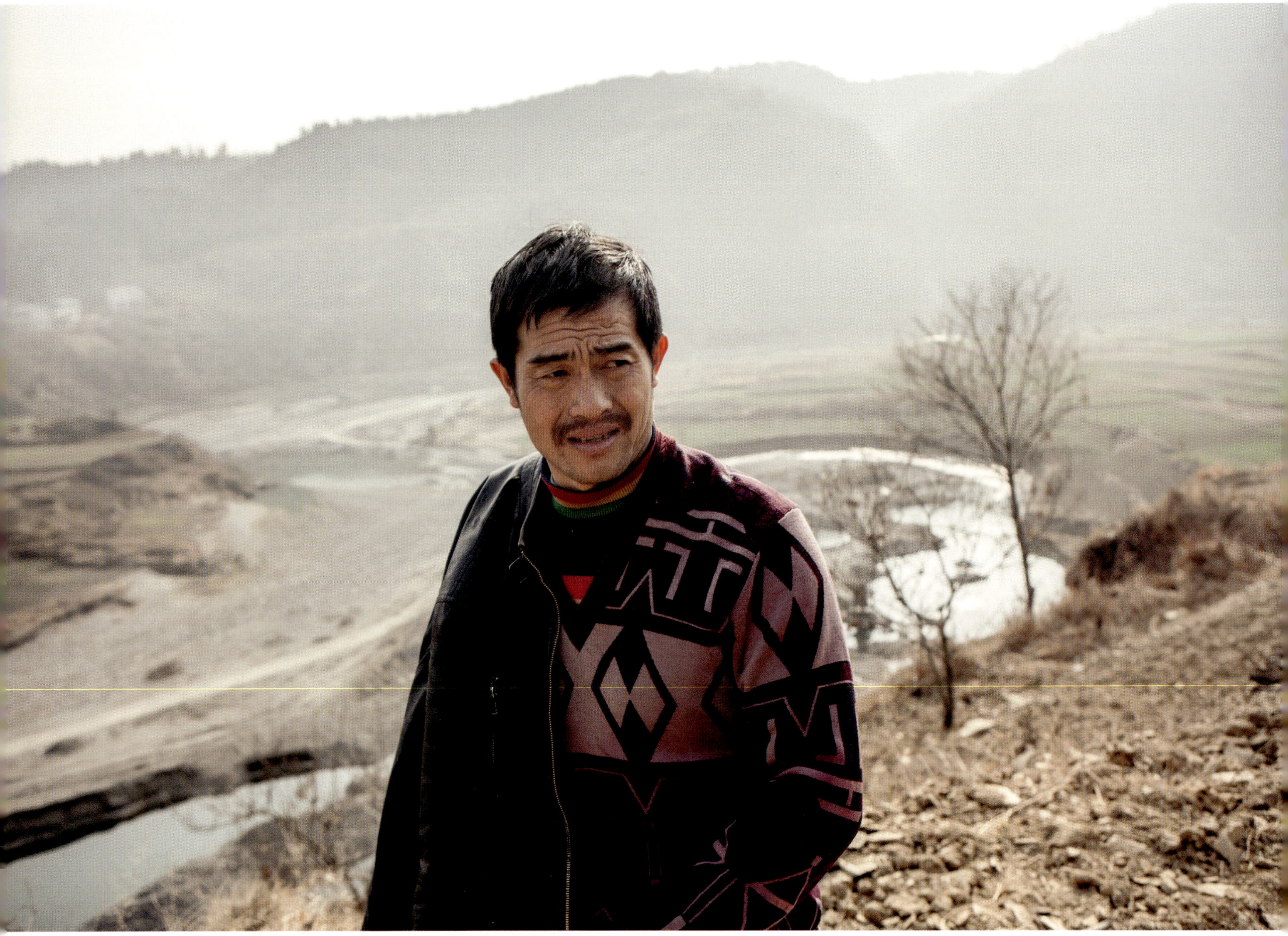

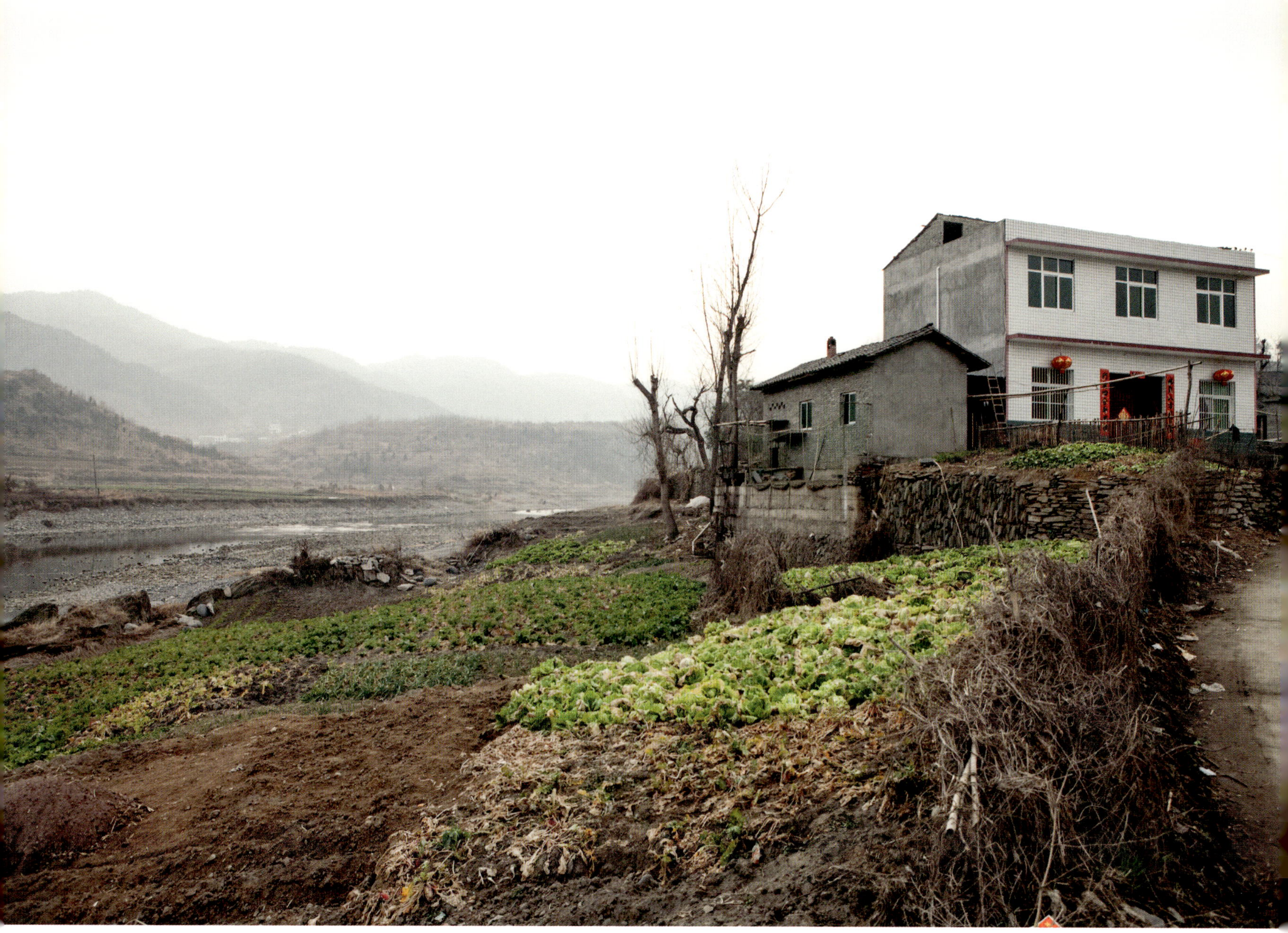

»Mit 40 ist gewöhnlich Schluss damit, sich auf einem Holzbrett an den Fassaden herunterzulassen und Fenster zu putzen. Die Konzentrationsfähigkeit lässt nach und der Job wird zu gefährlich.«

»When you turn forty, that usually means the end of lowering yourself down the facades on a wooden board to clean windows. That's when the ability to concentrate wanes and the job becomes too dangerous.«

Zhang Wei, 39

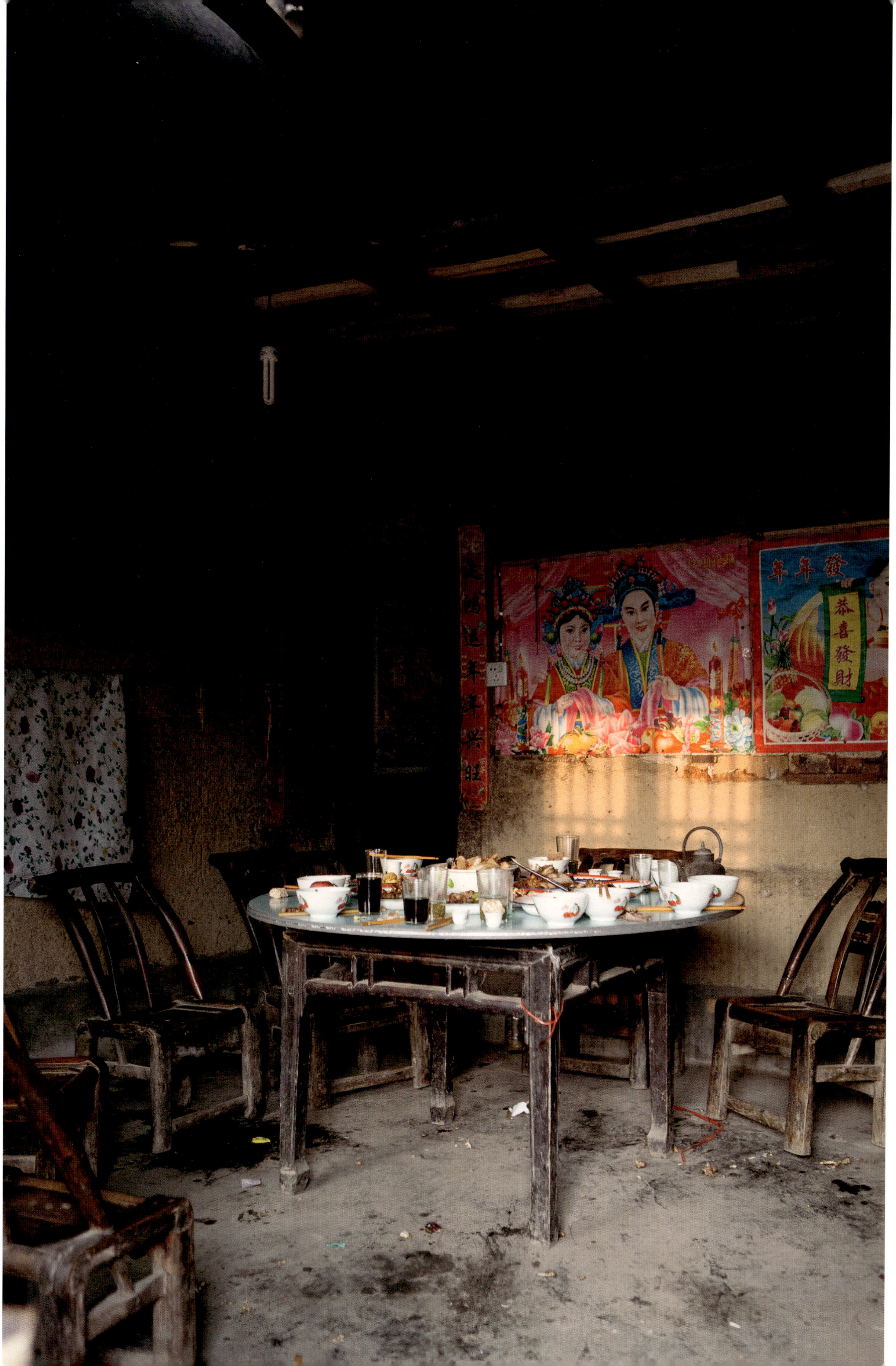

4

Xu Fang

Müllrecyclerin, Peking
Garbage Recycler, Beijing

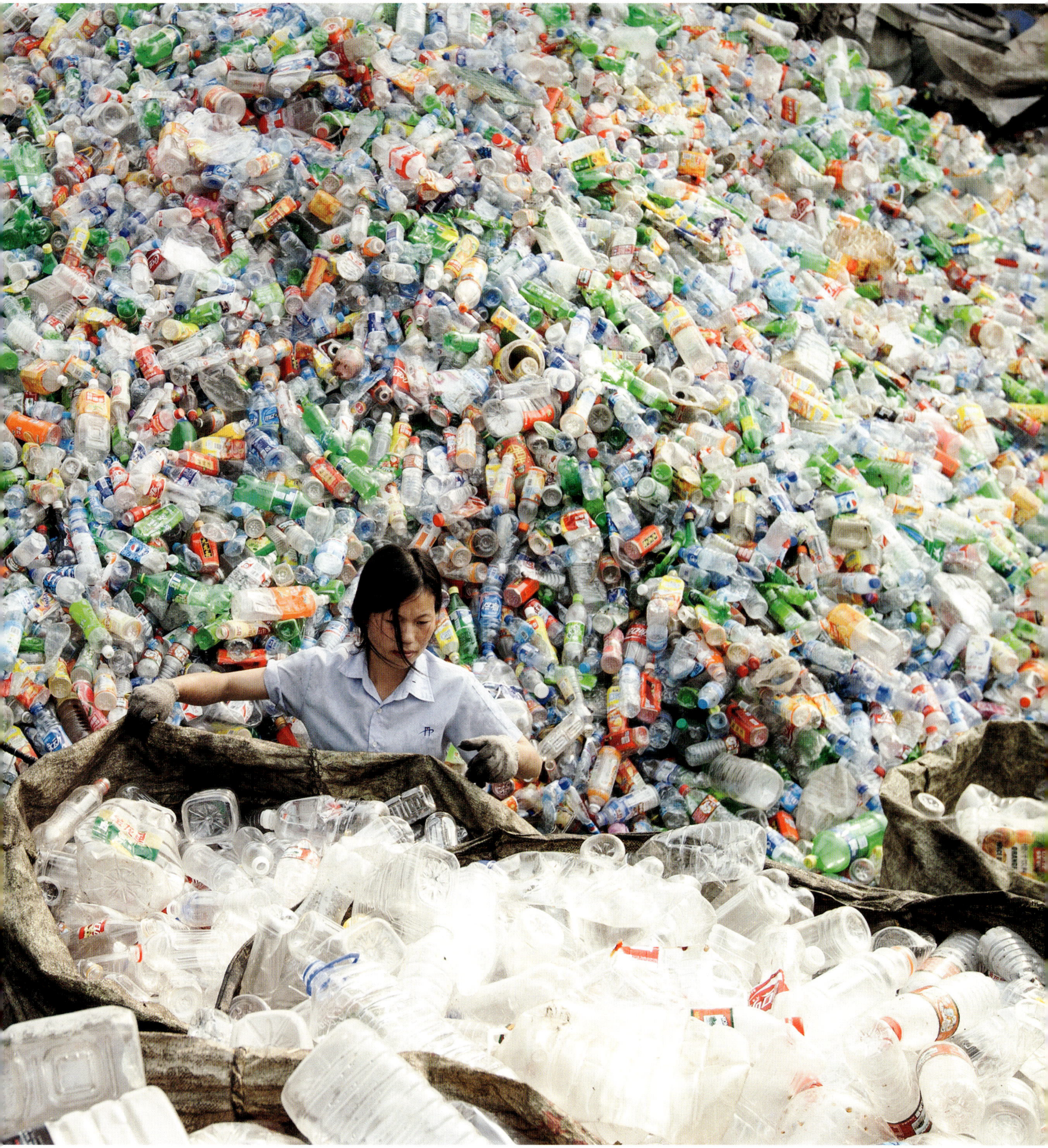

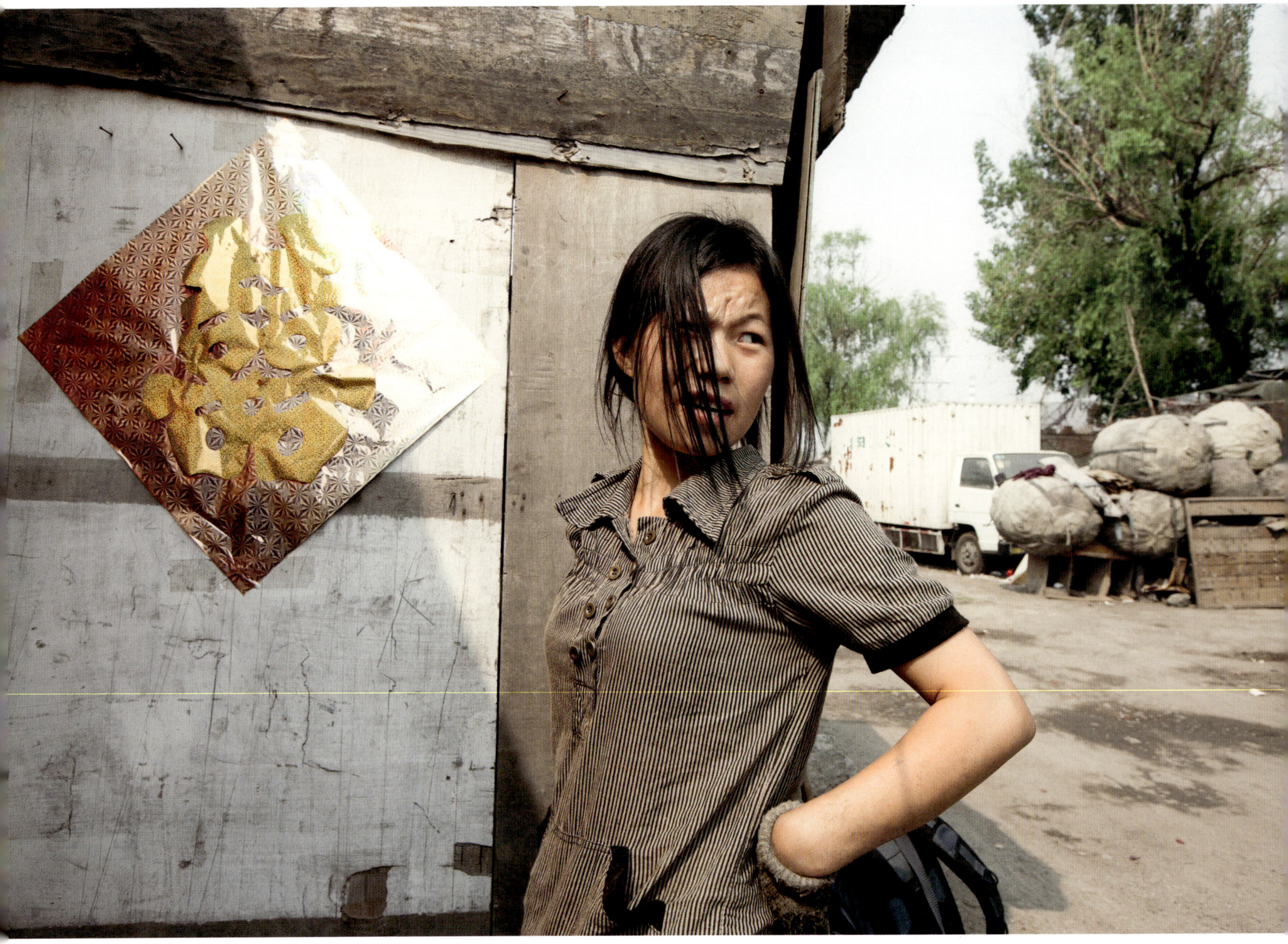

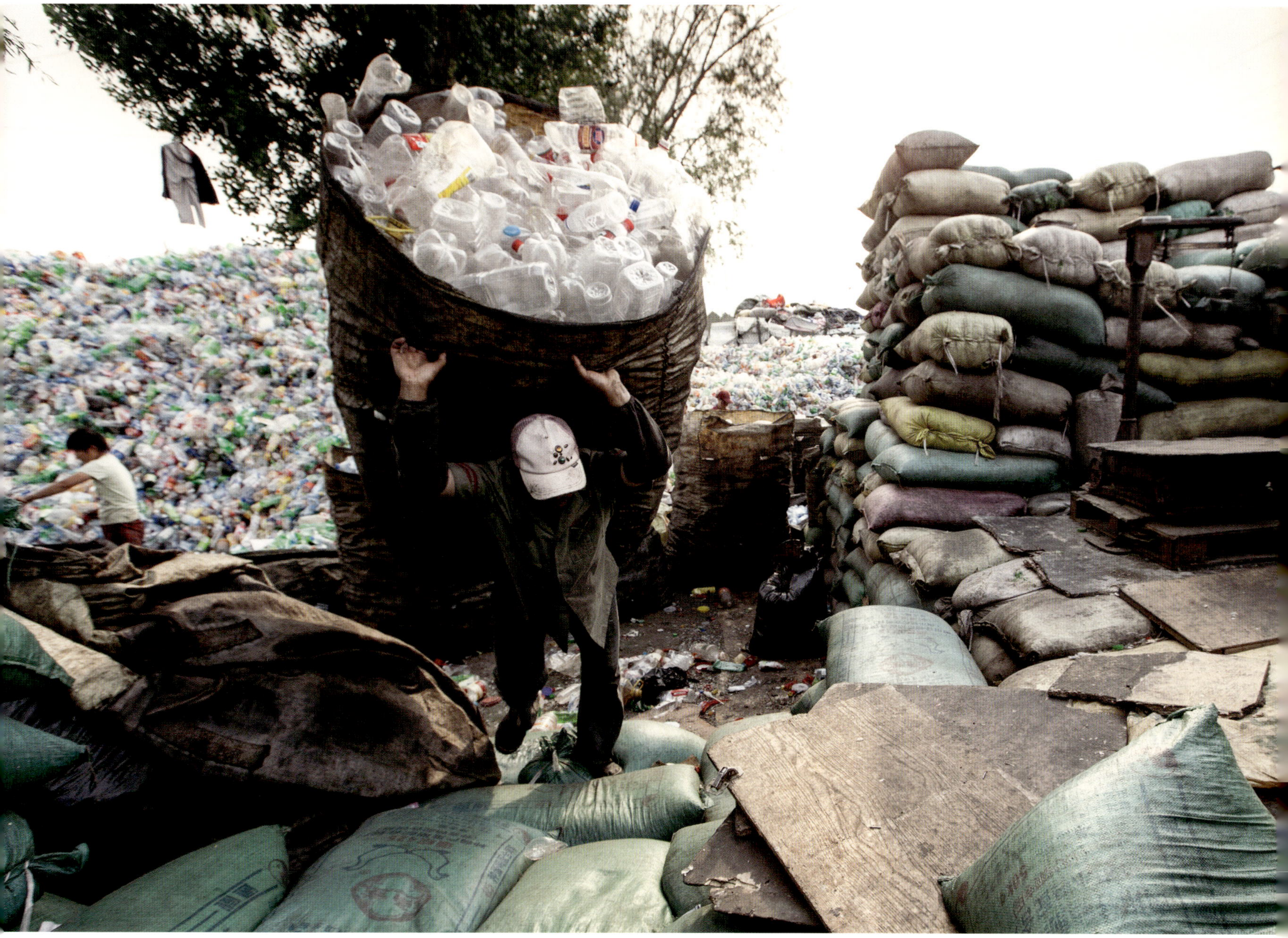

»Meinen Mann habe ich in einer Elektronikfabrik kennengelernt. Guangzhou war ein Ort voller Versuchungen. Wir waren viel unterwegs und haben unser ganzes Geld in Diskotheken und Karaoke-Bars ausgegeben.«

»I met my husband at an electronics factory. Guangzhou was a place full of temptations. We were out and about a lot and spent all our money in discos and karaoke bars.«

Xu Fang, 24

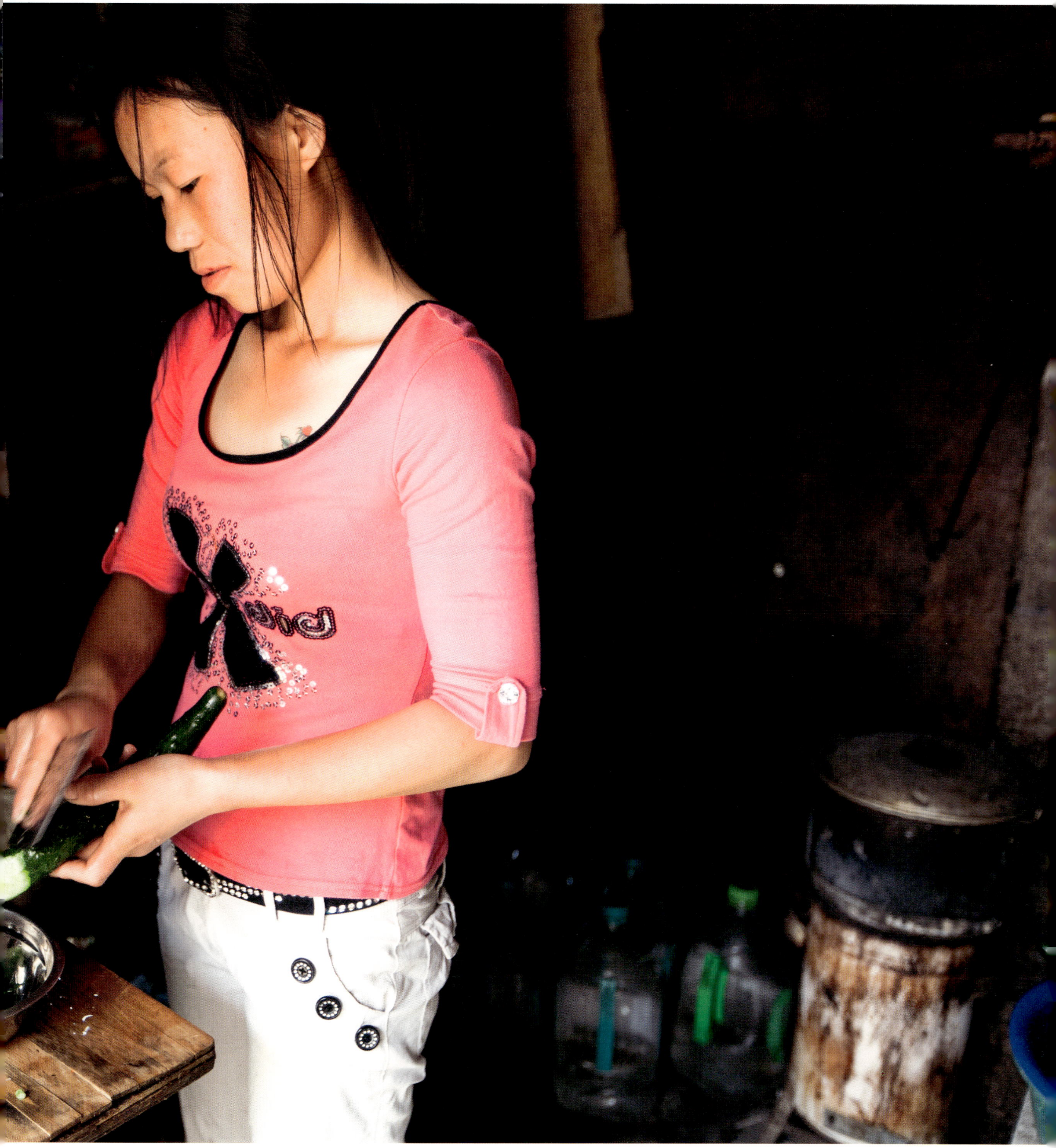

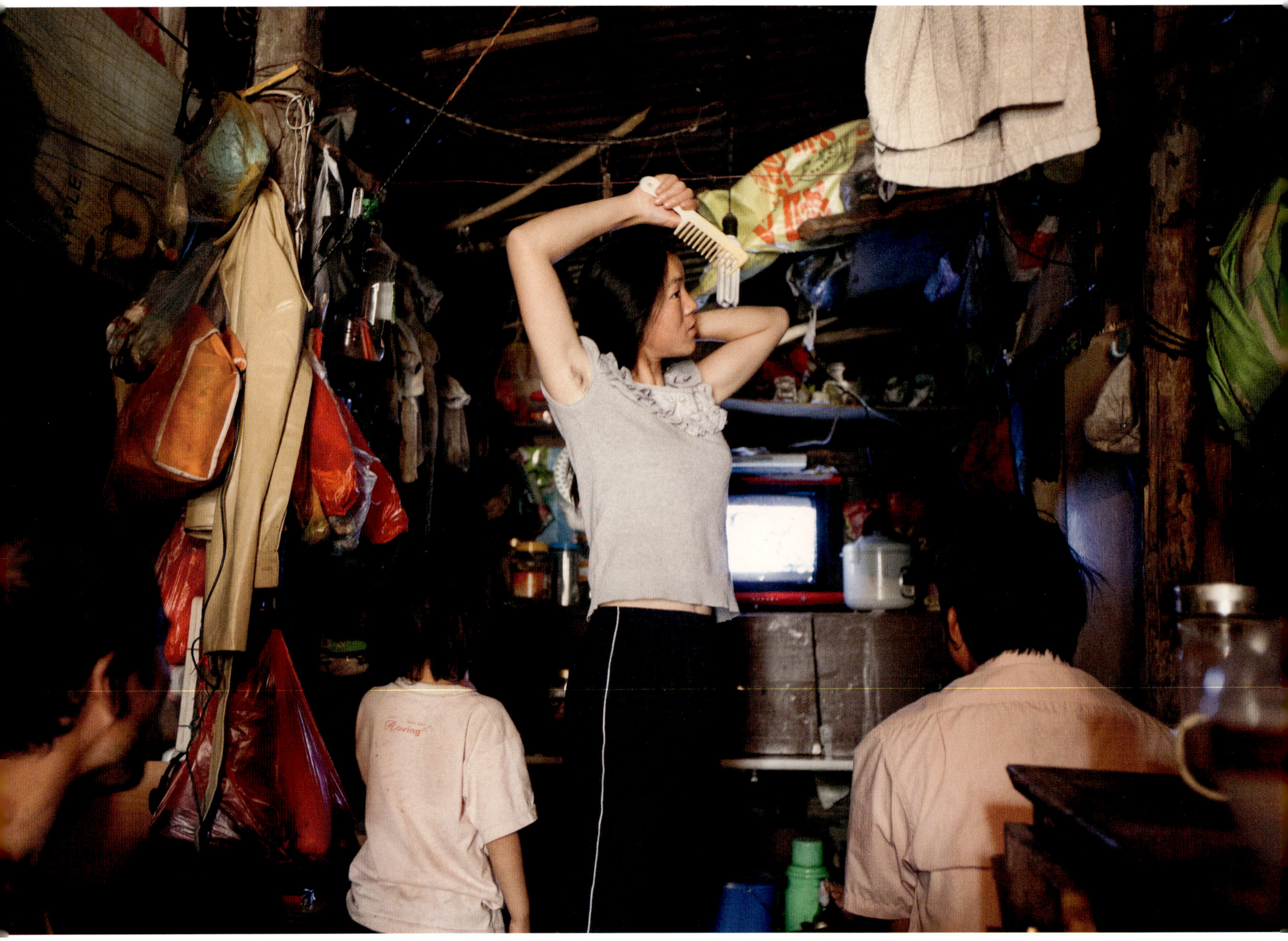
Roving

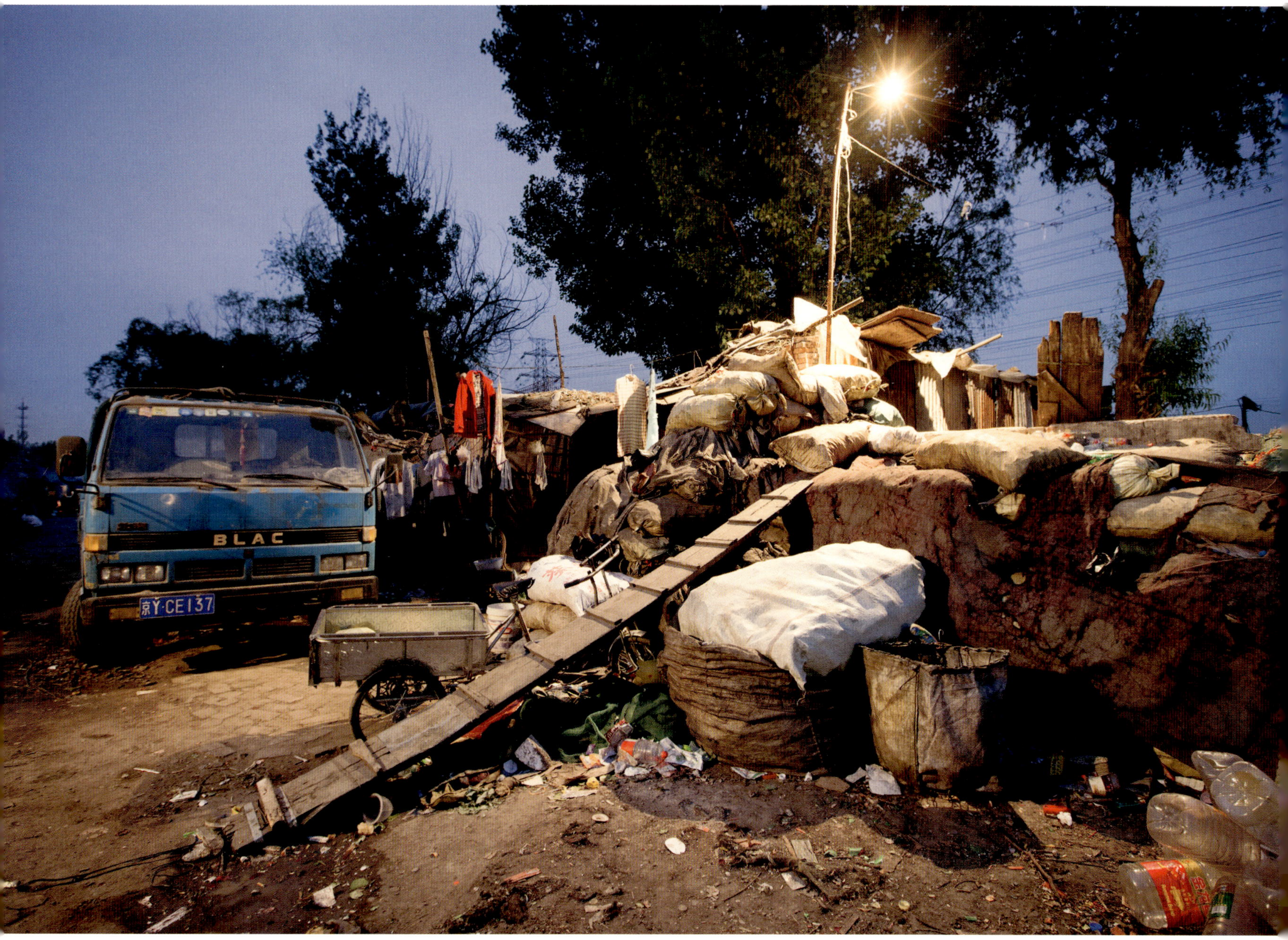
BLAC
京Y·CE137

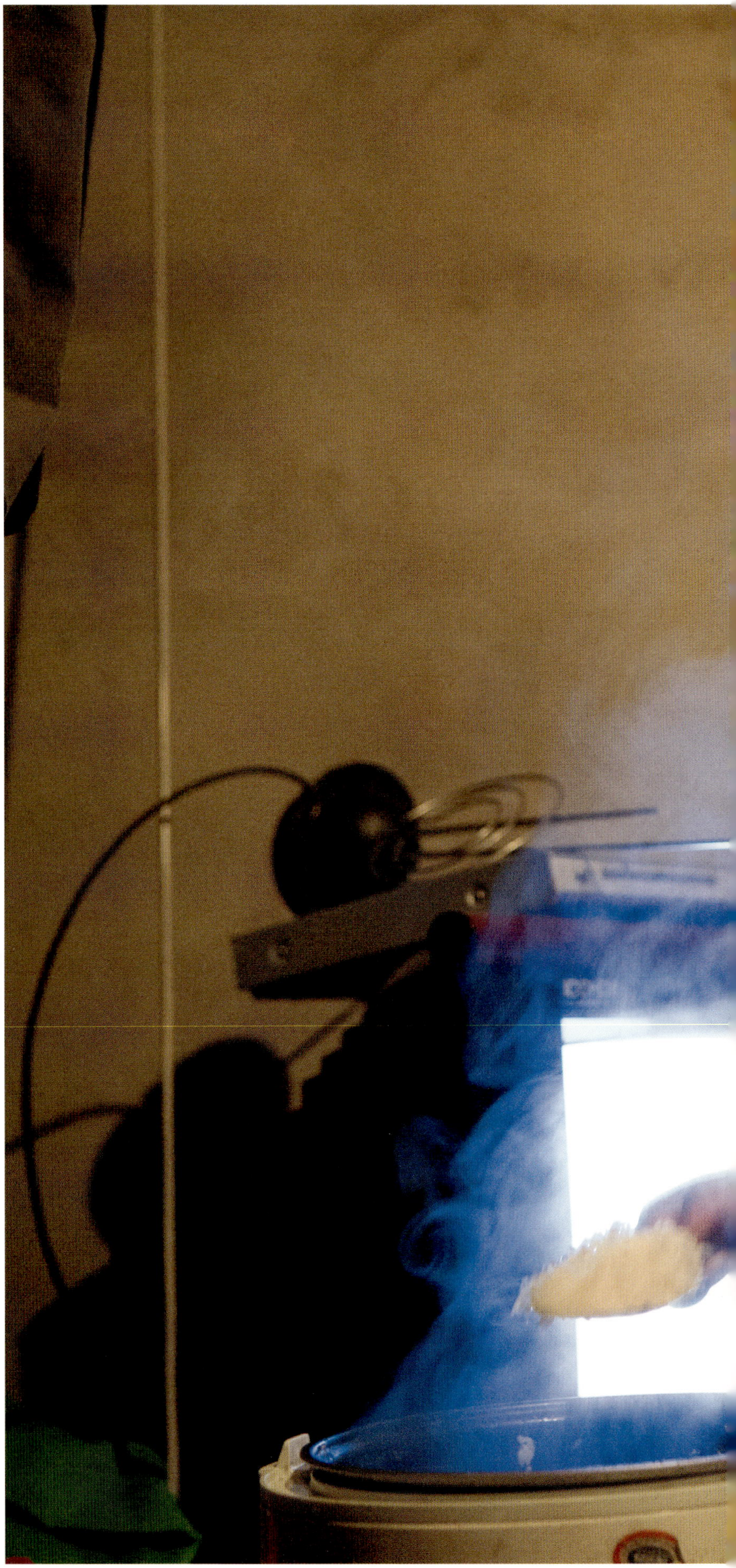

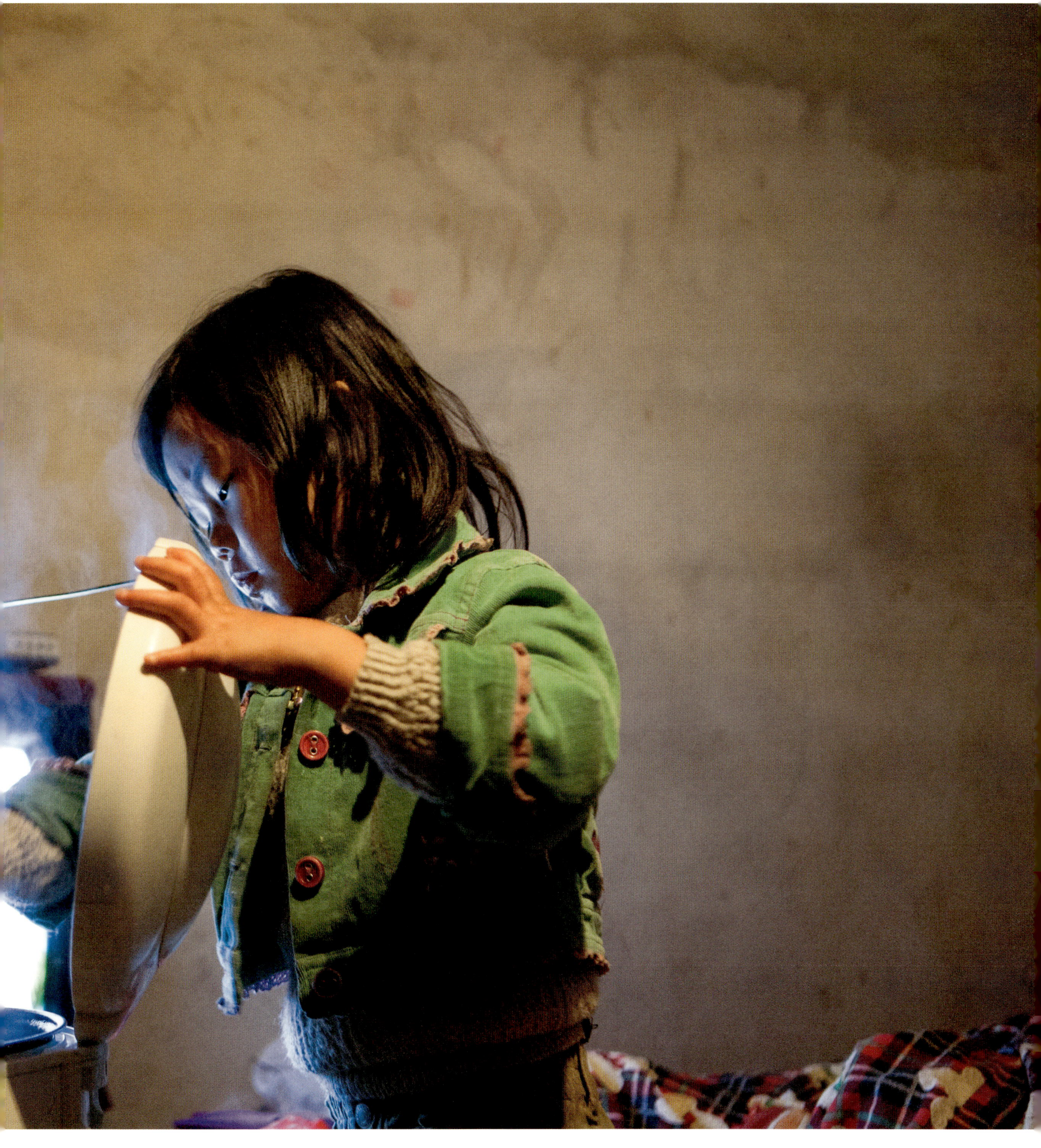

»Wir haben zu jung geheiratet, um unsere Ehe und unsere Kinder offiziell registrieren lassen zu können. In der Folge hatte ich oft Angst, dass es herauskommen und ich zwangssterilisiert werden könnte.«

»When we tied the knot, we were too young to have our marriage and our children officially registered. As a result, I was later often afraid that it would come out and I would be forced to undergo sterilization.«

Xu Fang, 26

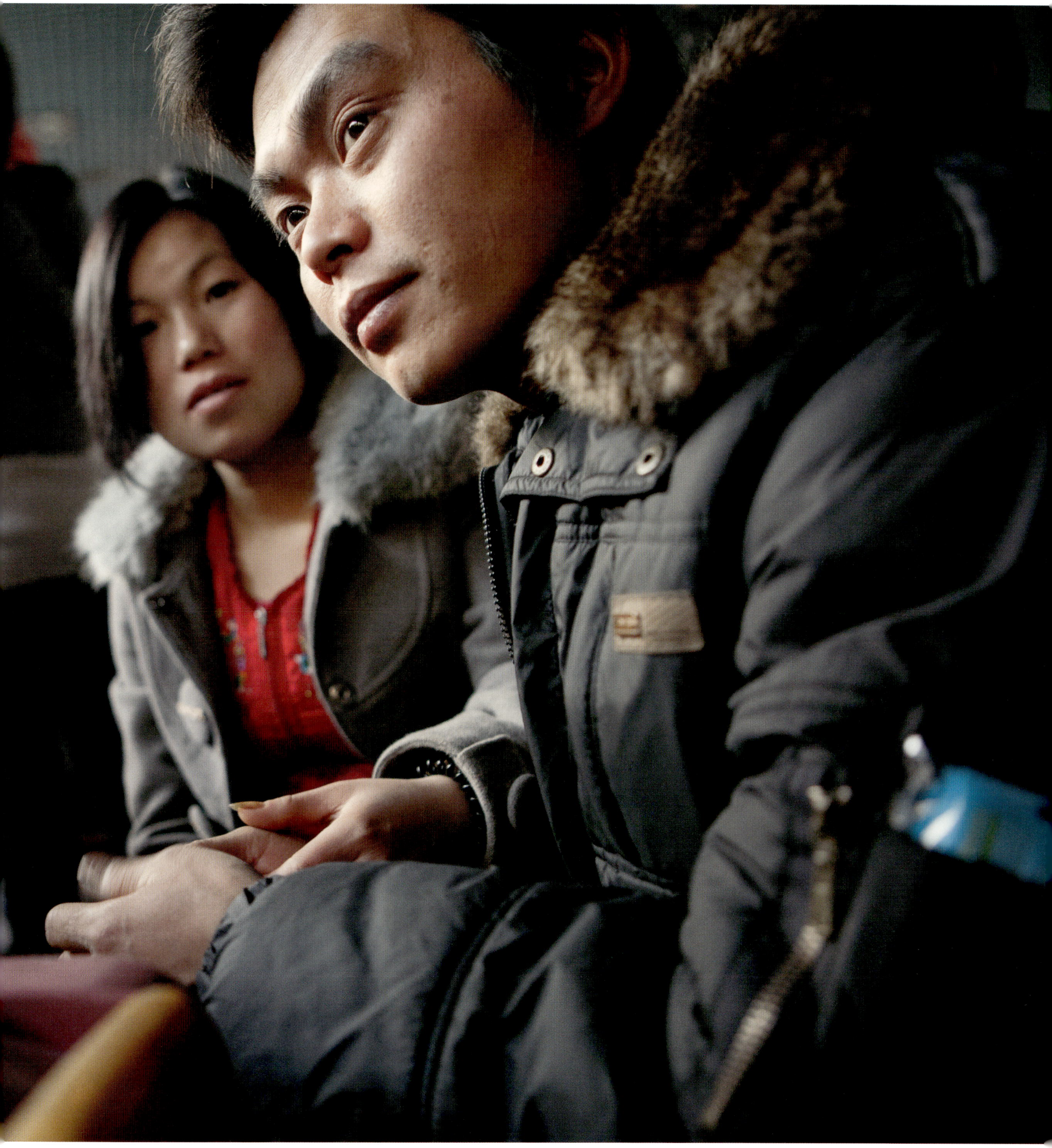

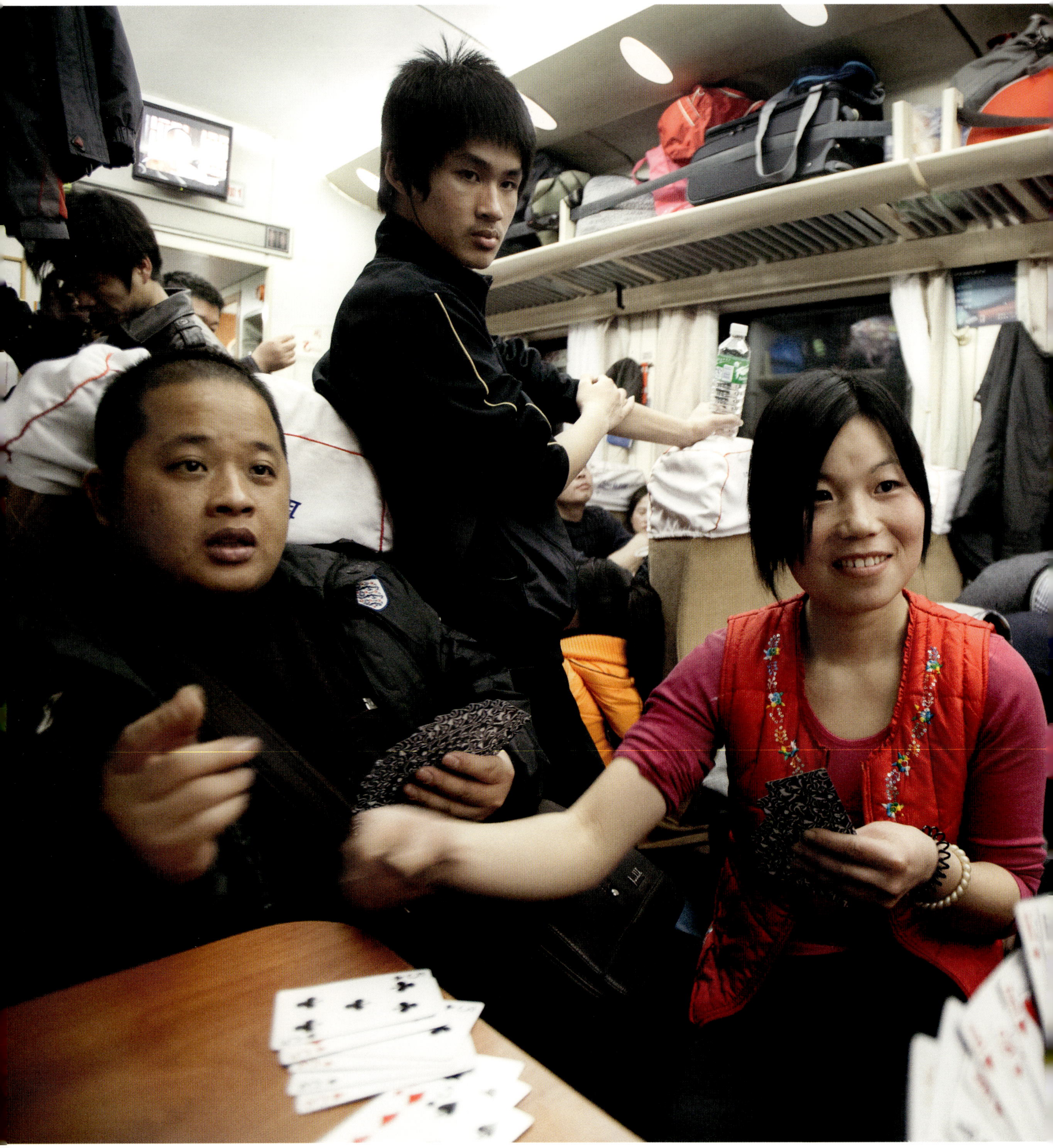

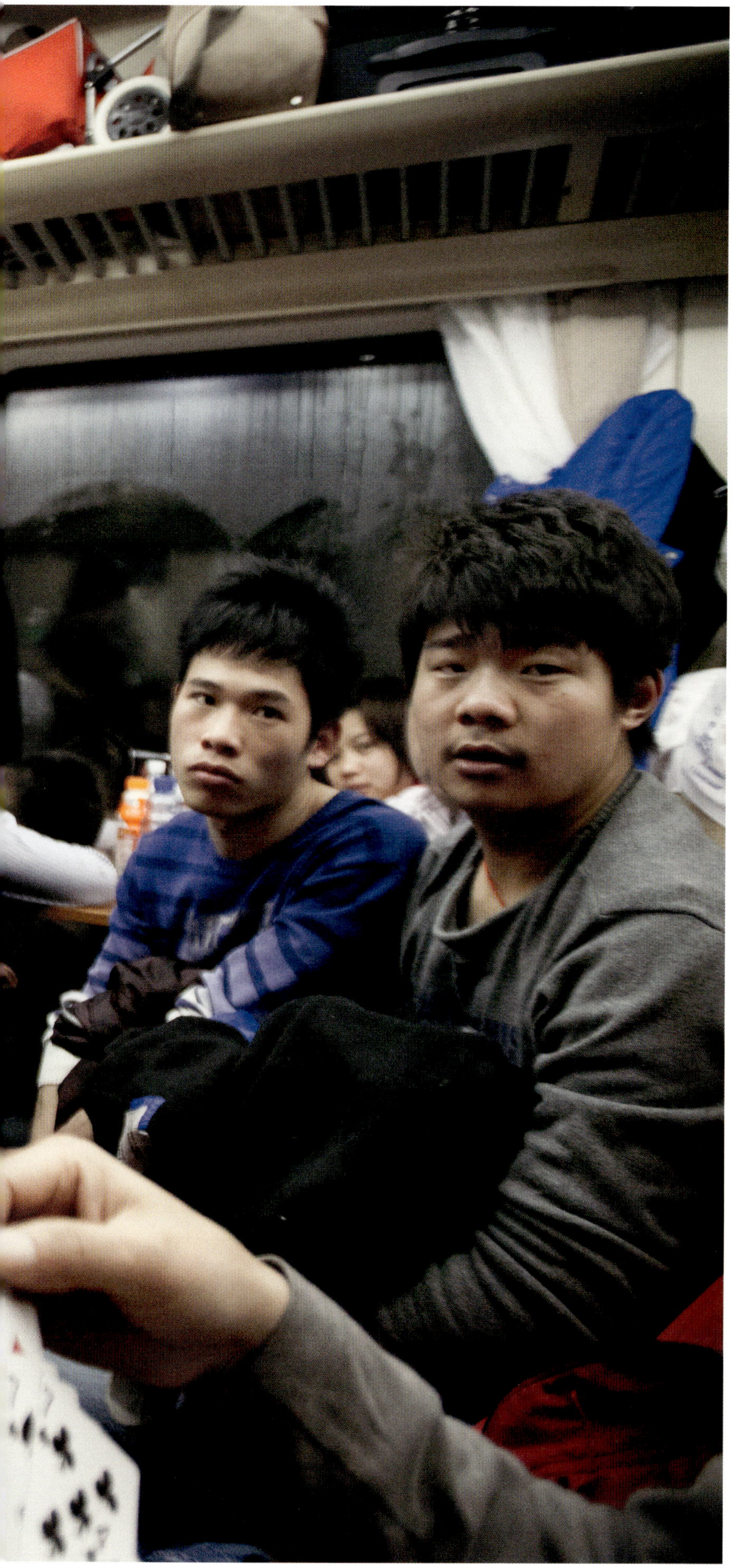

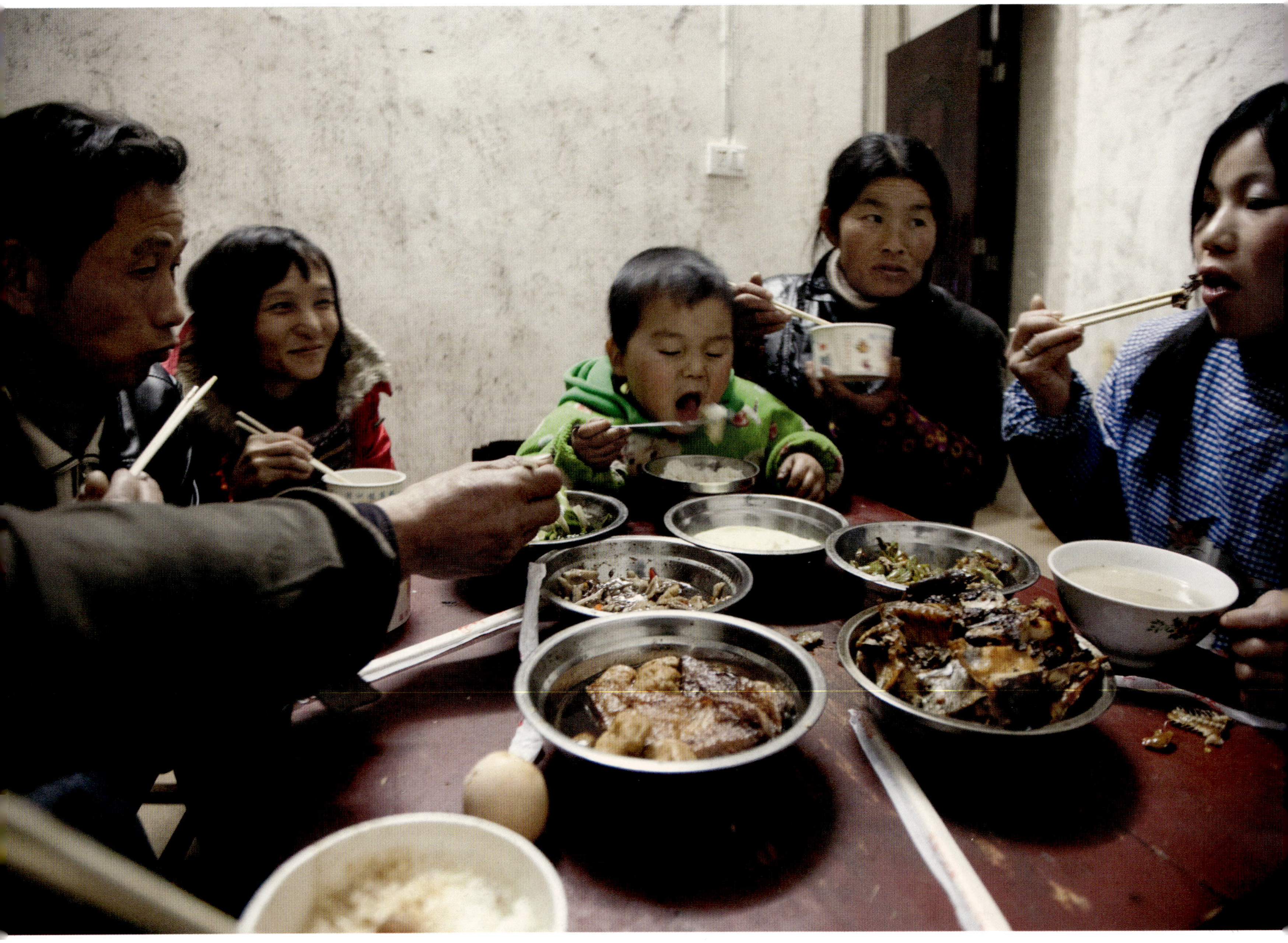

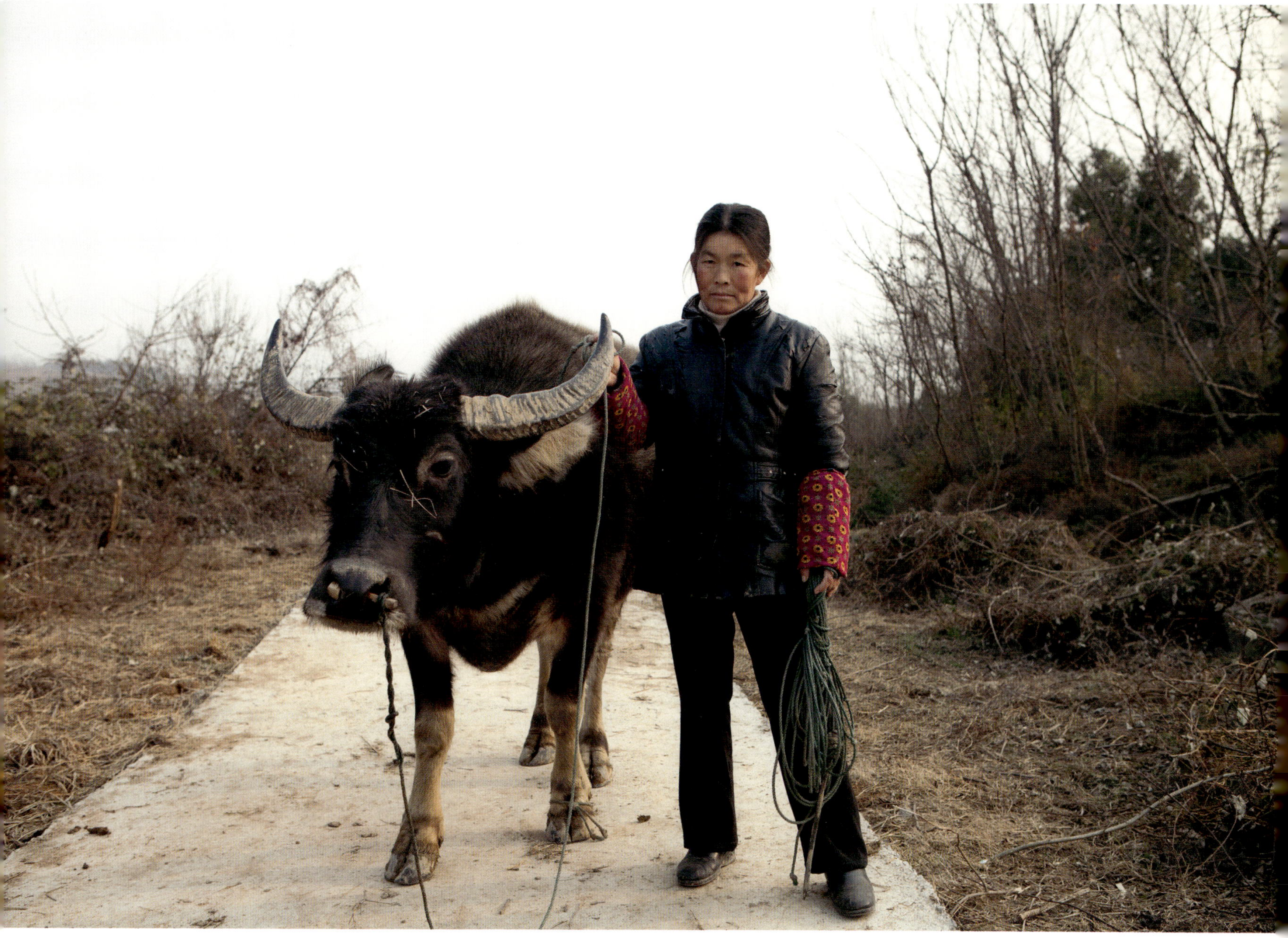

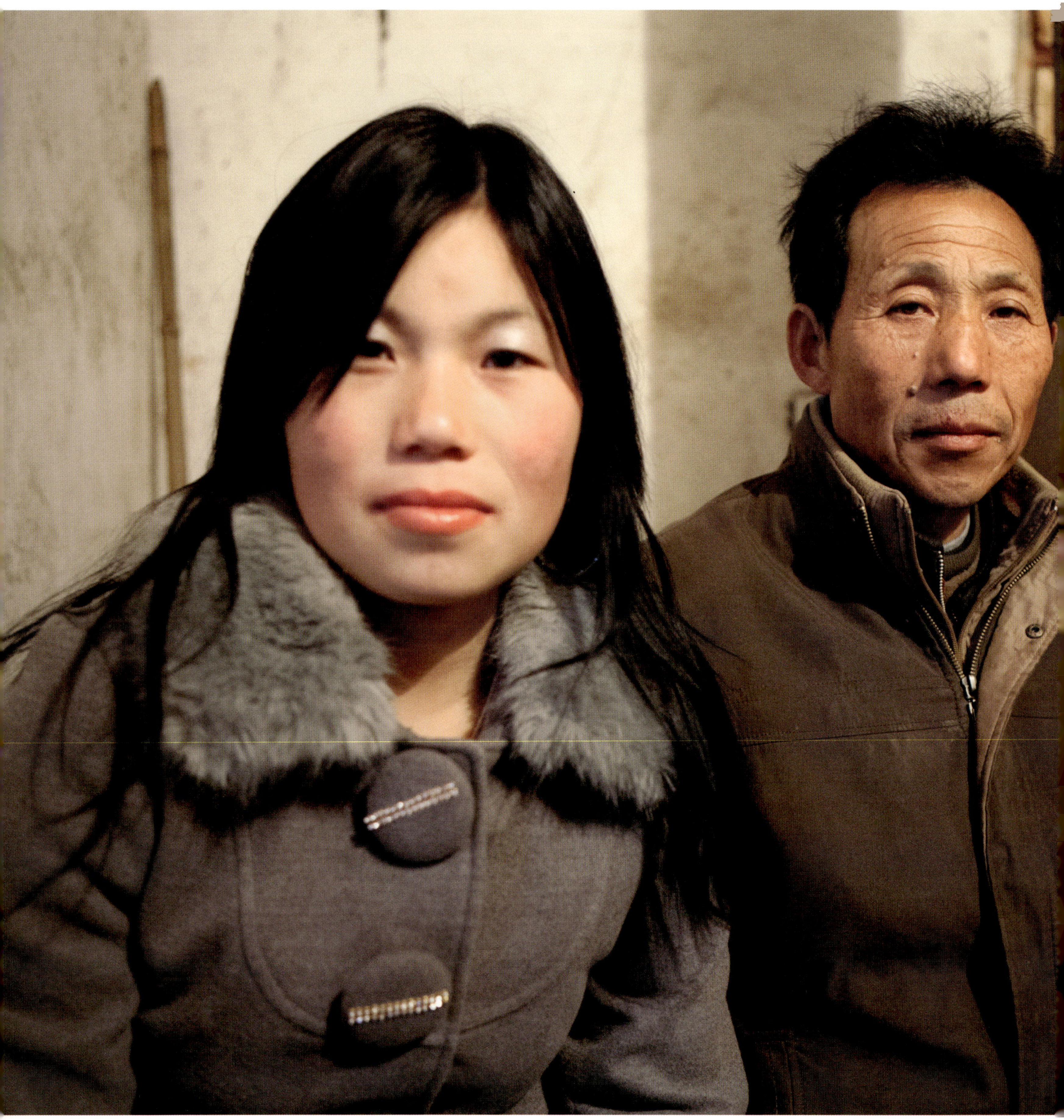

»Als mich mein Vater im Zimmer einsperrte, um meine Rückkehr in die Fabrik zu verhindern, habe ich ihm die Scheibe eingeschlagen, mir 200 Yuan geschnappt und bin abgehauen.«

»When my father locked me into a room to keep me from returning to the factory, I broke one of his window panes, grabbed 200 yuan, and took off.«

Xu Fang, 26

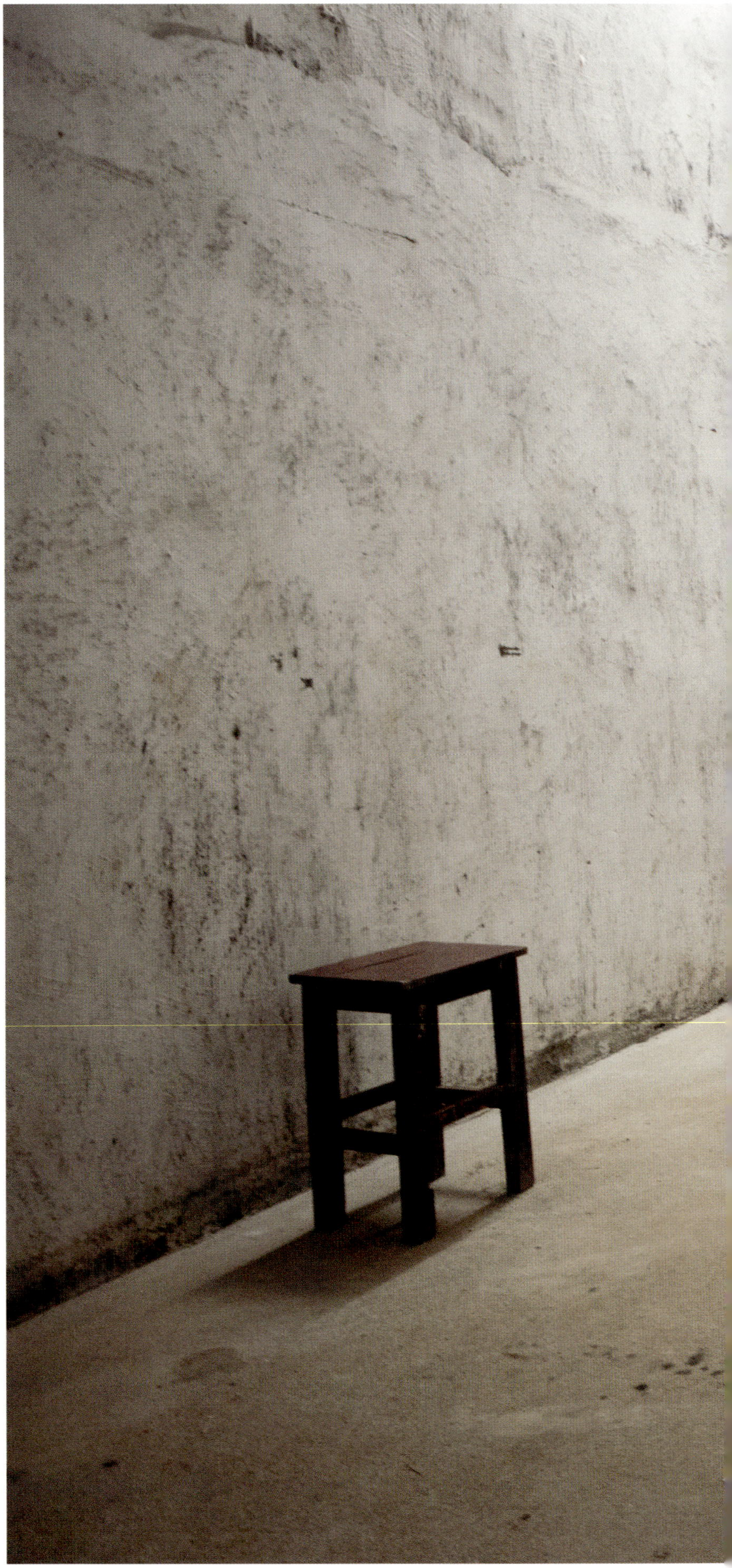

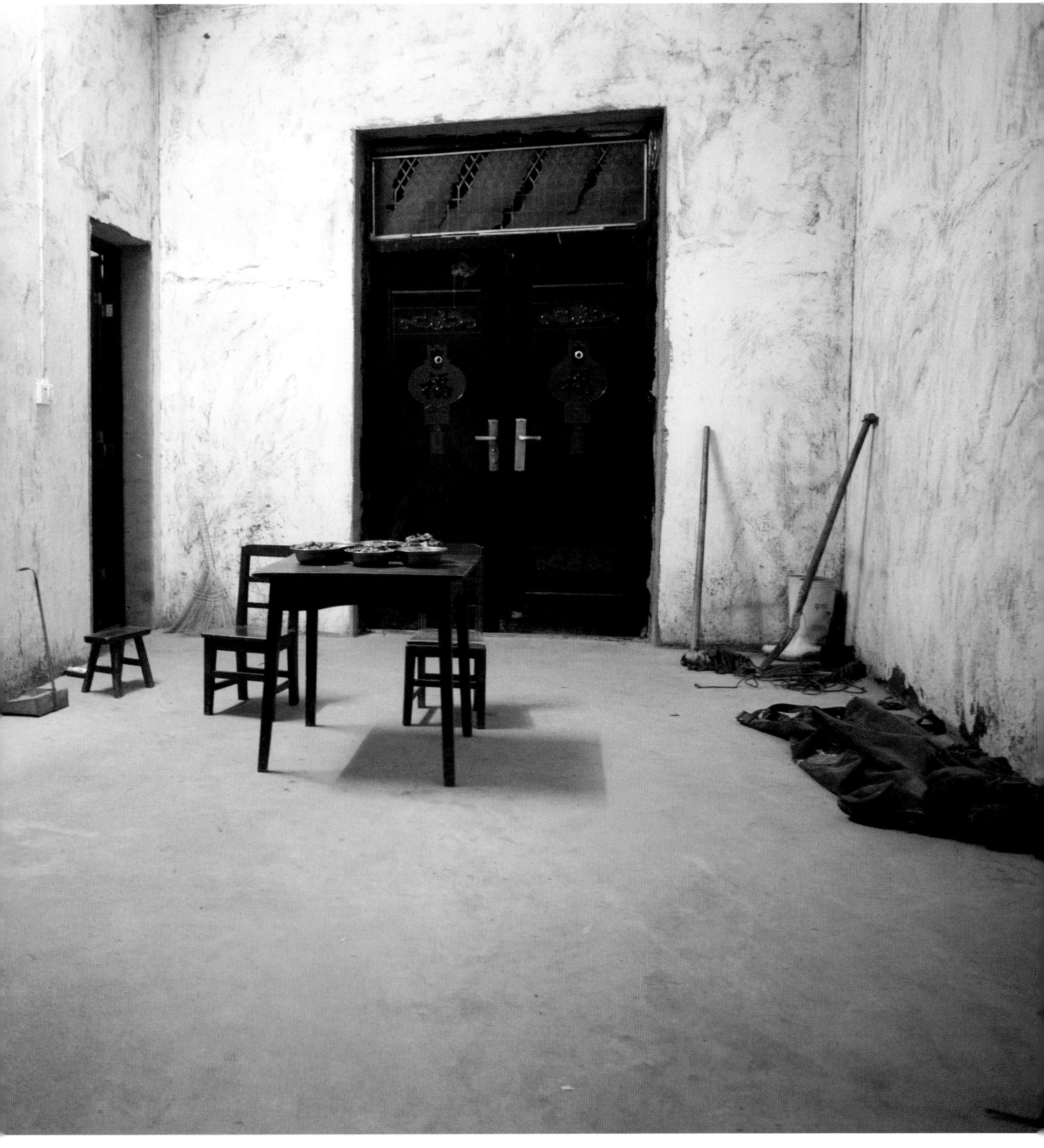

5

Spielzeugfabrik, Shenzhen
Toy Factory, Shenzhen

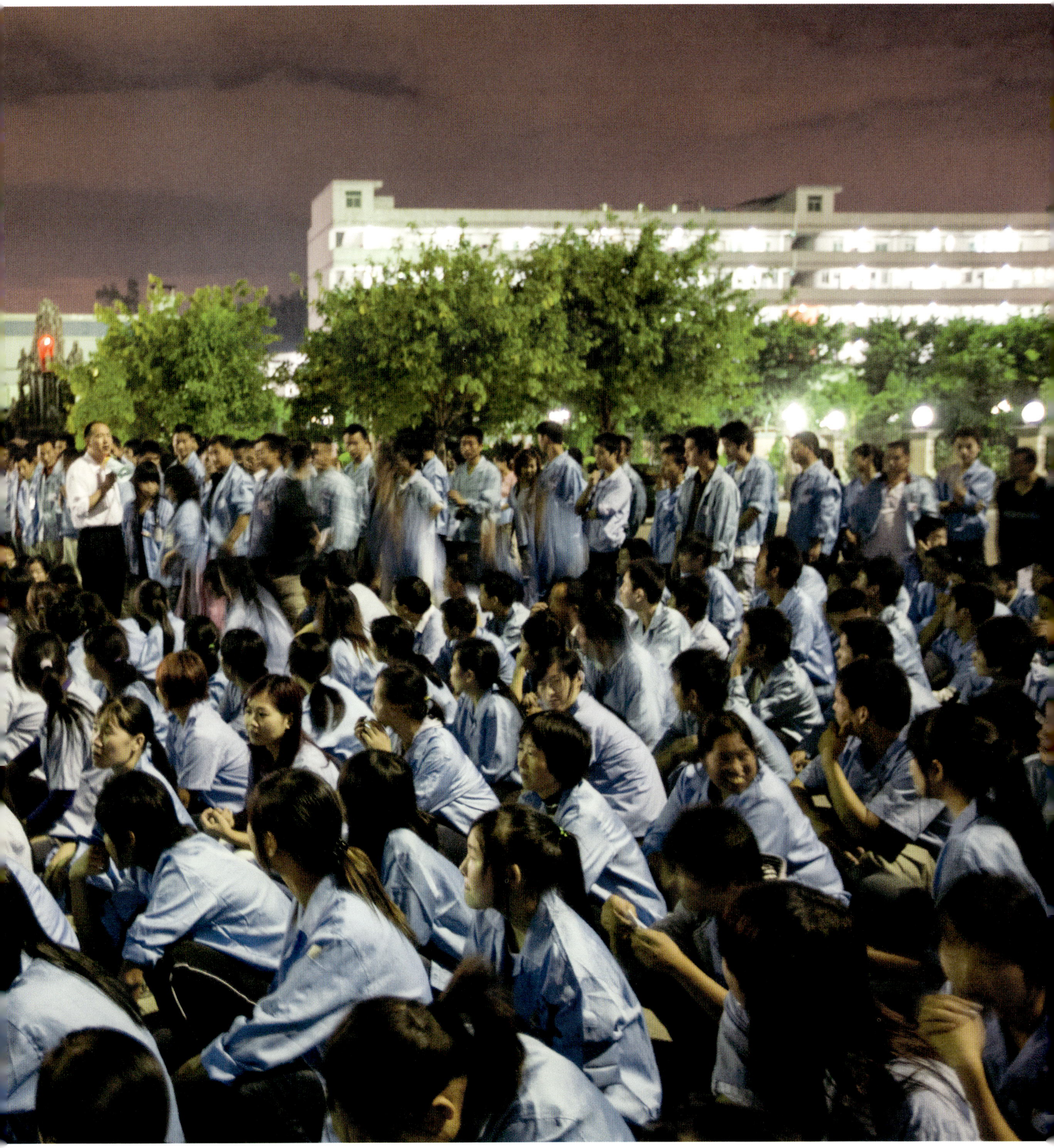

»Wir arbeiten hier in Schichten von 9 bis 11 Stunden pro Tag. In den letzten 2 Monaten habe ich nicht einen Tag frei bekommen.«

»We work 9 to 11 hour shifts each day here. I haven't had a single day off over the last two months.«

Tan Yaru, 20

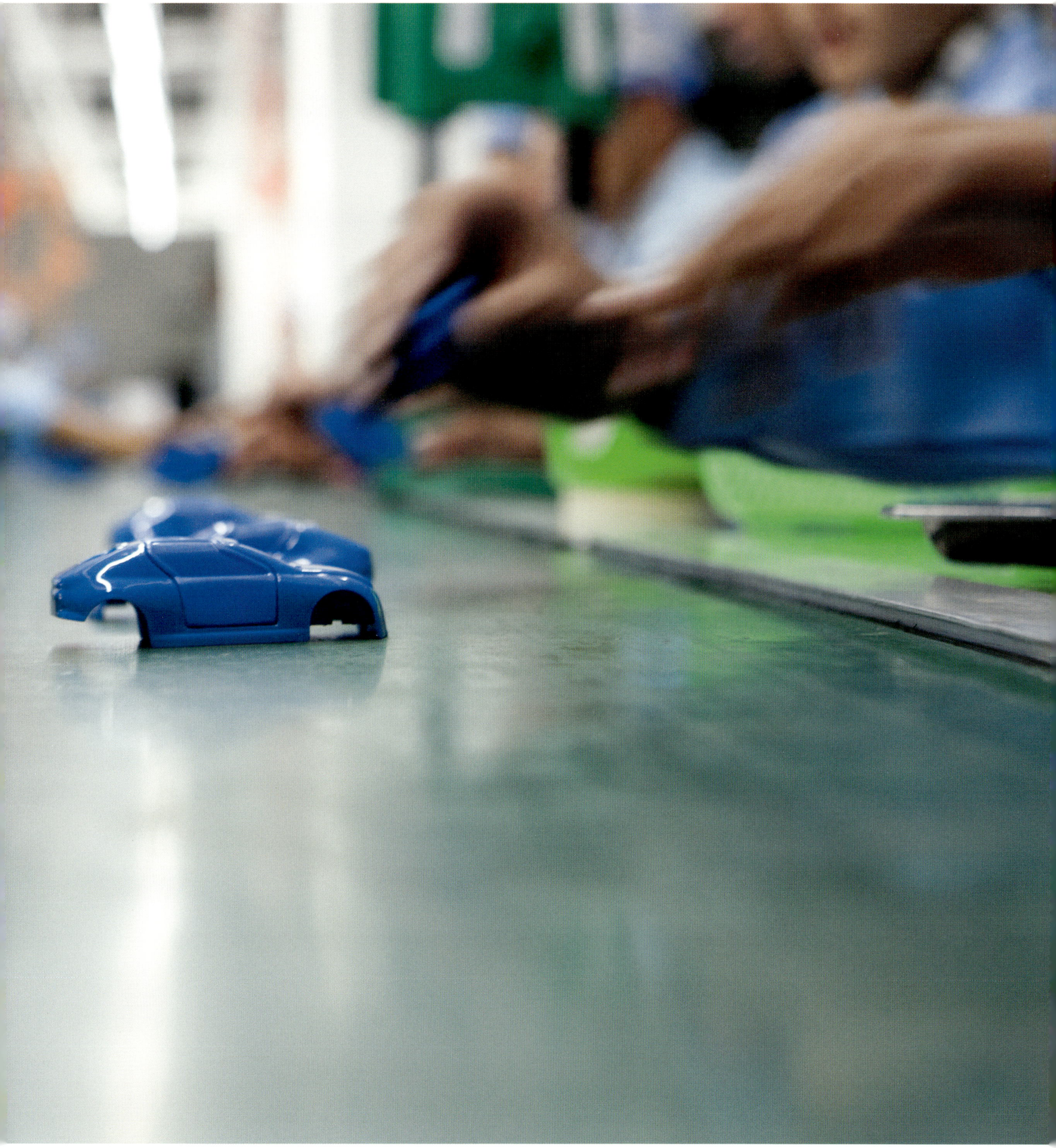

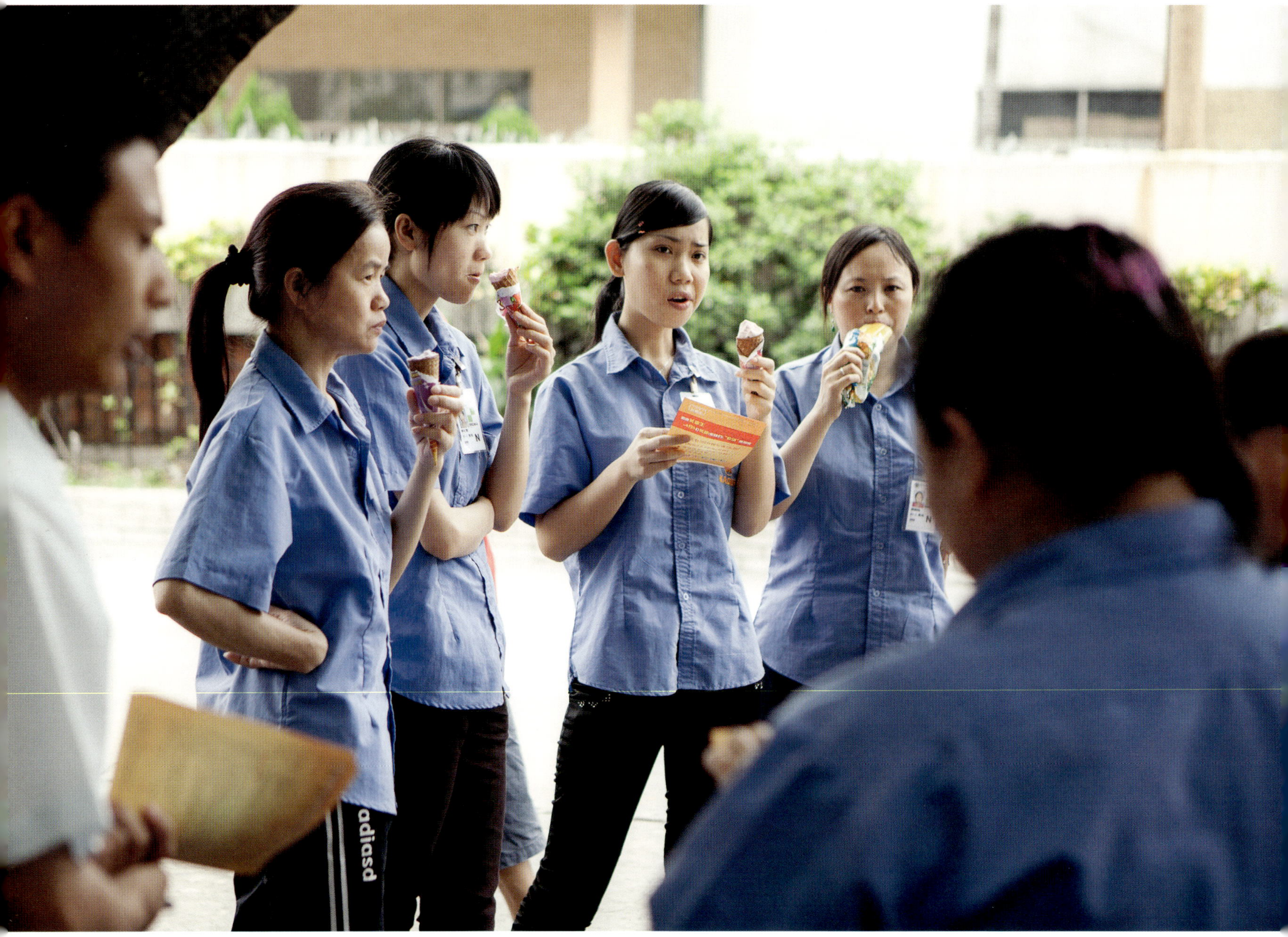
adiasd

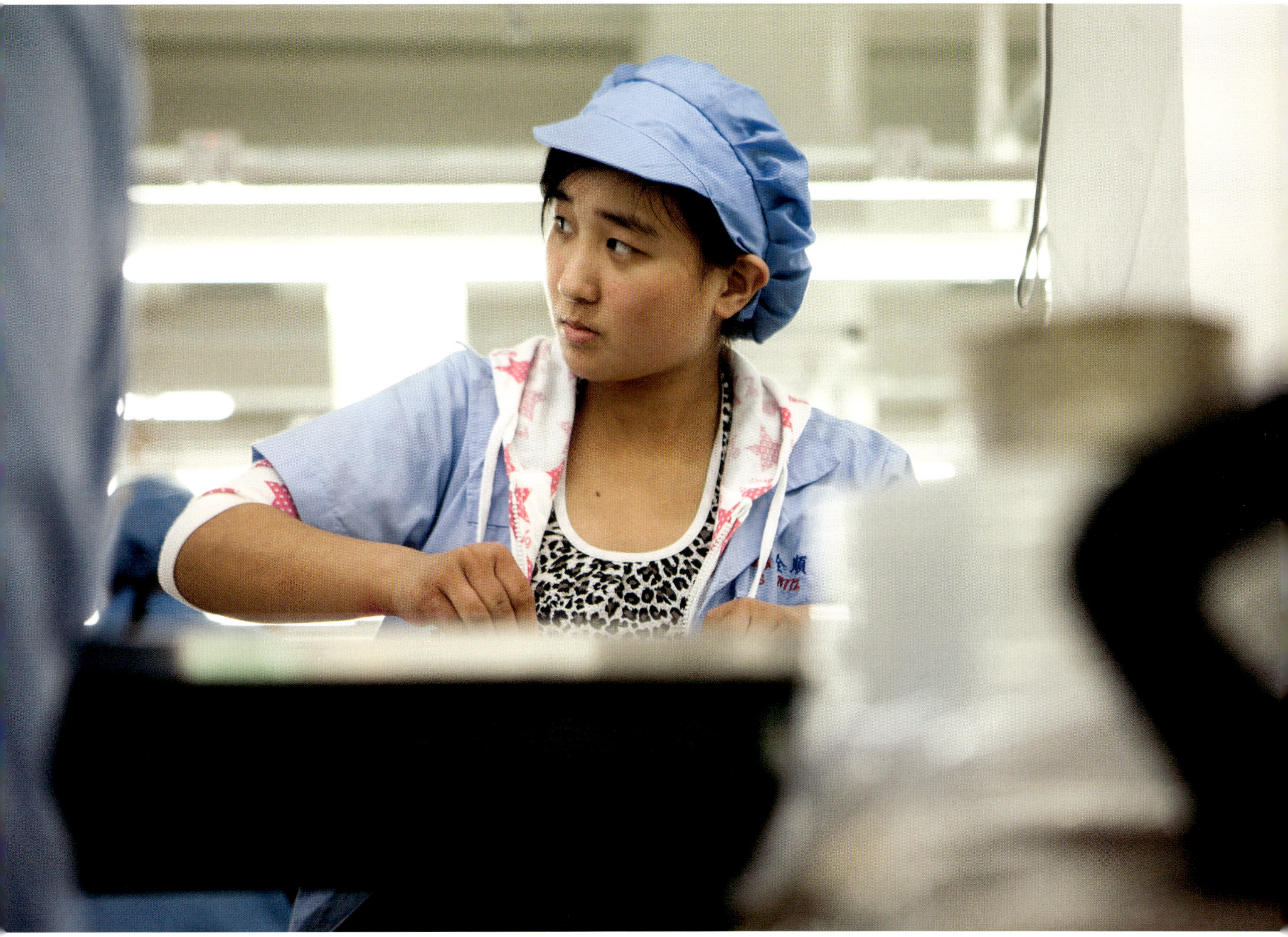

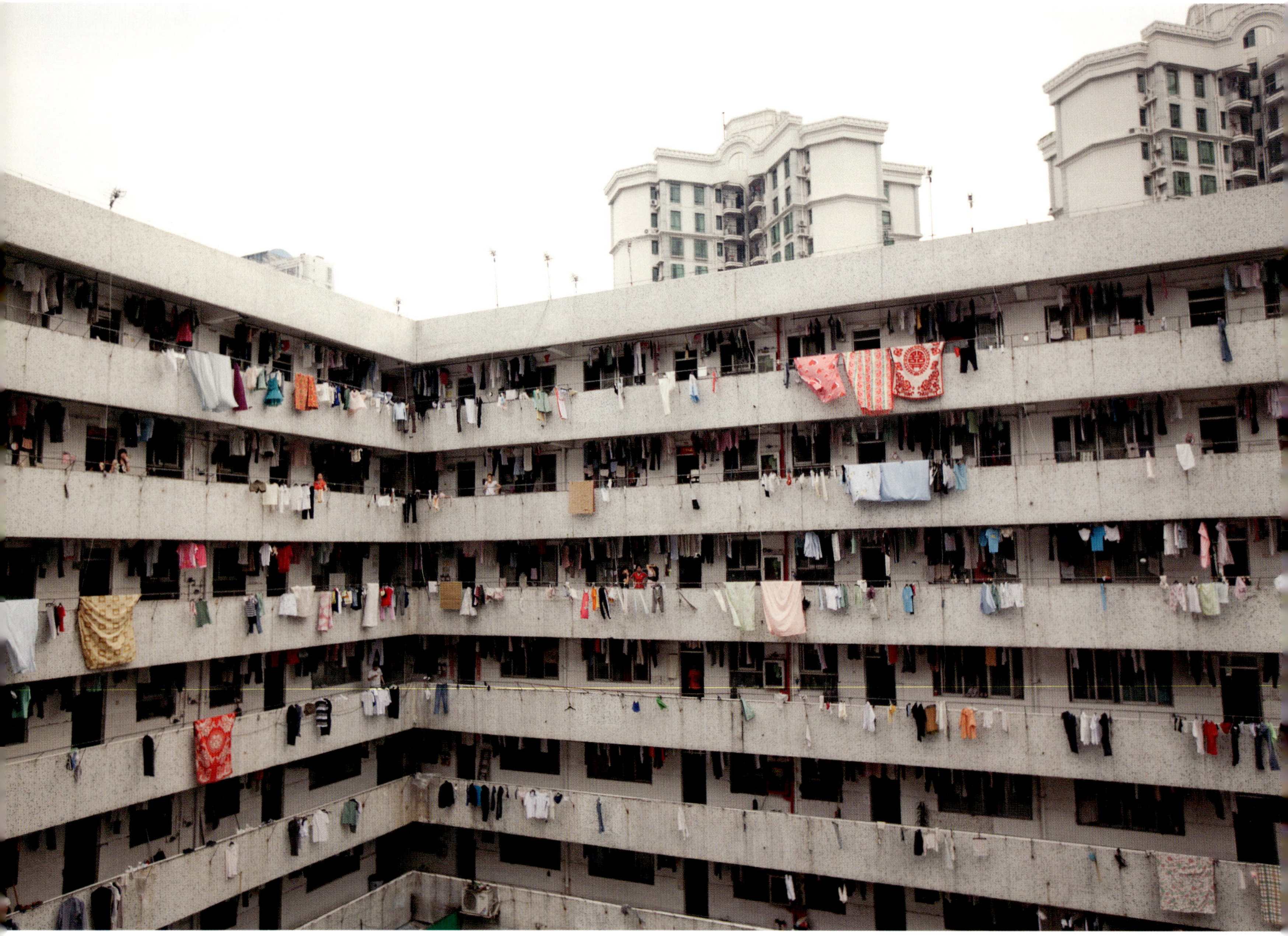

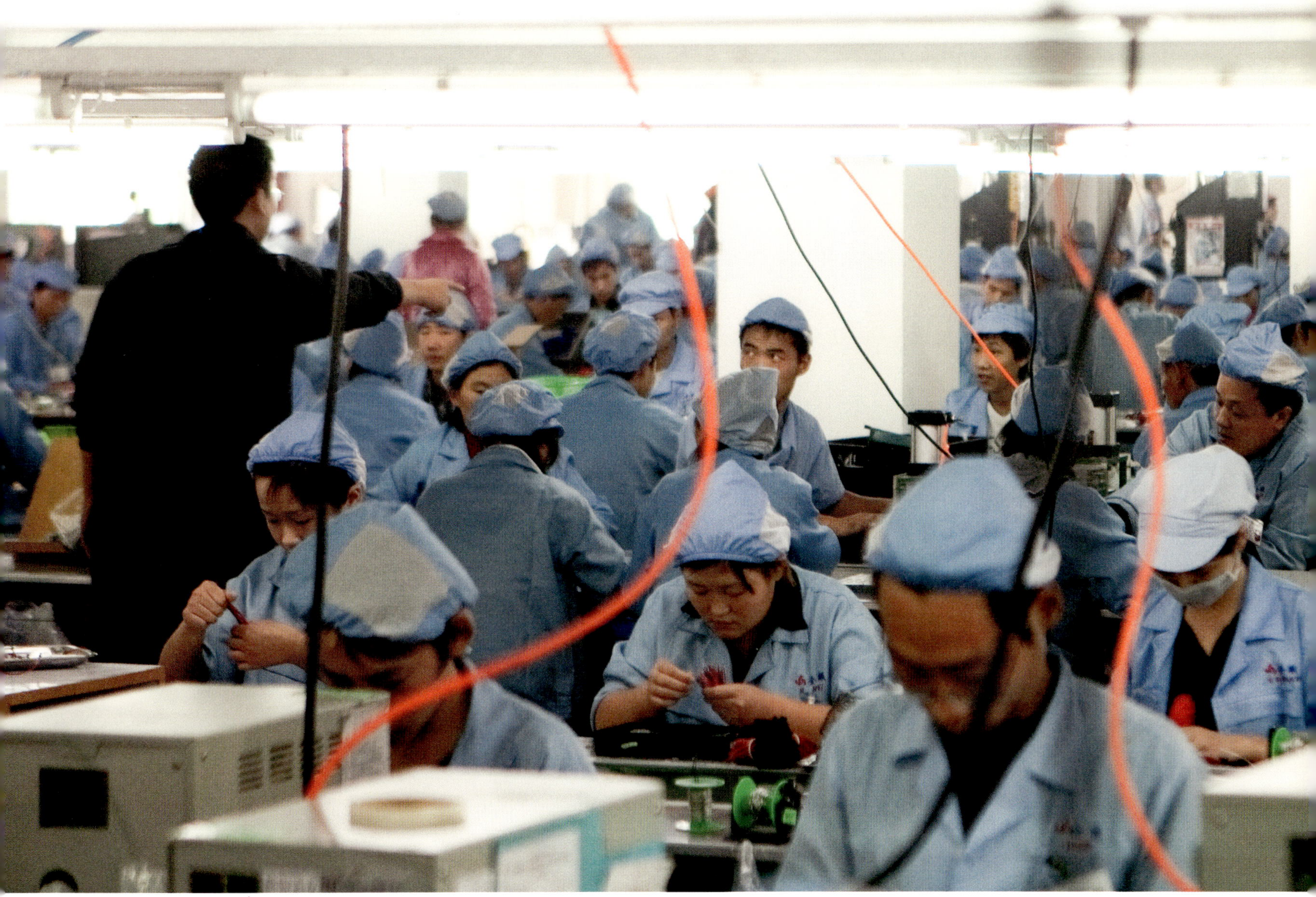

»Nach dem Neujahrsfest fällt es mir immer sehr schwer, mich von meiner Familie und meinen Freunden zu verabschieden. So bin ich manchmal erst mit 1 oder 2 Wochen Verspätung wieder auf der Arbeit erschienen.«

»After the New Year celebrations, I always had a hard time saying goodbye to my family and friends. So, sometimes I was one or two weeks late when I arrived back at work.«

Tan Yaru, 20

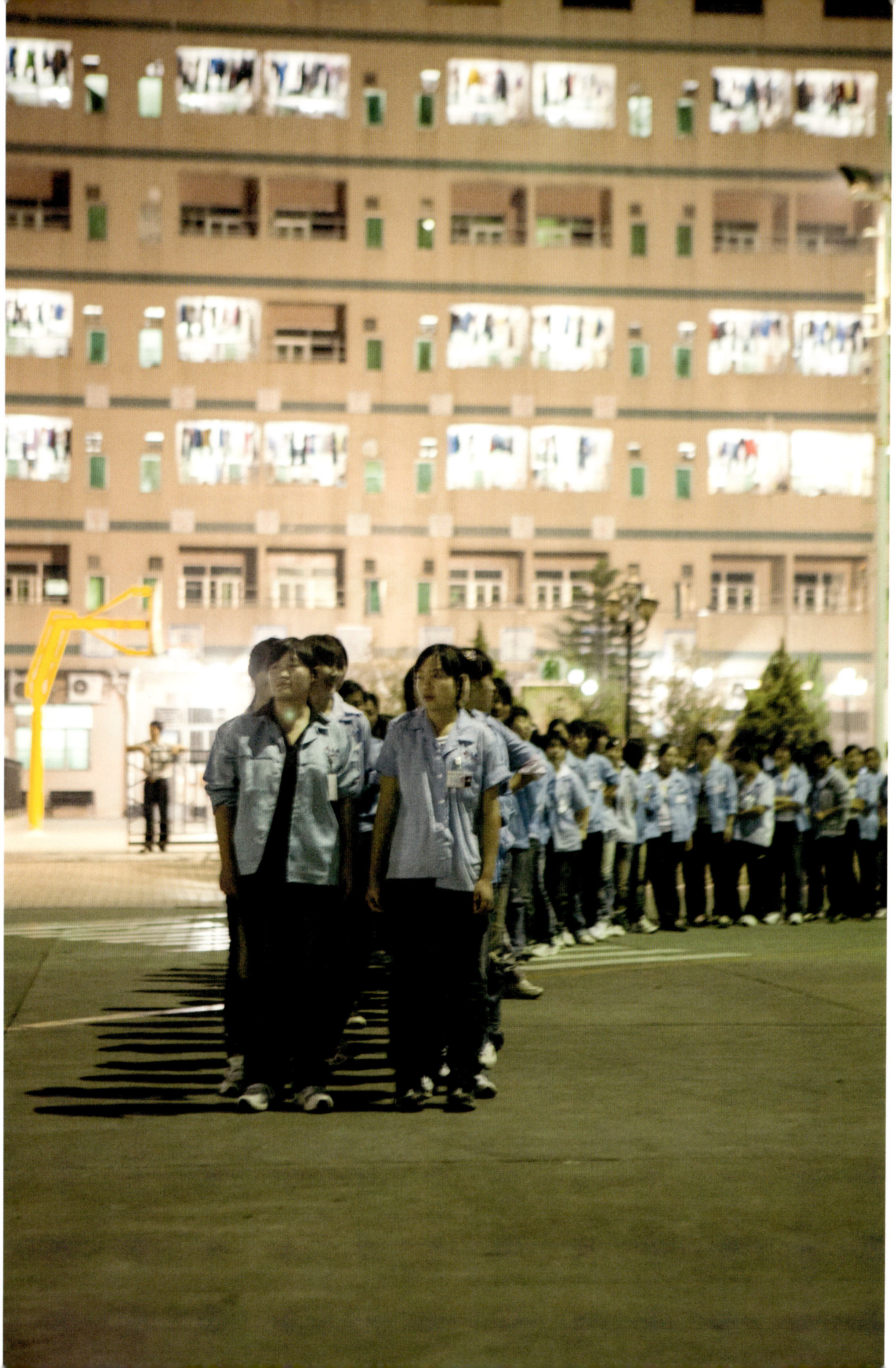

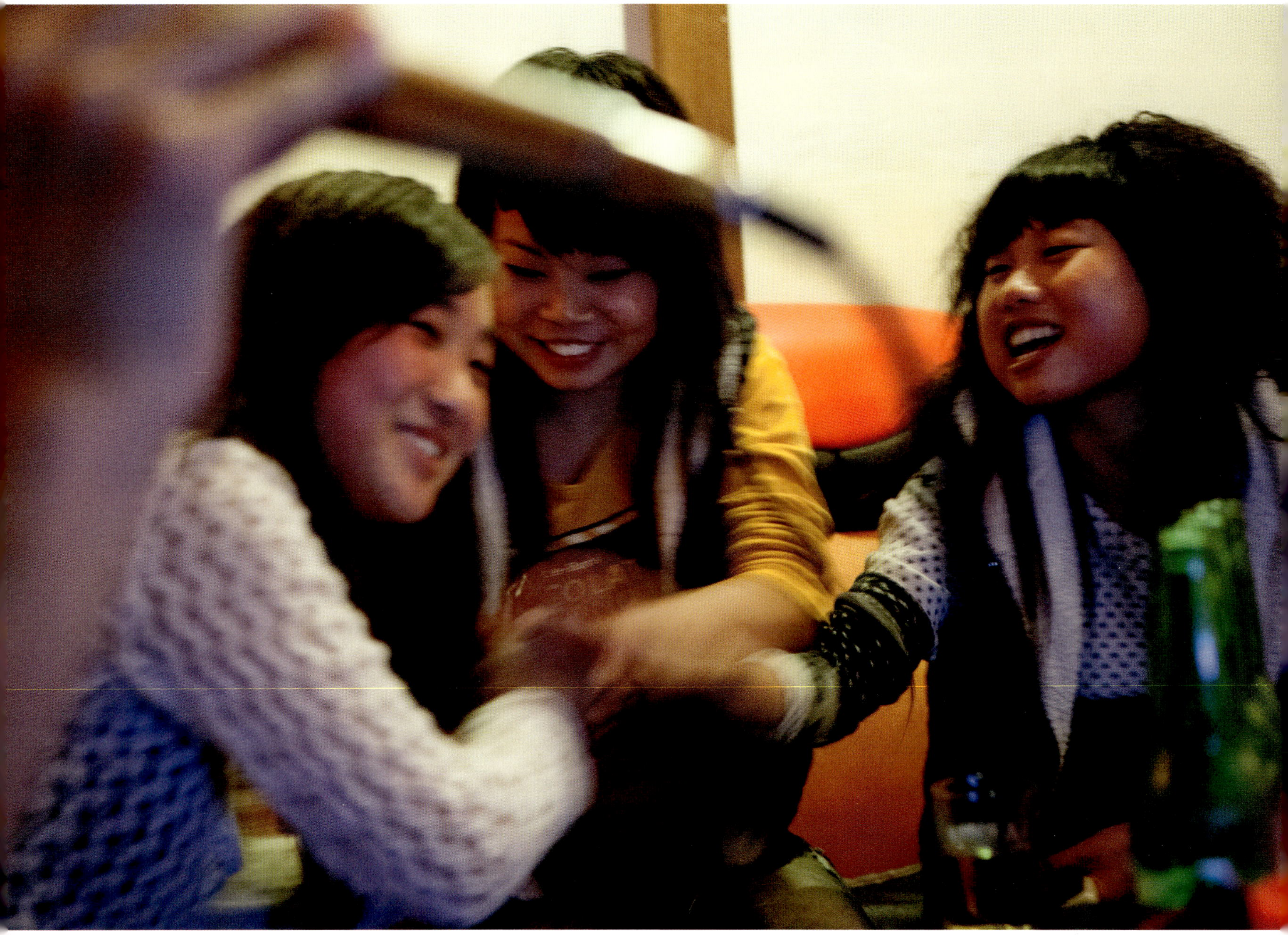

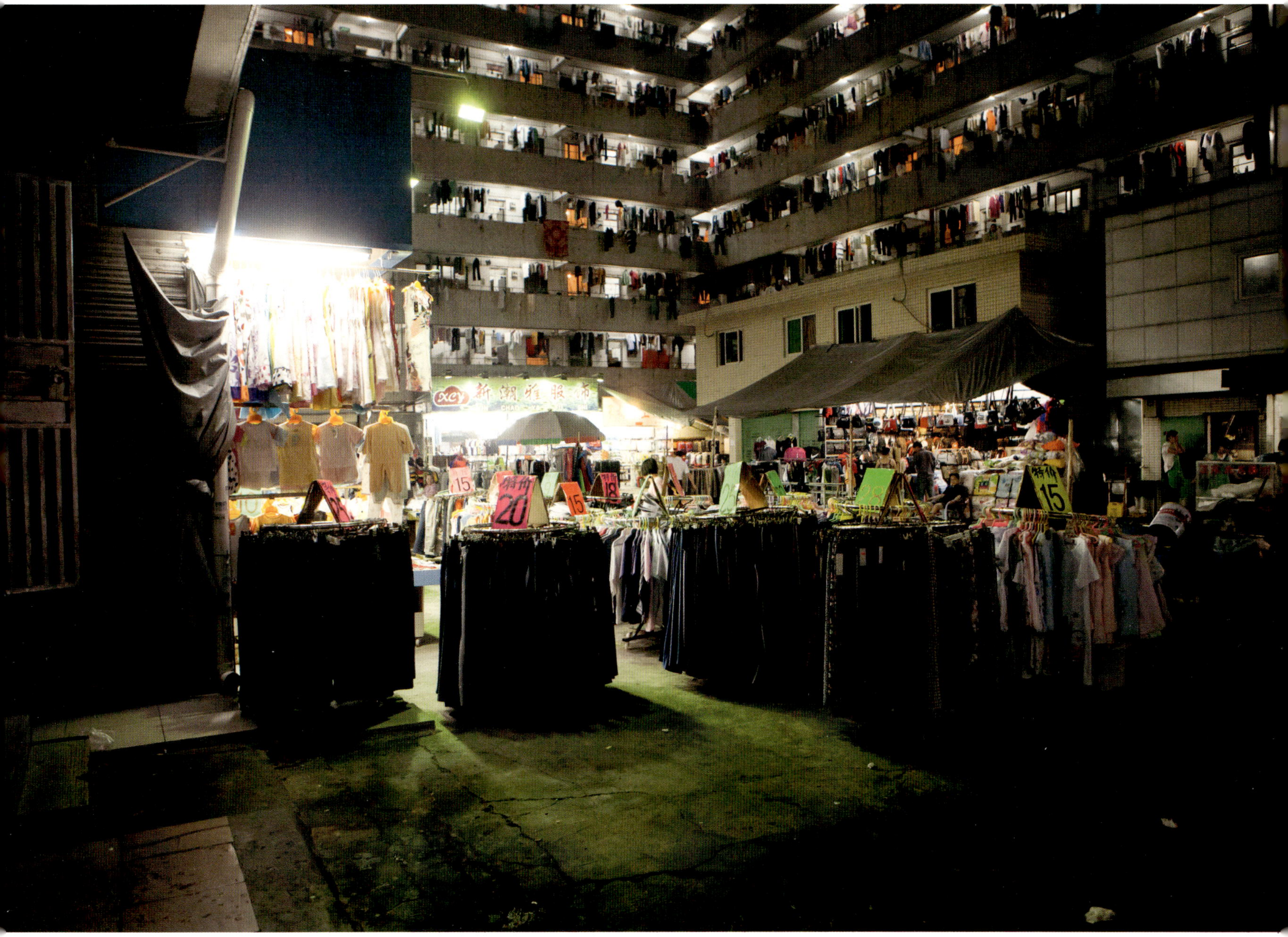

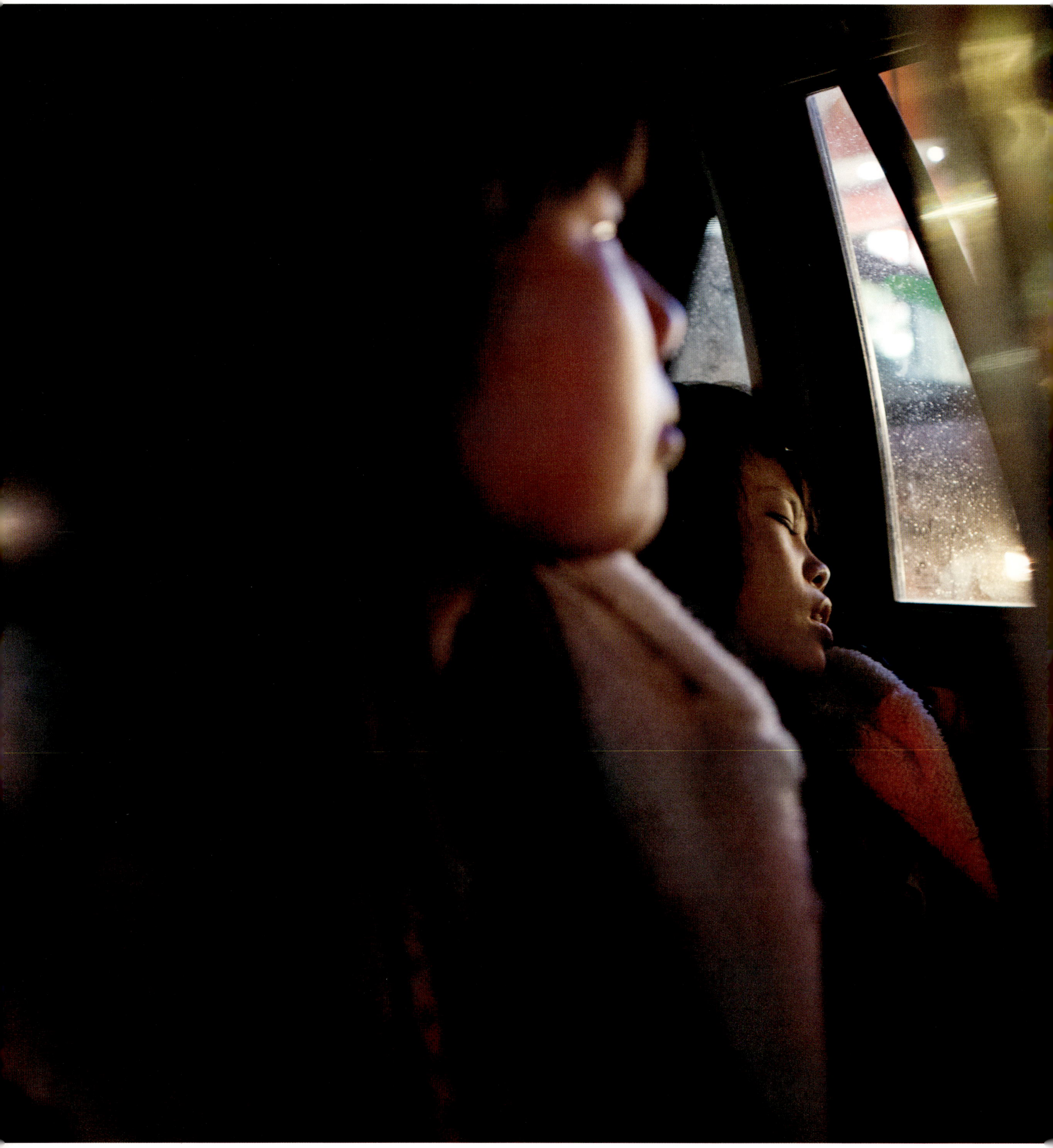

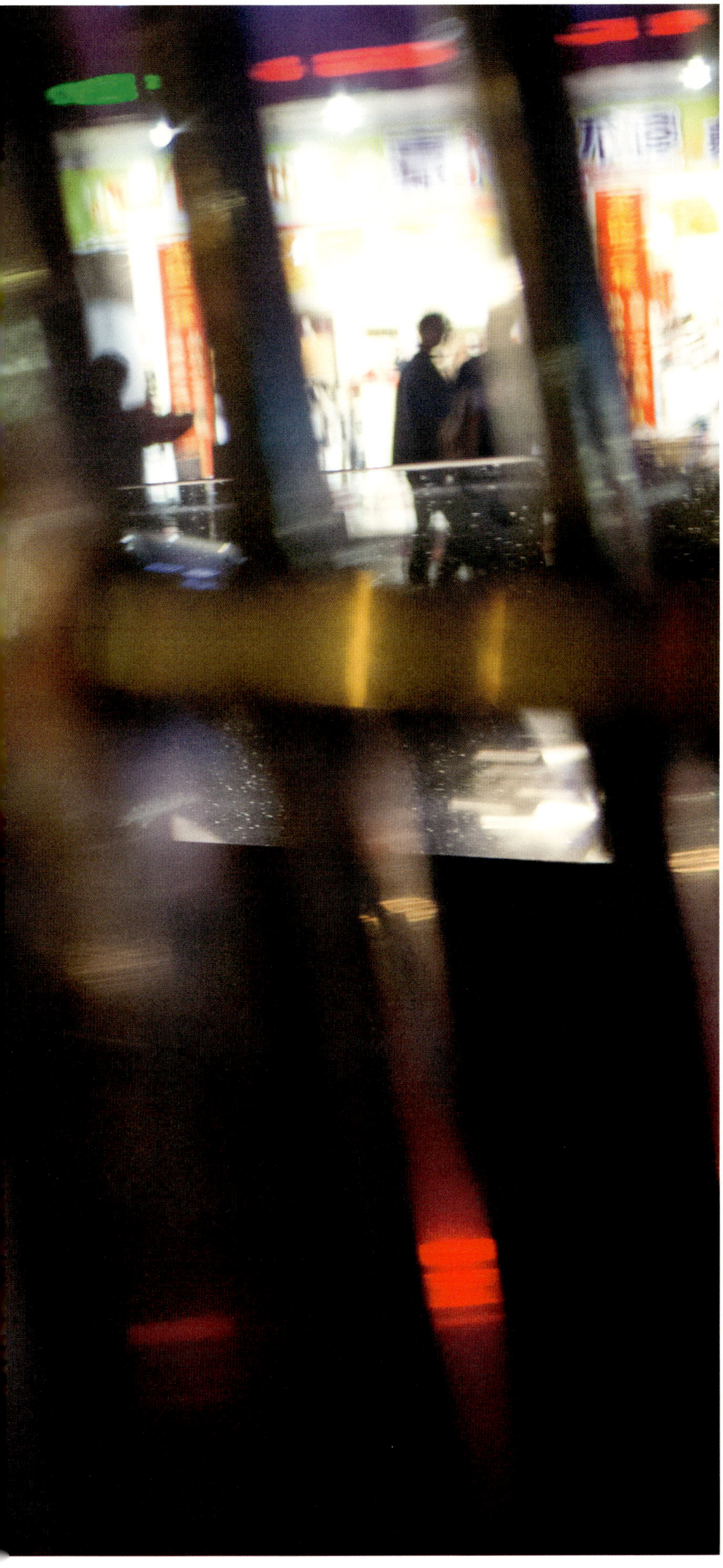

6

Wang Xiuxiu

Hostess, Dongguan
Hostess, Dongguan

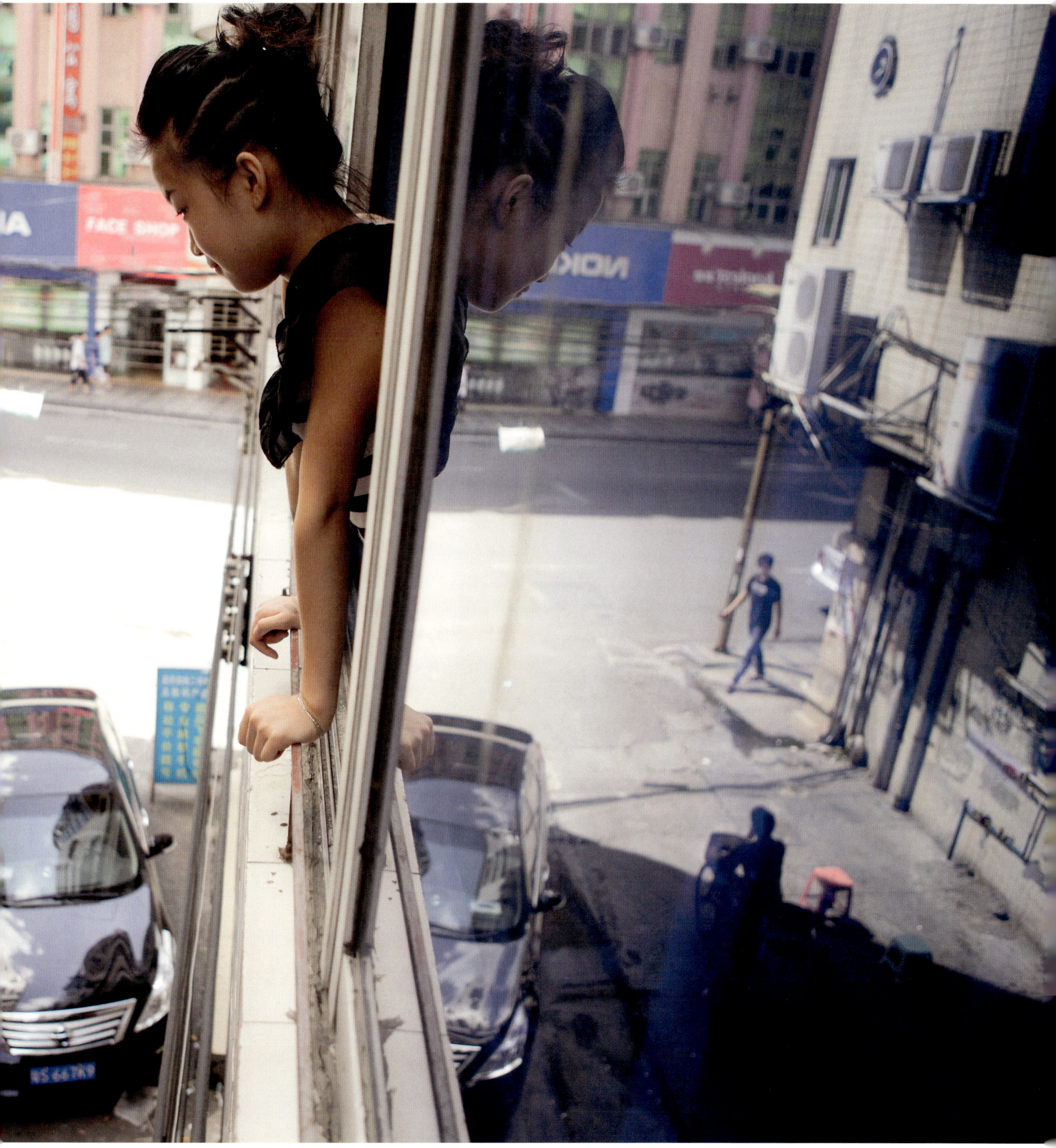
FACE SHOP

»Ich bin nicht wegen des Geldes von zu Hause abgehauen. Nachdem meine Stiefmutter eingezogen war, gab es für mich dort einfach keinen Platz mehr.«

»I didn't run away from home for the money. After my stepmother moved in, there was simply no room for me there anymore.«

Wang Xiuxiu, 21

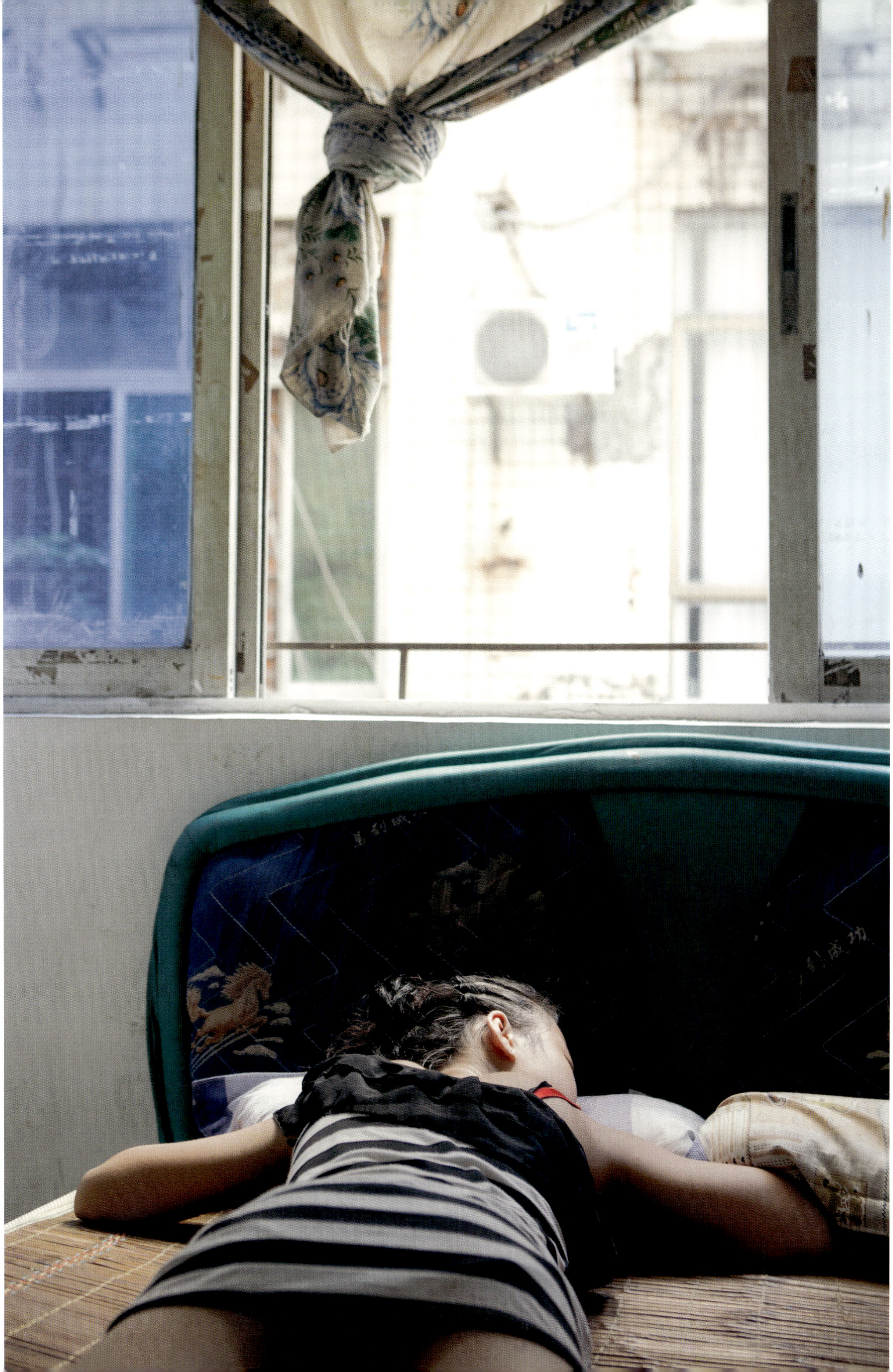

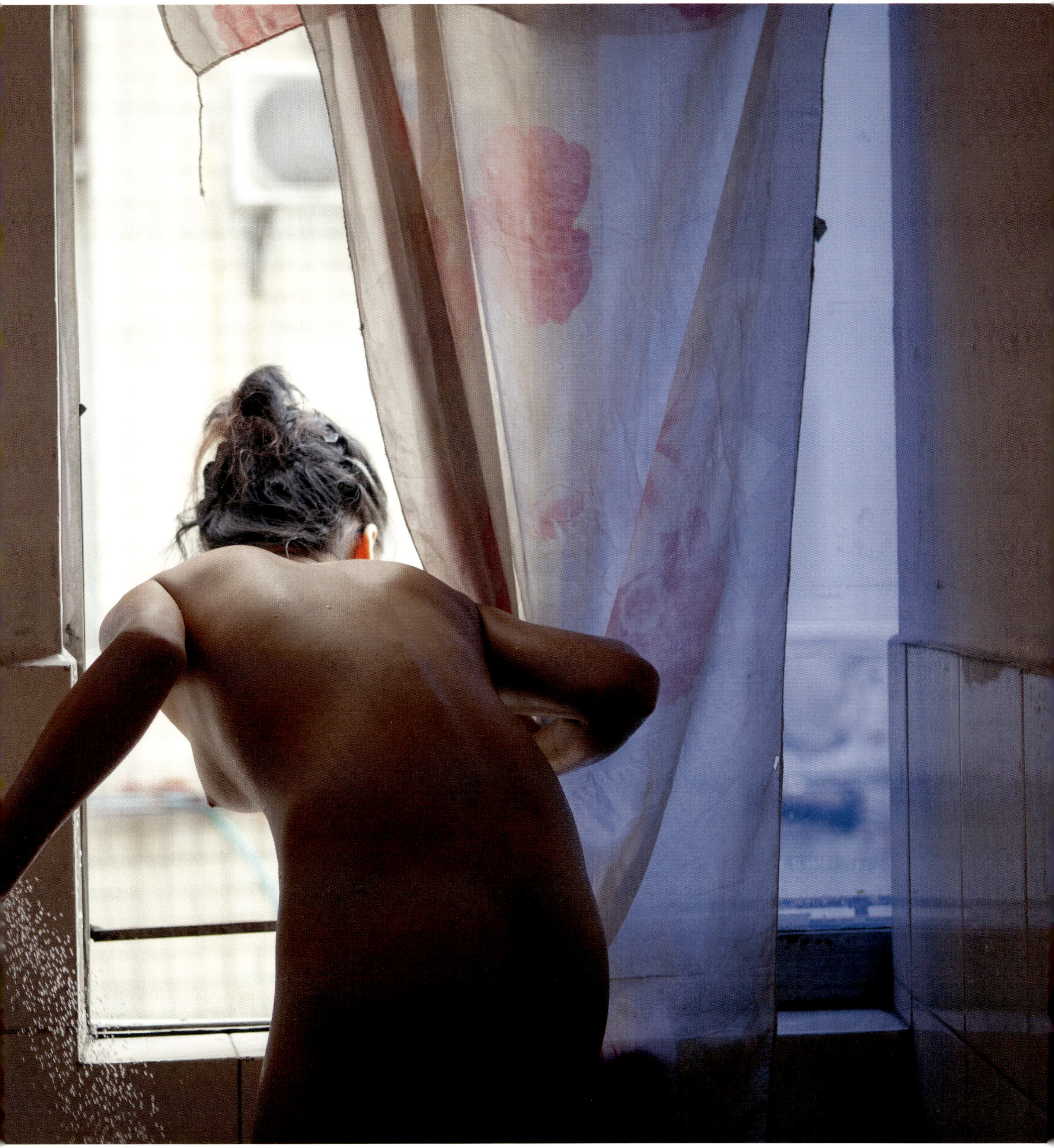

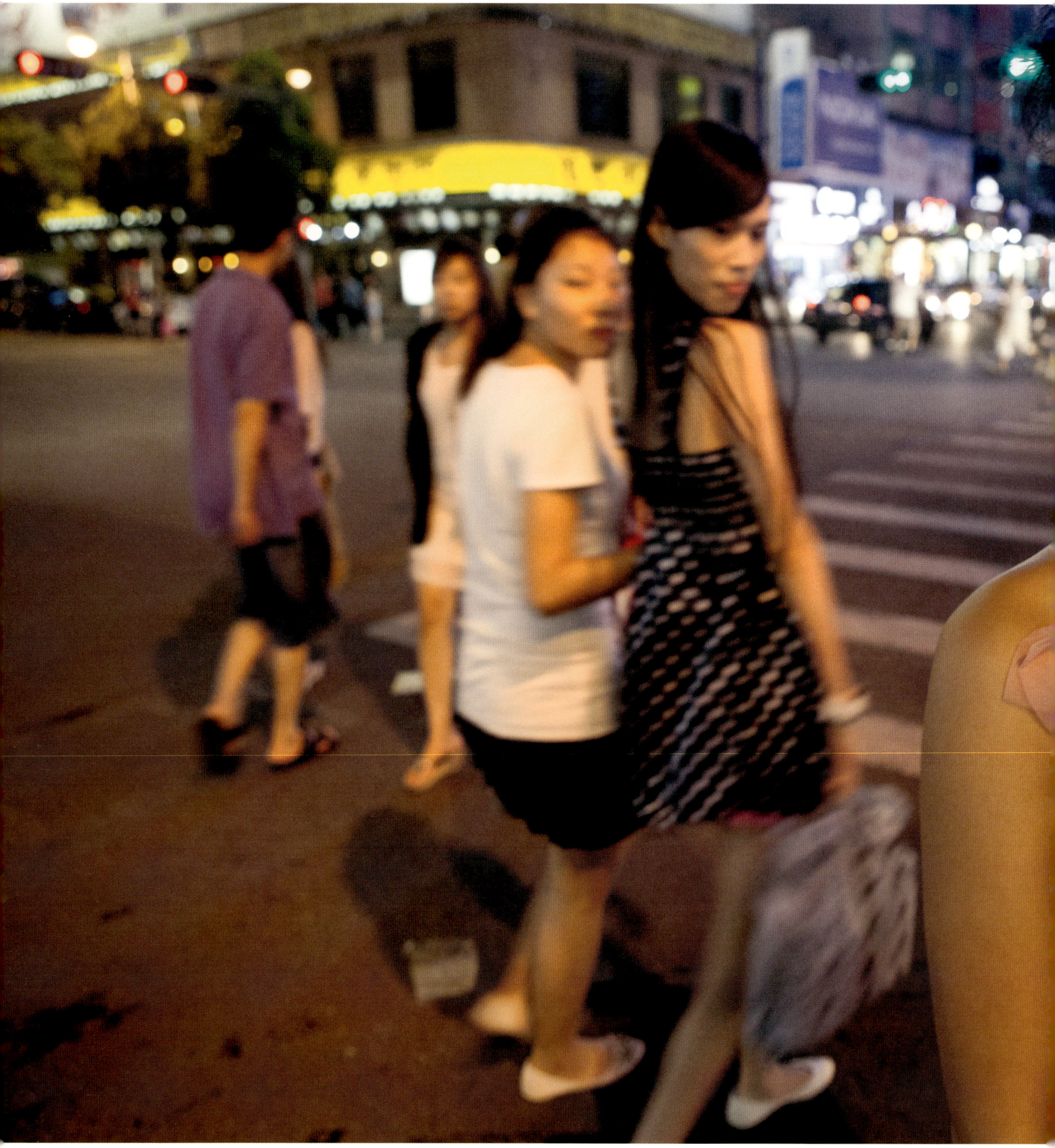

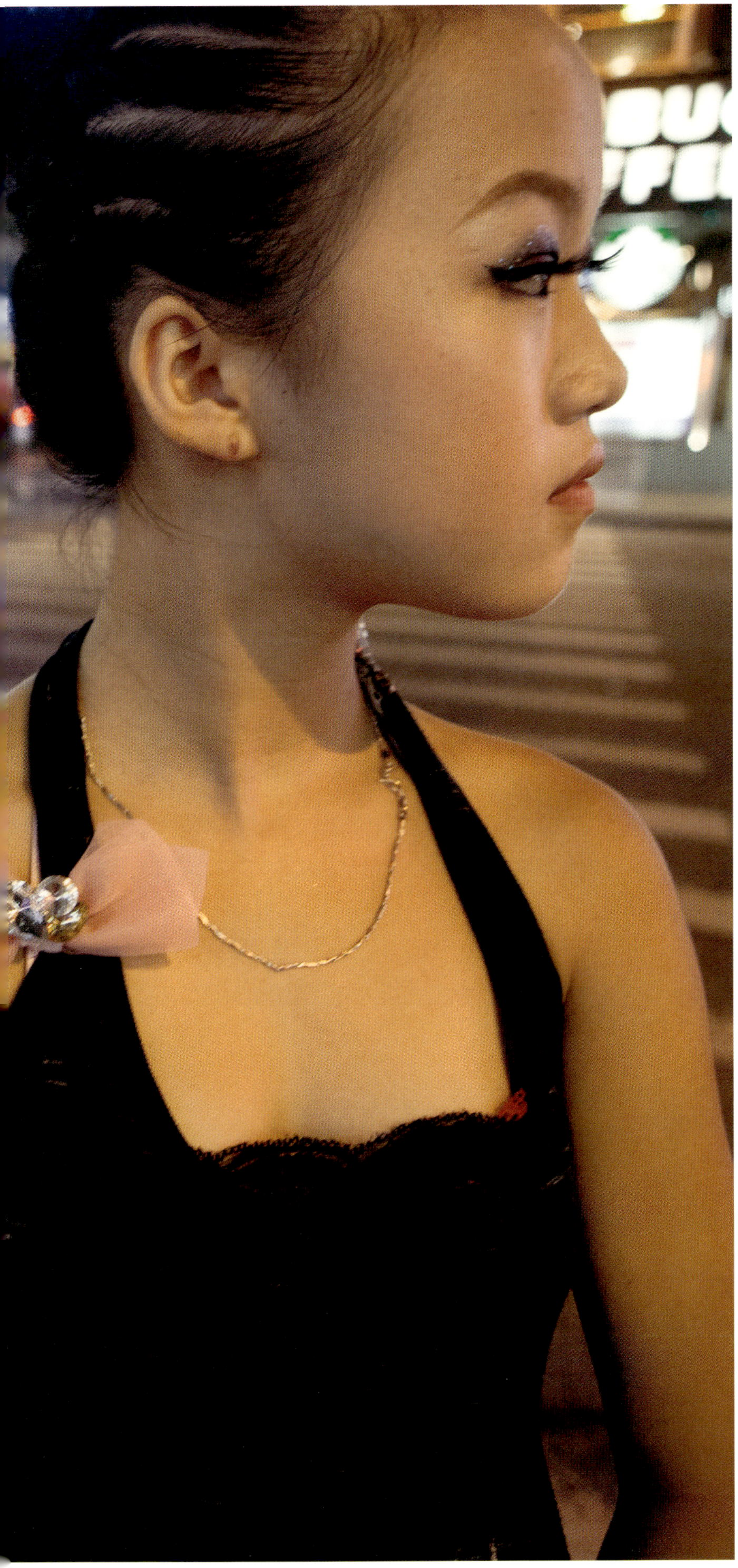

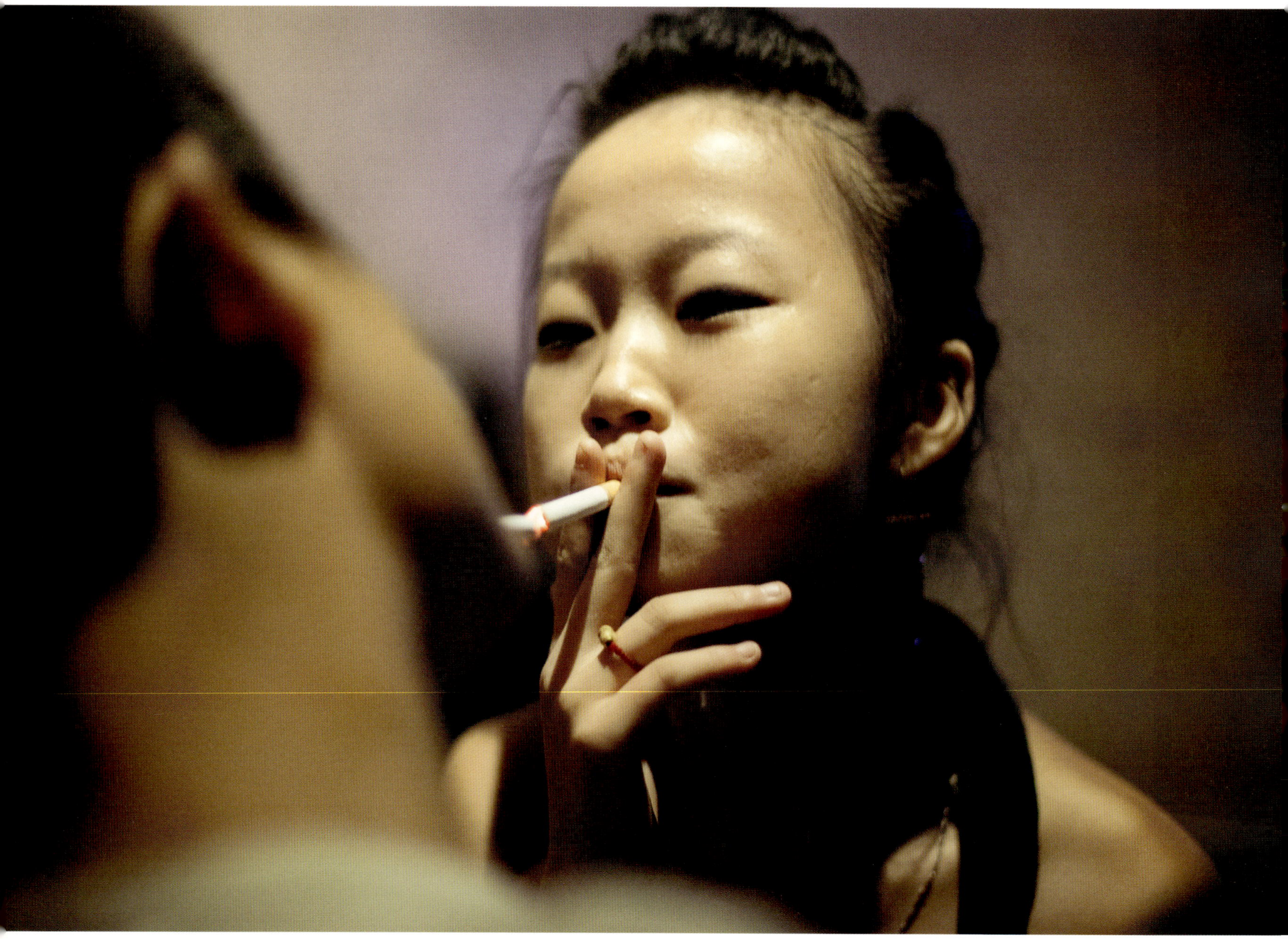

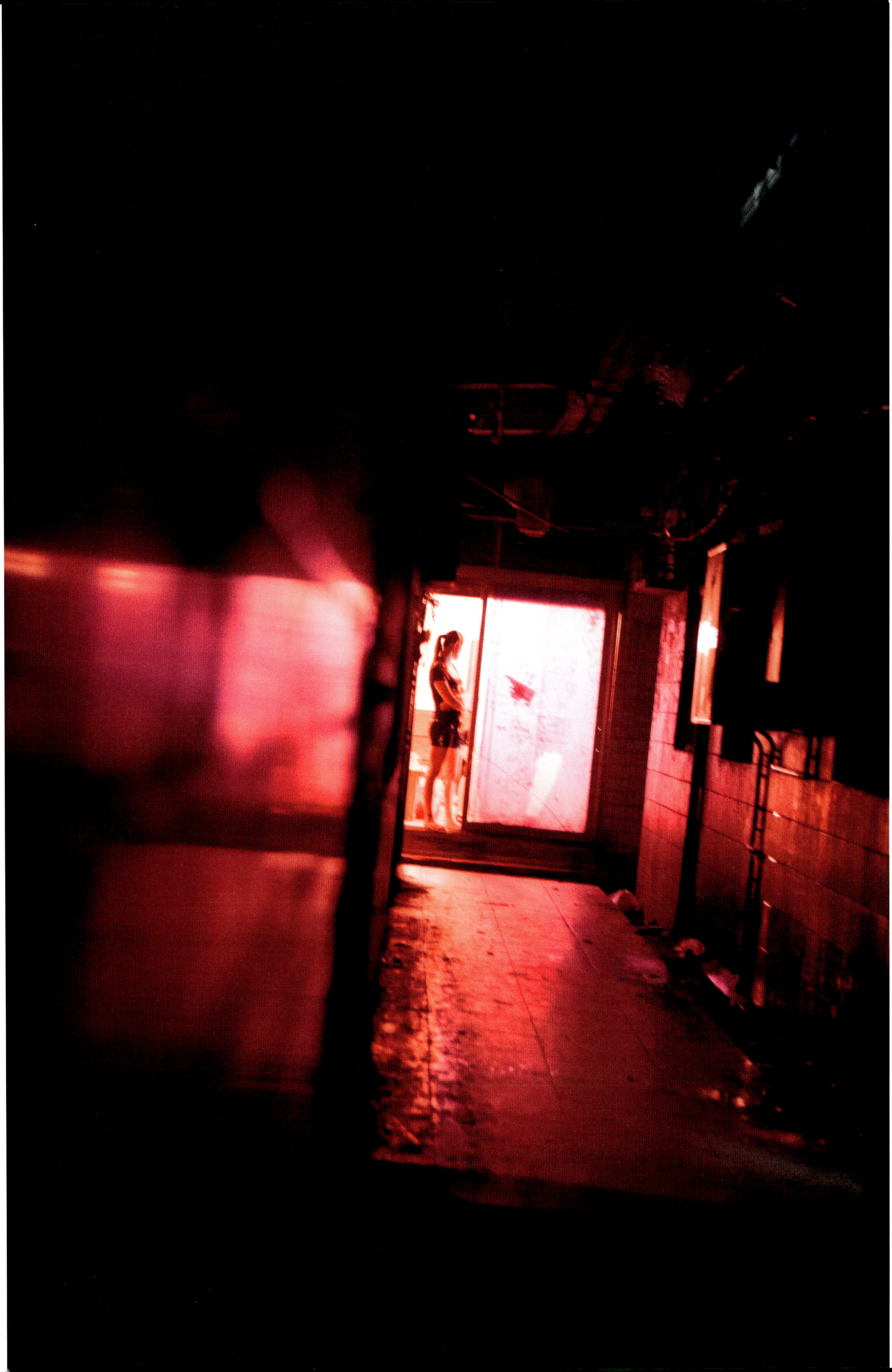

»Je mehr Geld so ein Kerl hat, desto schwieriger ist es, sein Herz zu gewinnen.«

»The more money a guy has, the harder it is to win his heart.«

Wang Xiuxiu, 21

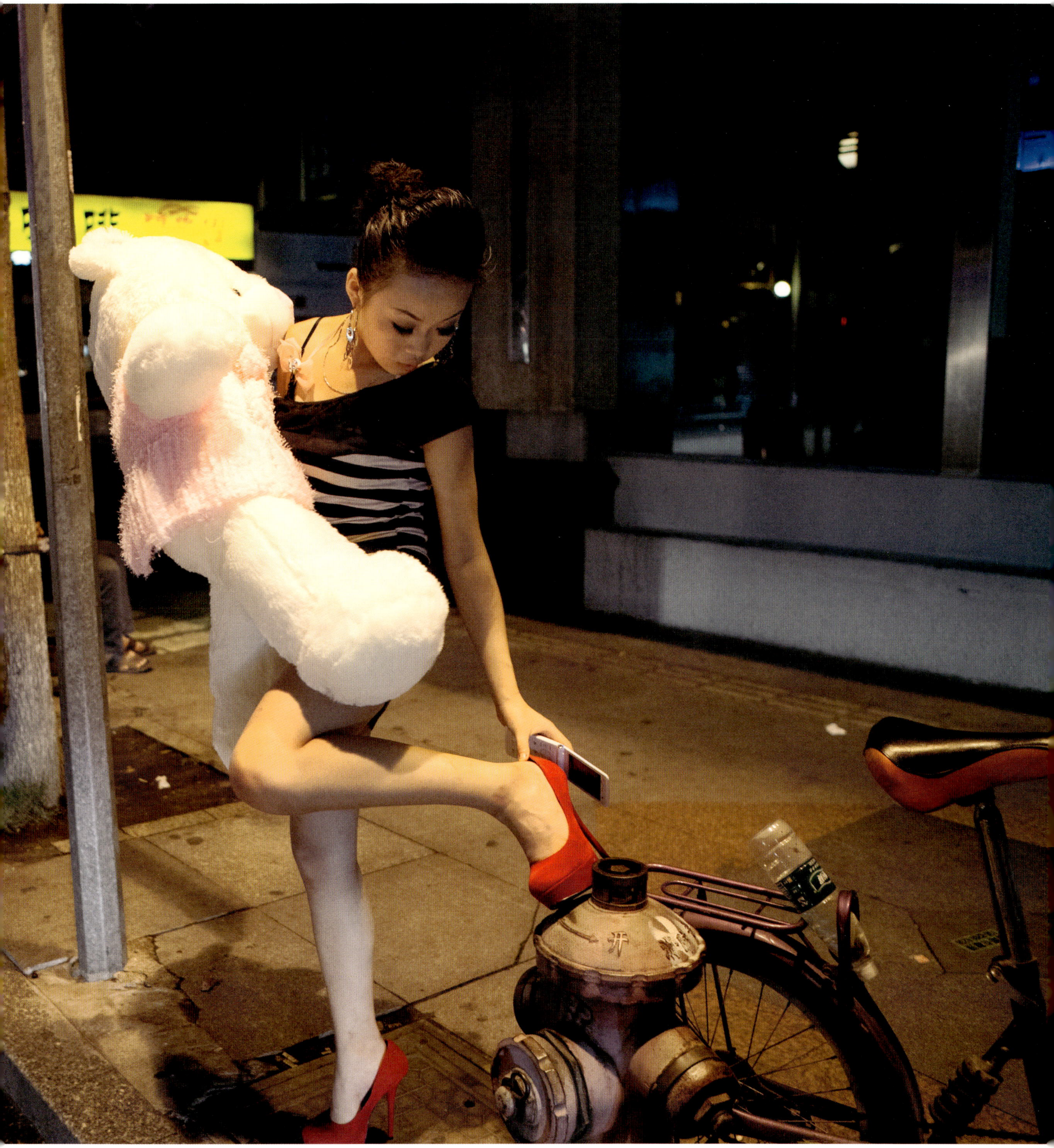

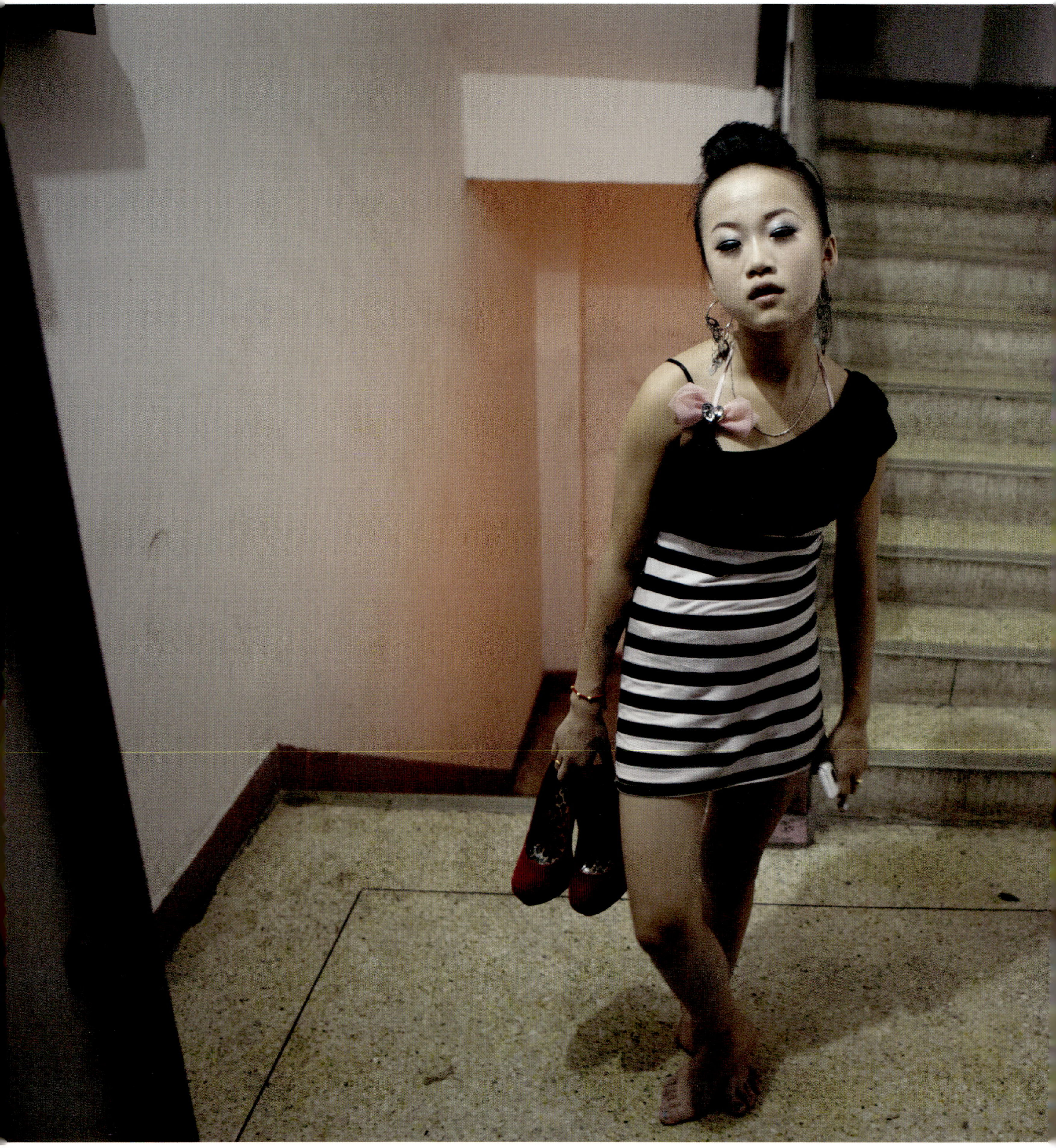

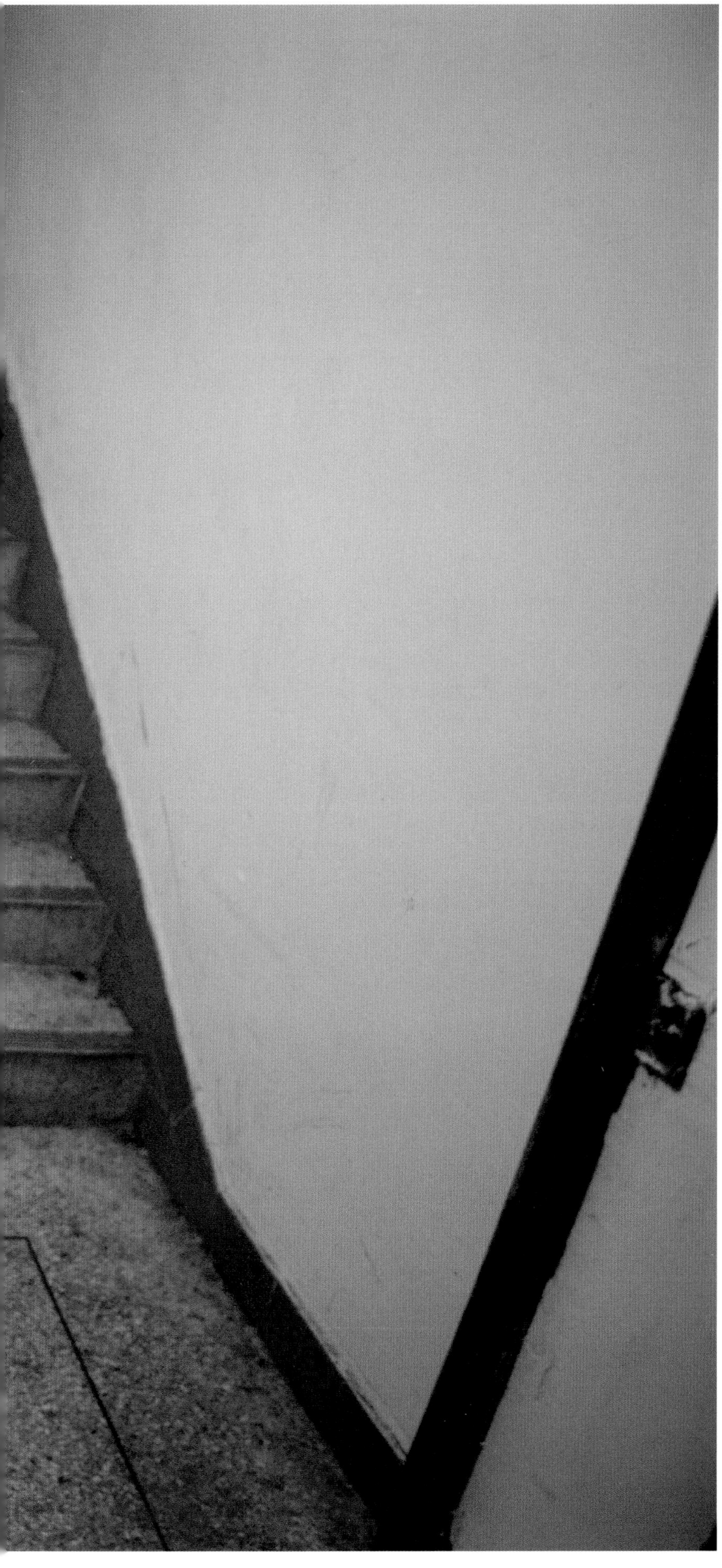

7

Li Bo, Zhou Dong

Müllsammler, Peking
Garbage Collectors, Beijing

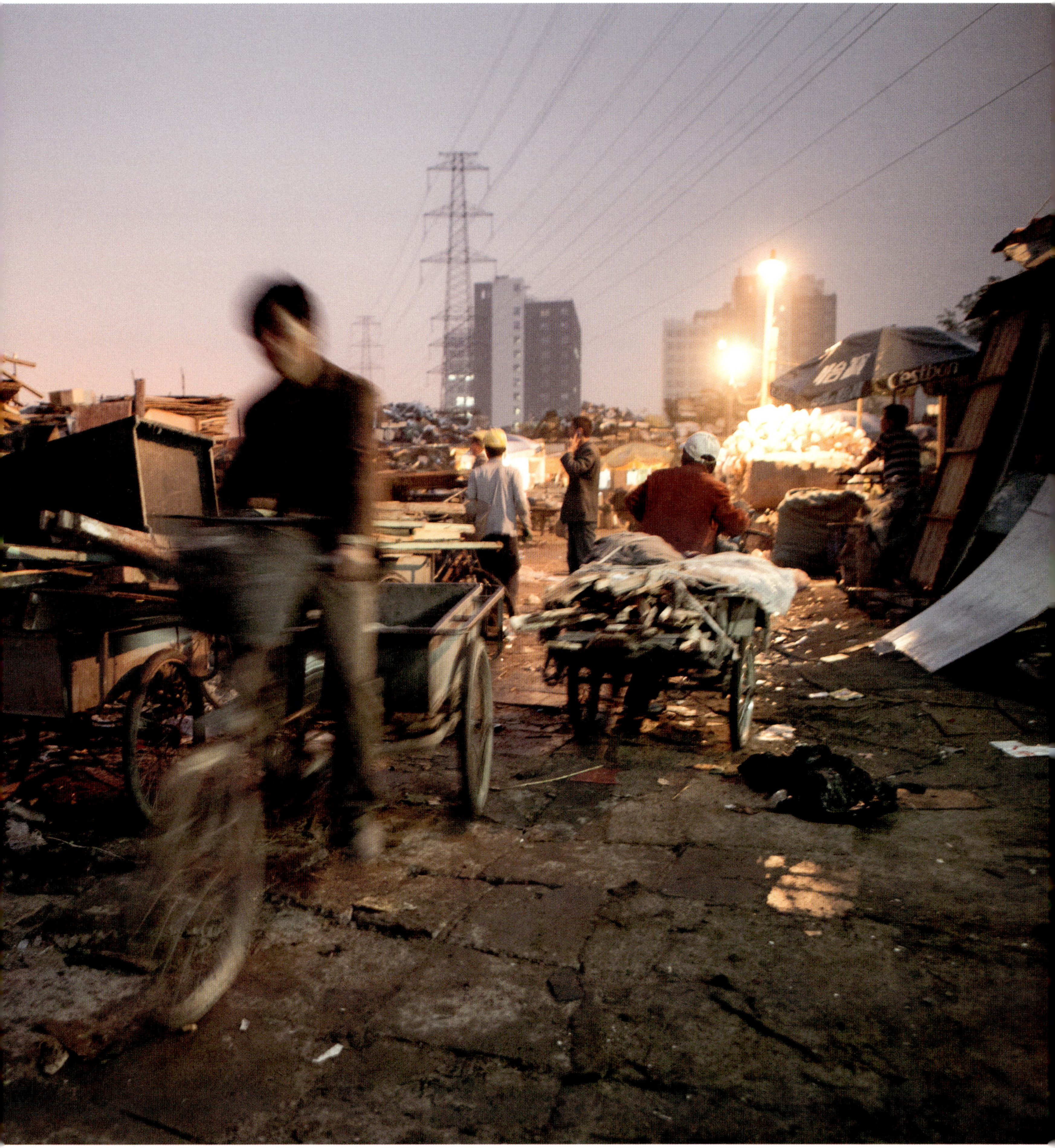
Cestbon

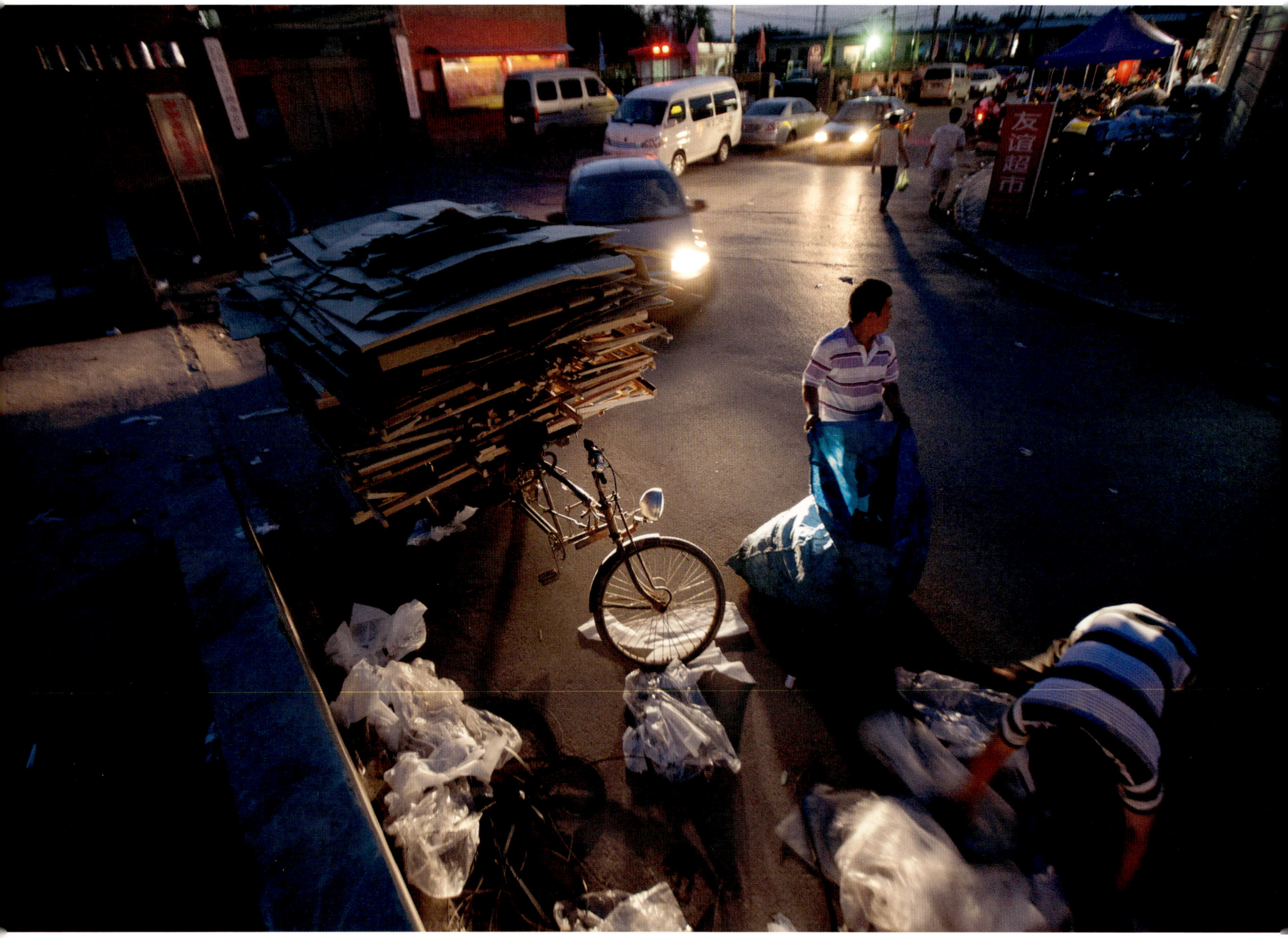
友谊超市

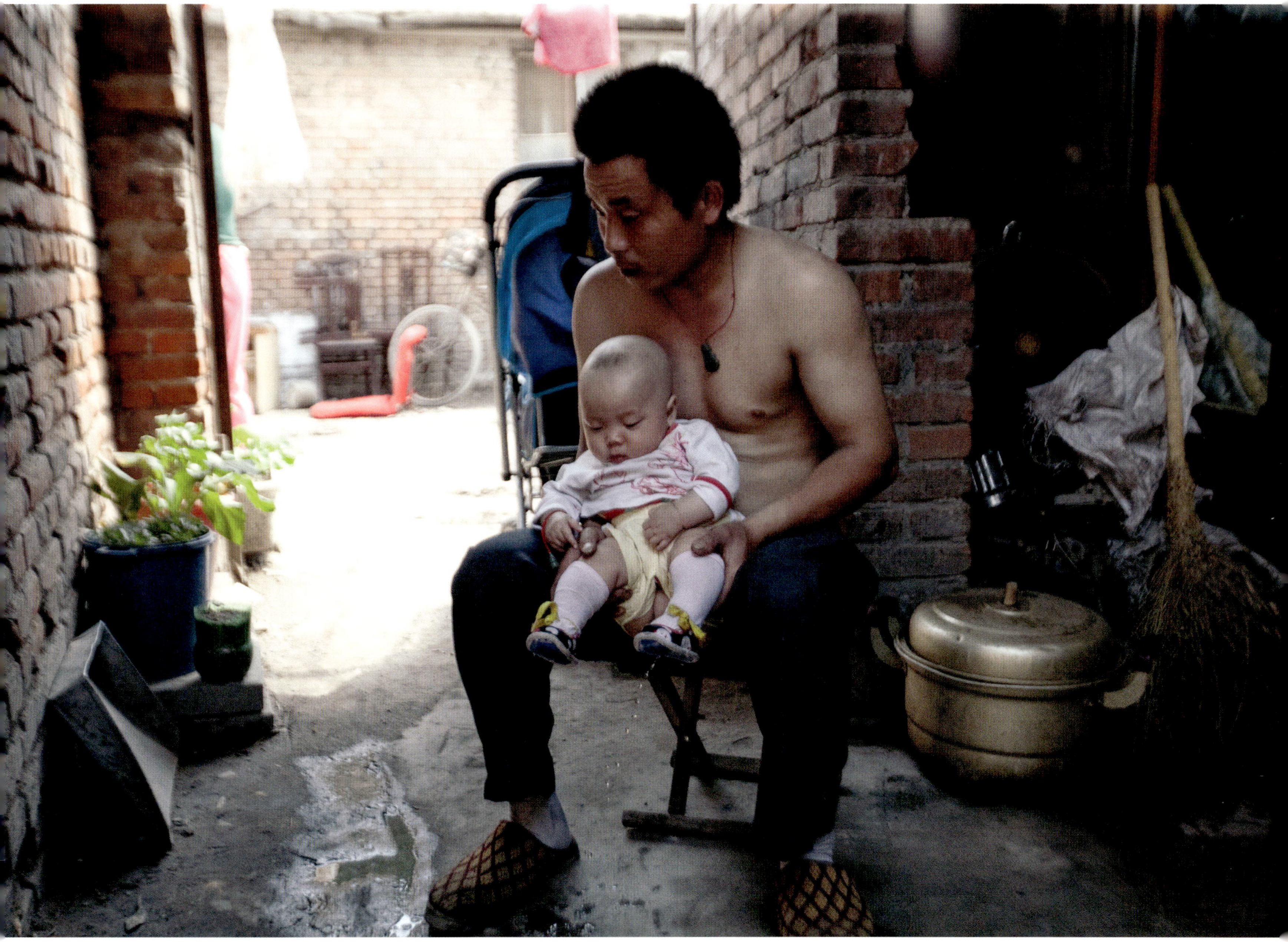

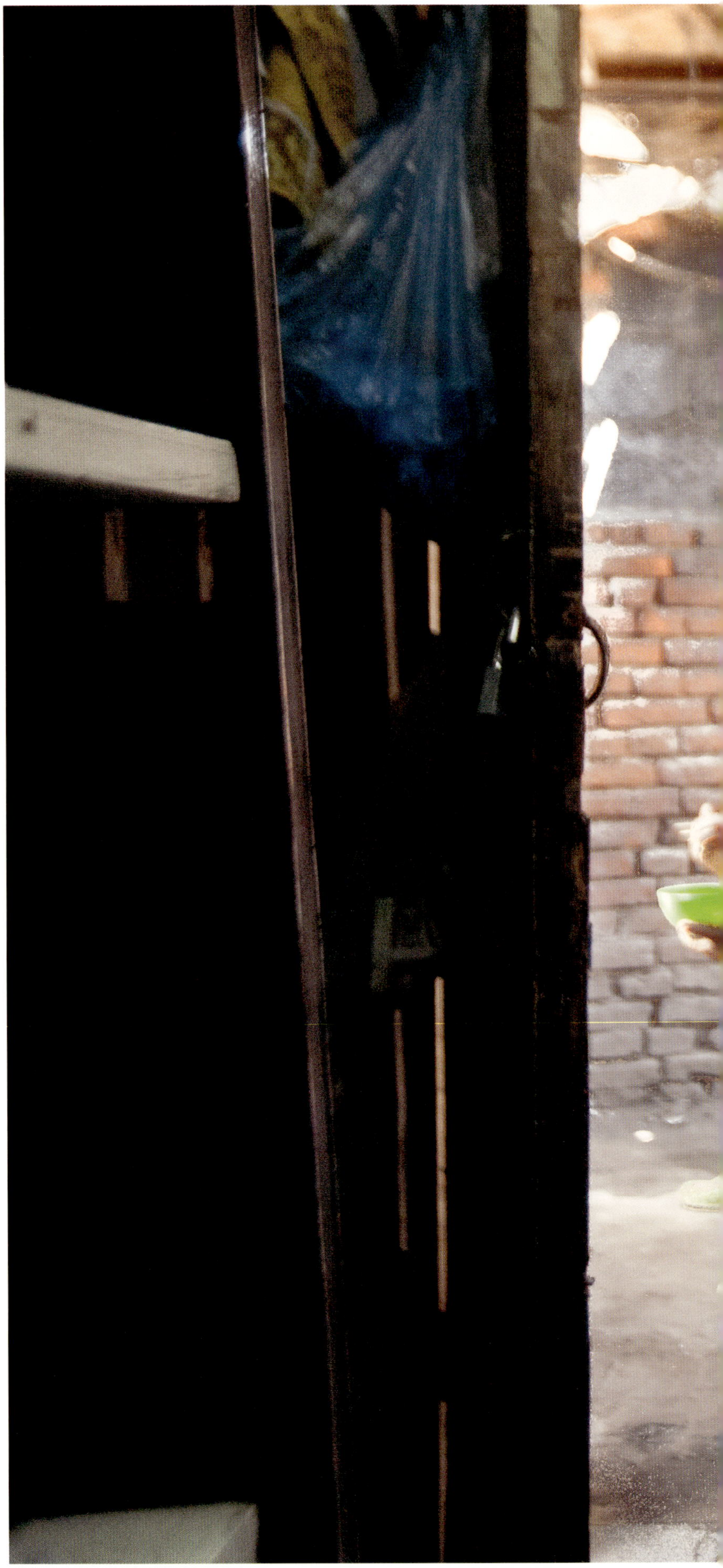

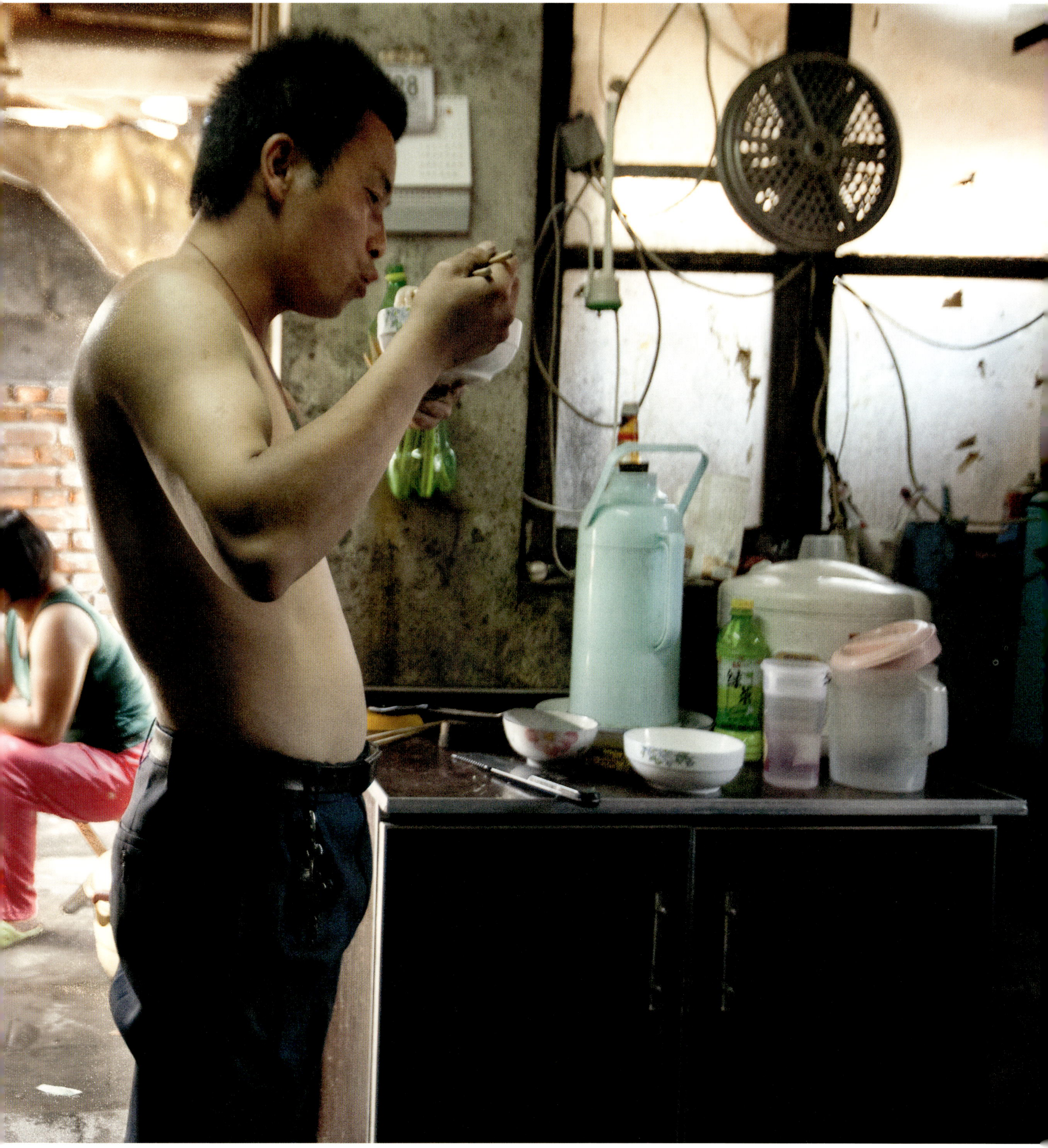

»Viele Wanderarbeiter ohne Ausbildung versuchen sich mit dem Sammeln von Müll eine Existenz aufzubauen. Deshalb ist die Konkurrenz riesengroß.«

»Many migrant workers with no education try to build a new life as garbage collectors. But competition is tough in this business.«

Zhou Dong, 40

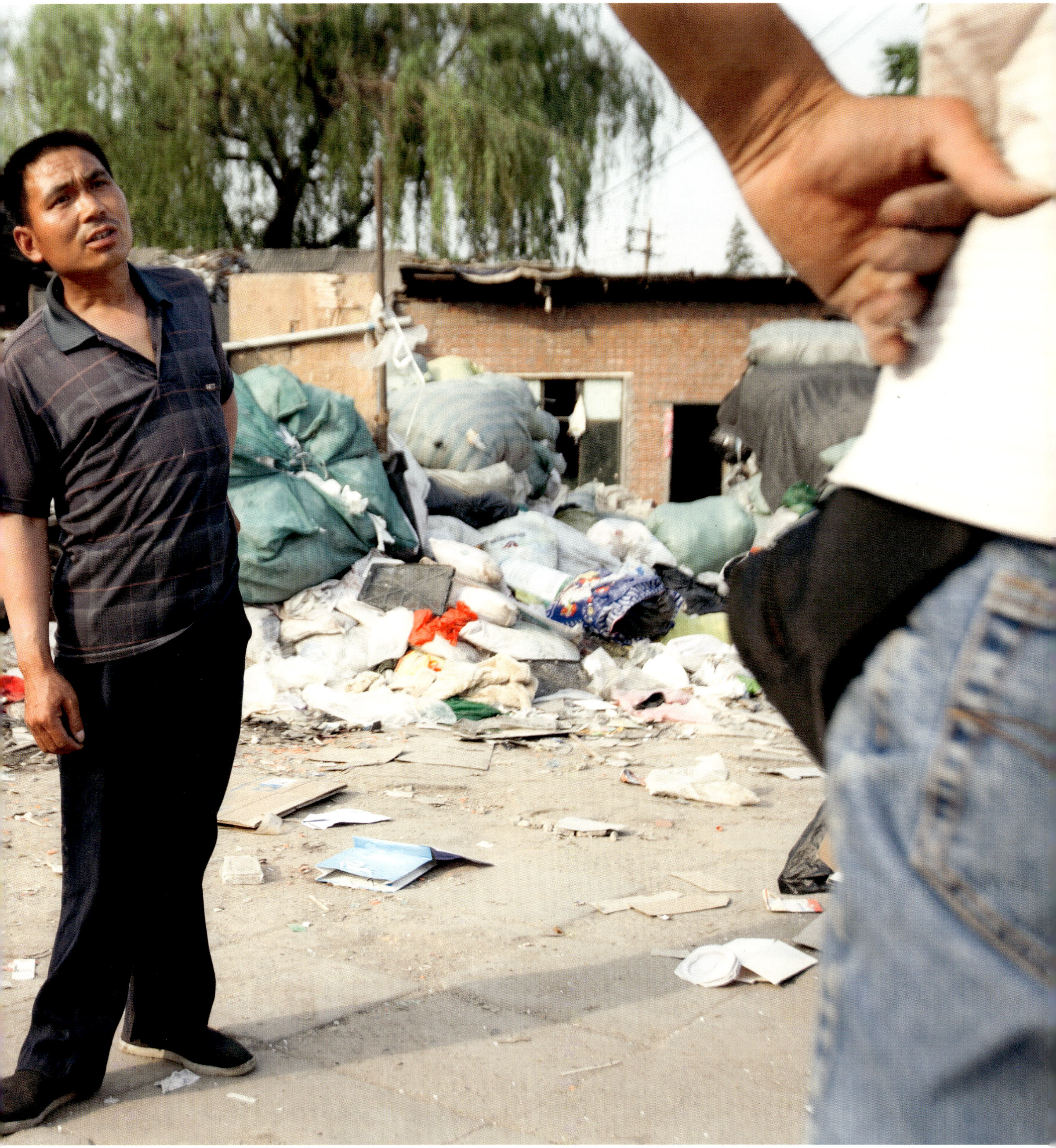

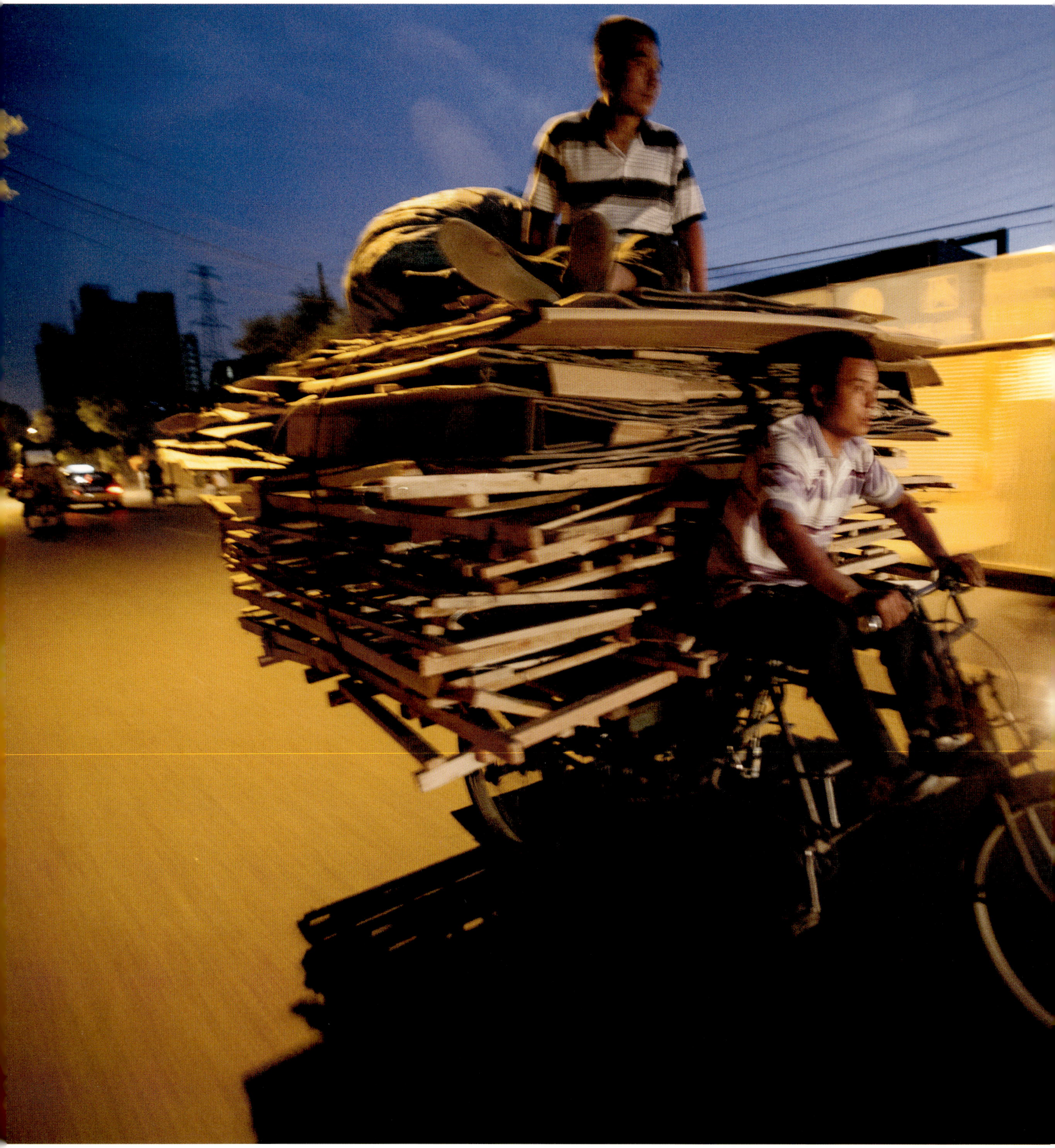

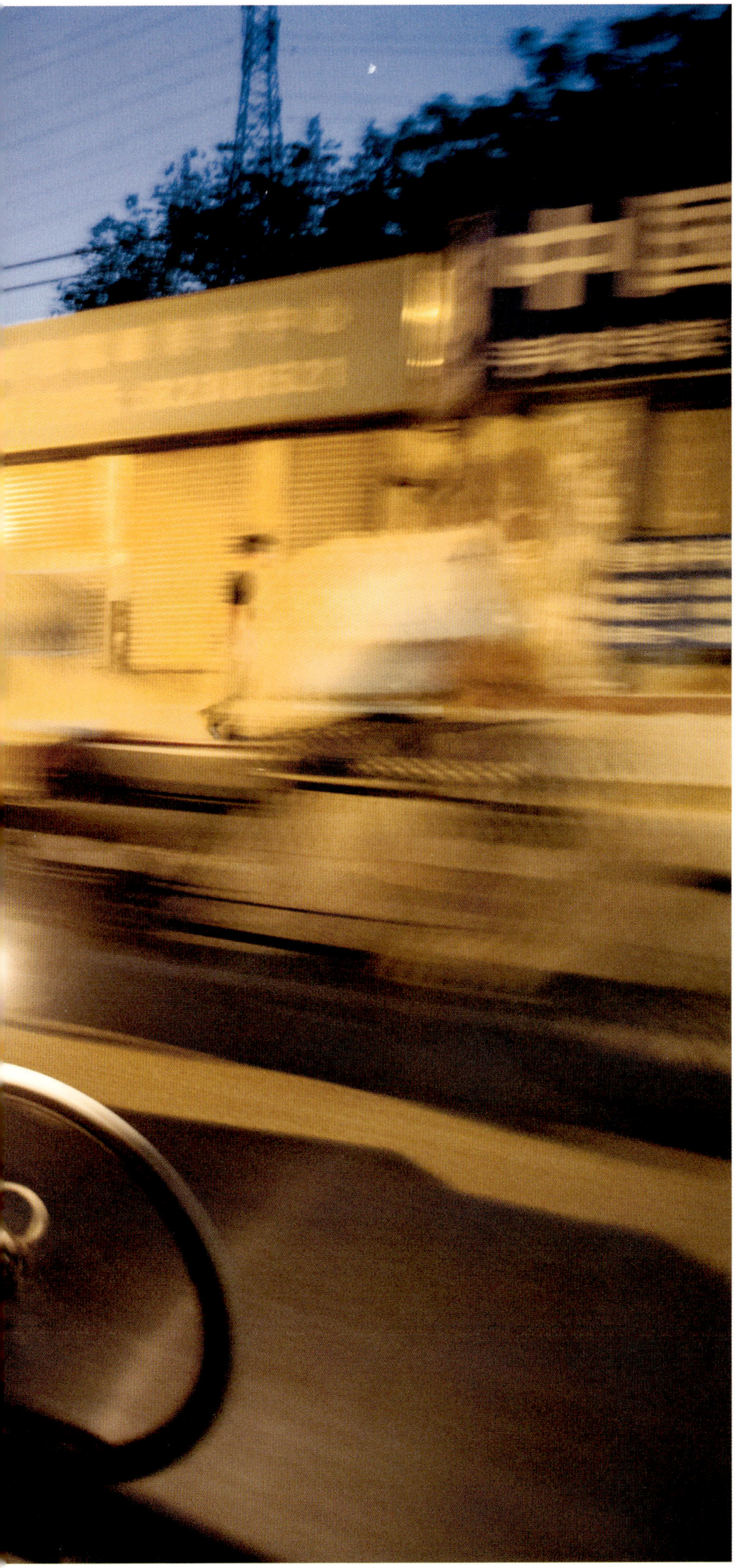

8

Su Feng
Bettler, Guangzhou
Beggar, Guangzhou

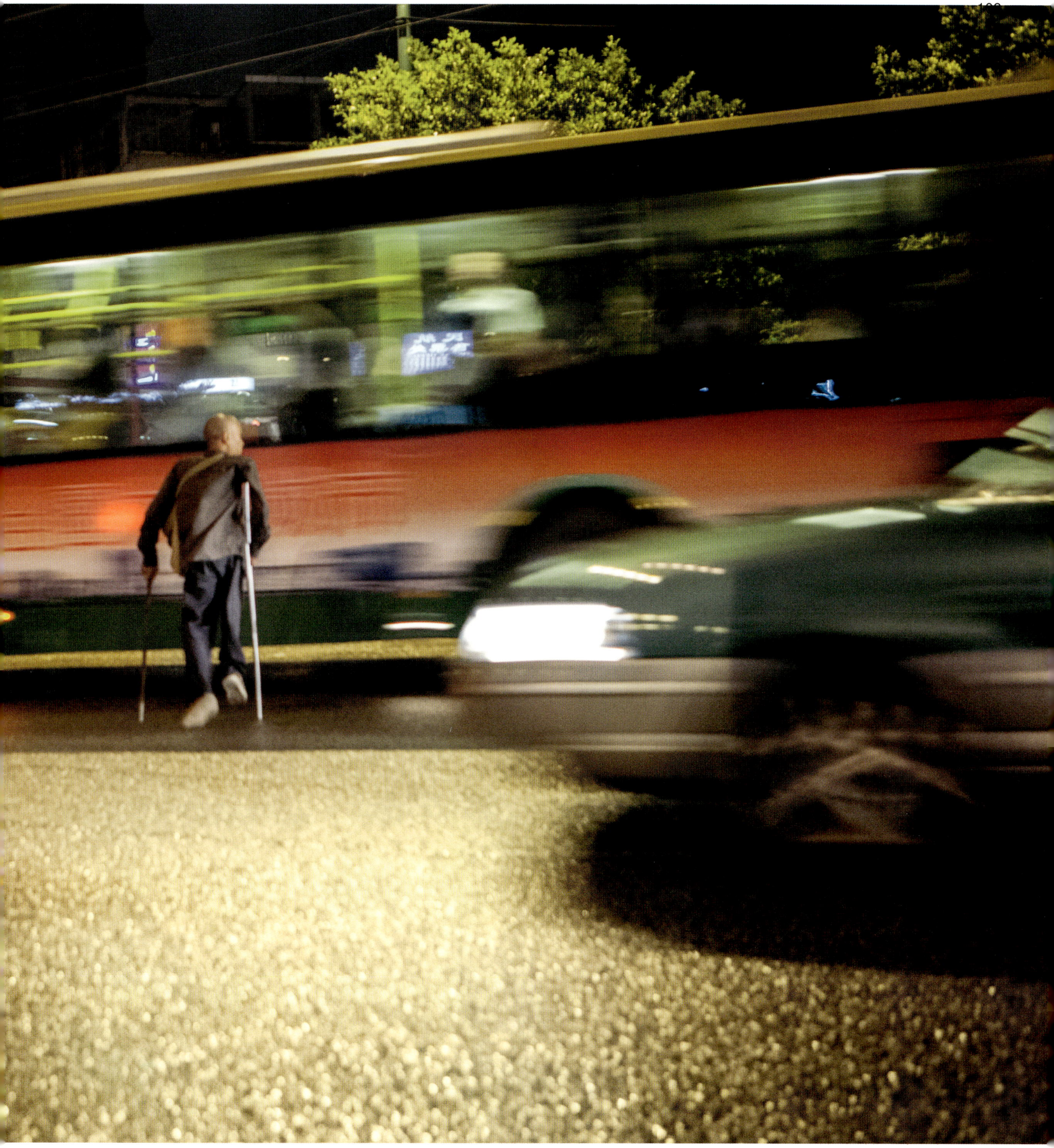

»Als Schwarzfahrer mit der Bahn unterwegs bin
ich schon in fast allen Provinzen Chinas gewesen.«

»I have ridden trains as a fare dodger around
almost all of China's provinces.«

Su Feng, 38

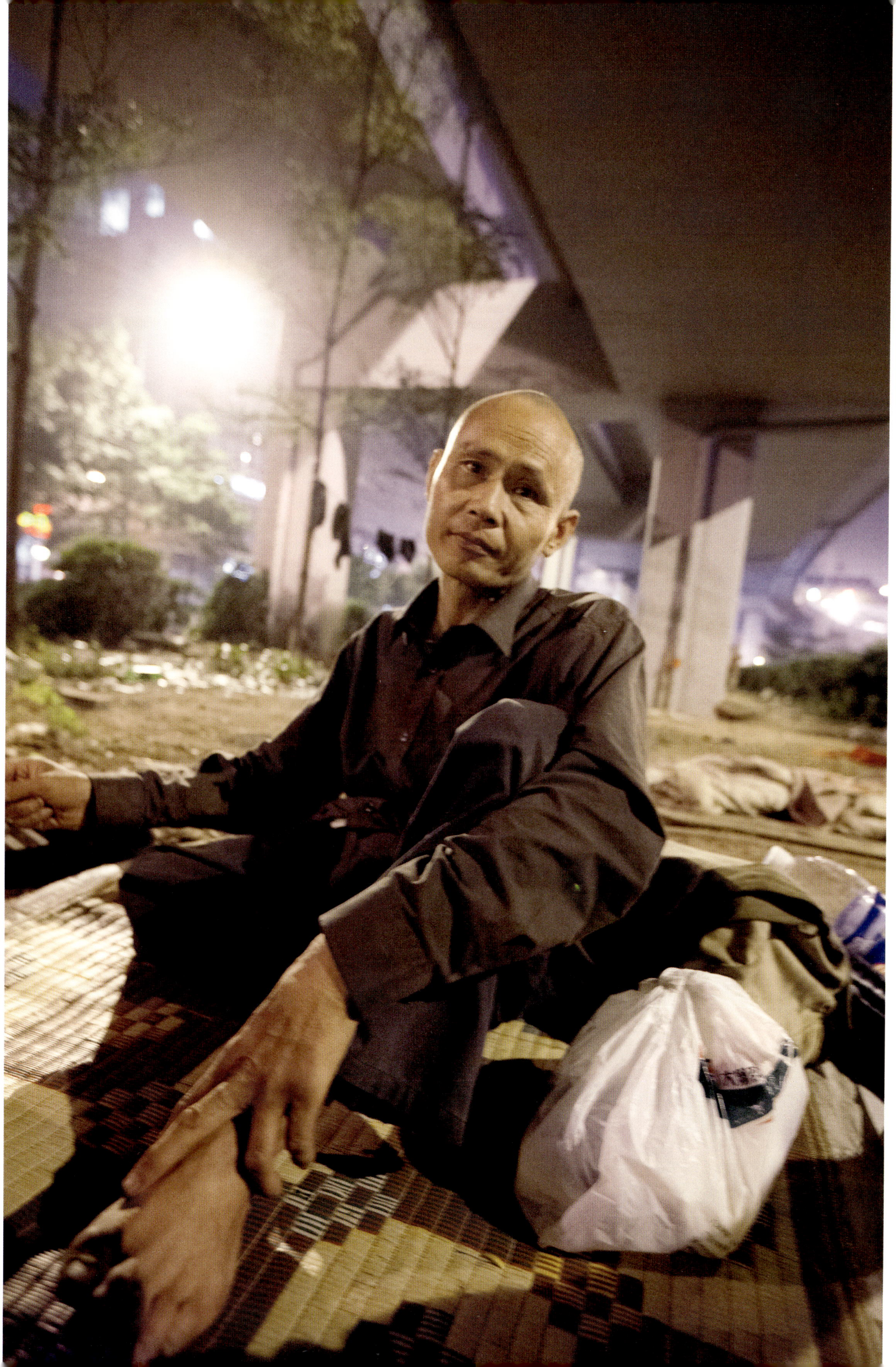

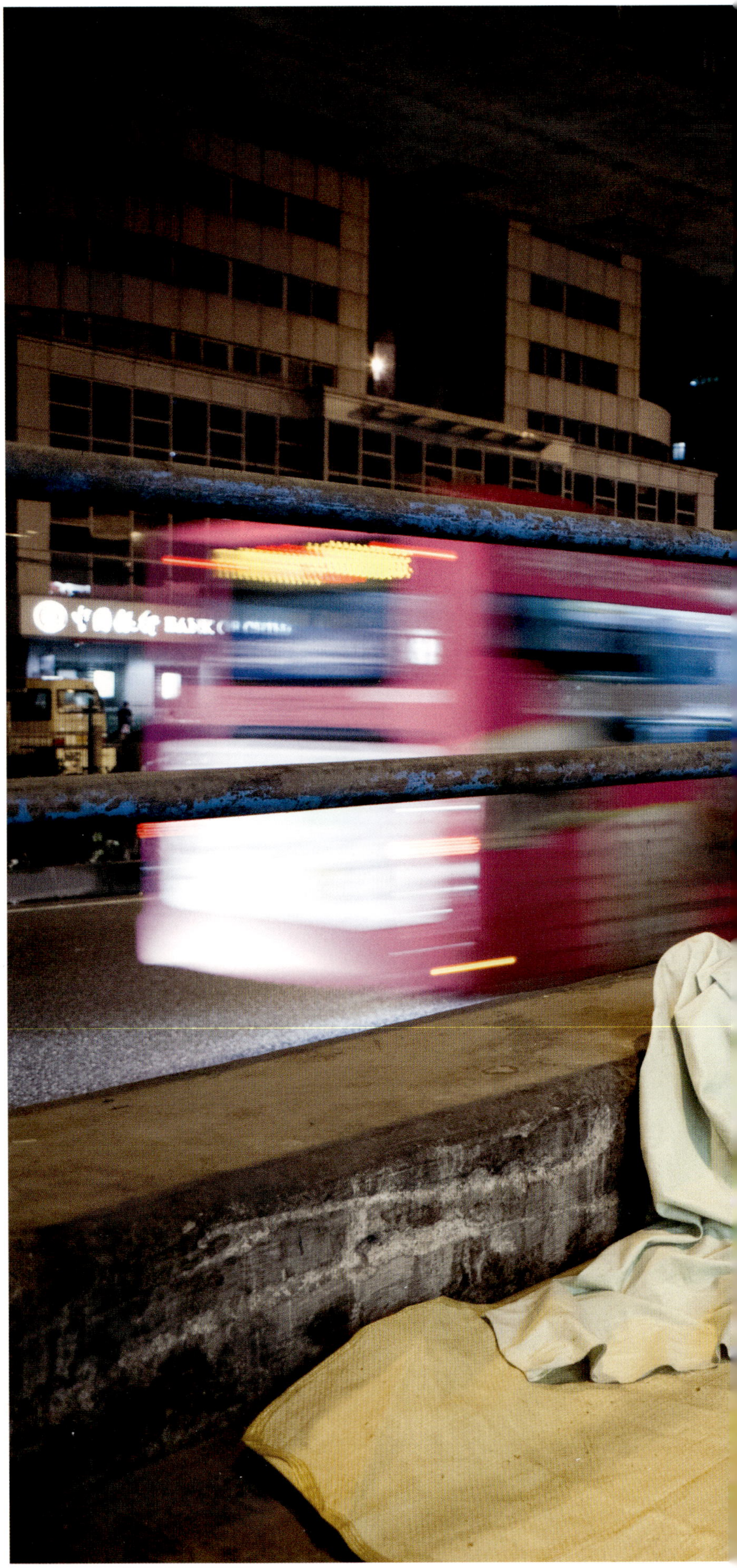

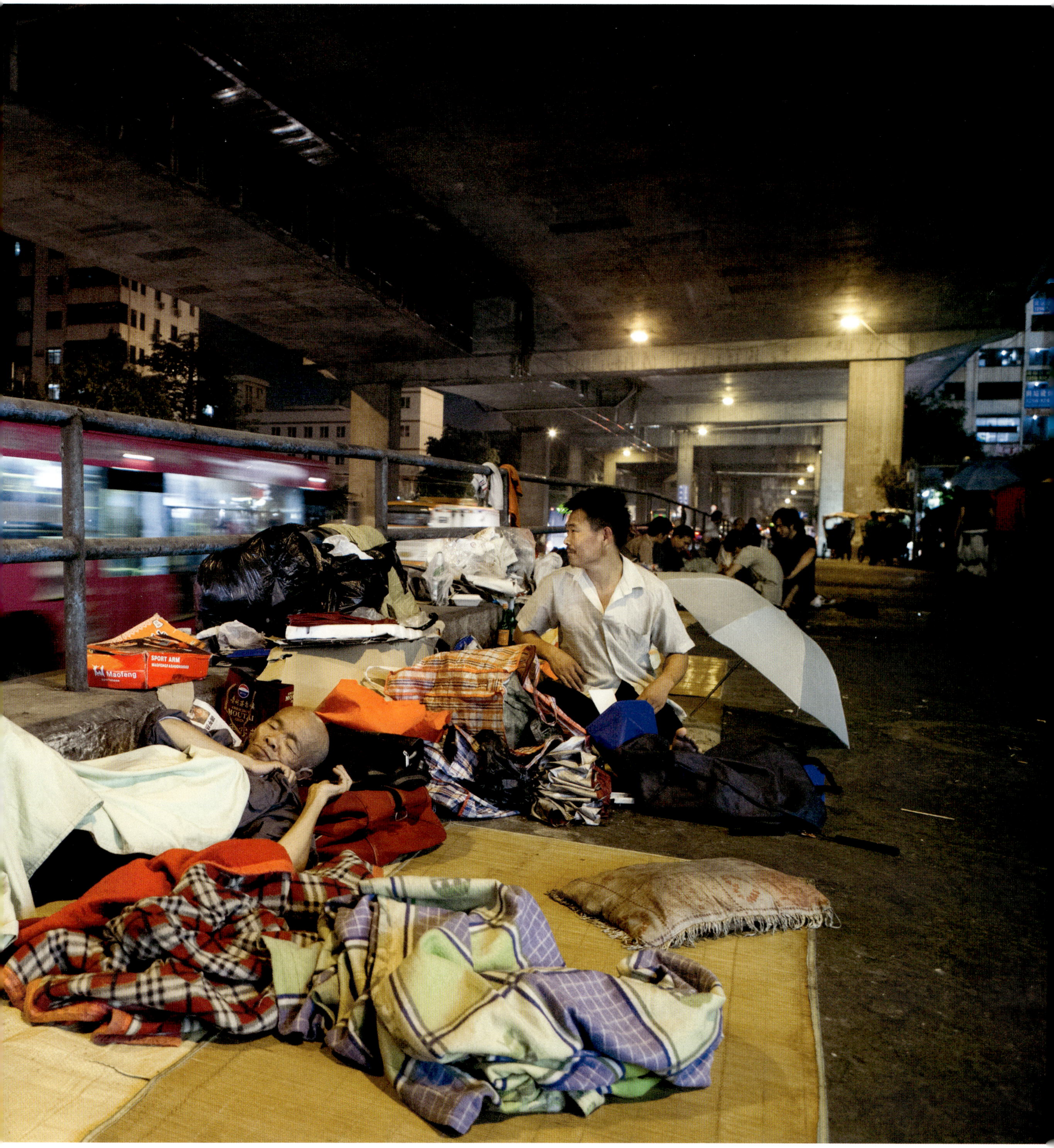
SPORT ARM
Maofeng
MOUTAI

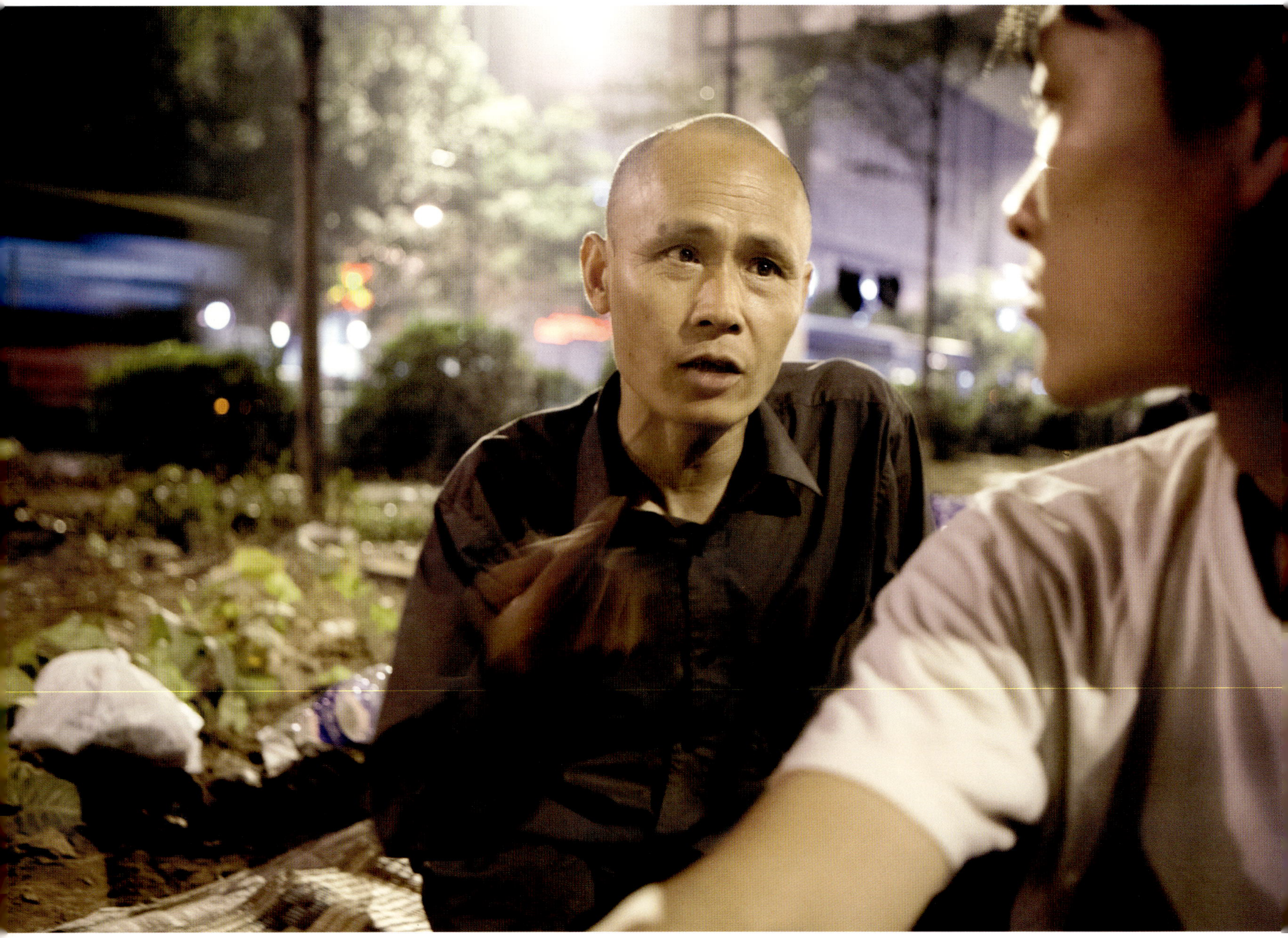

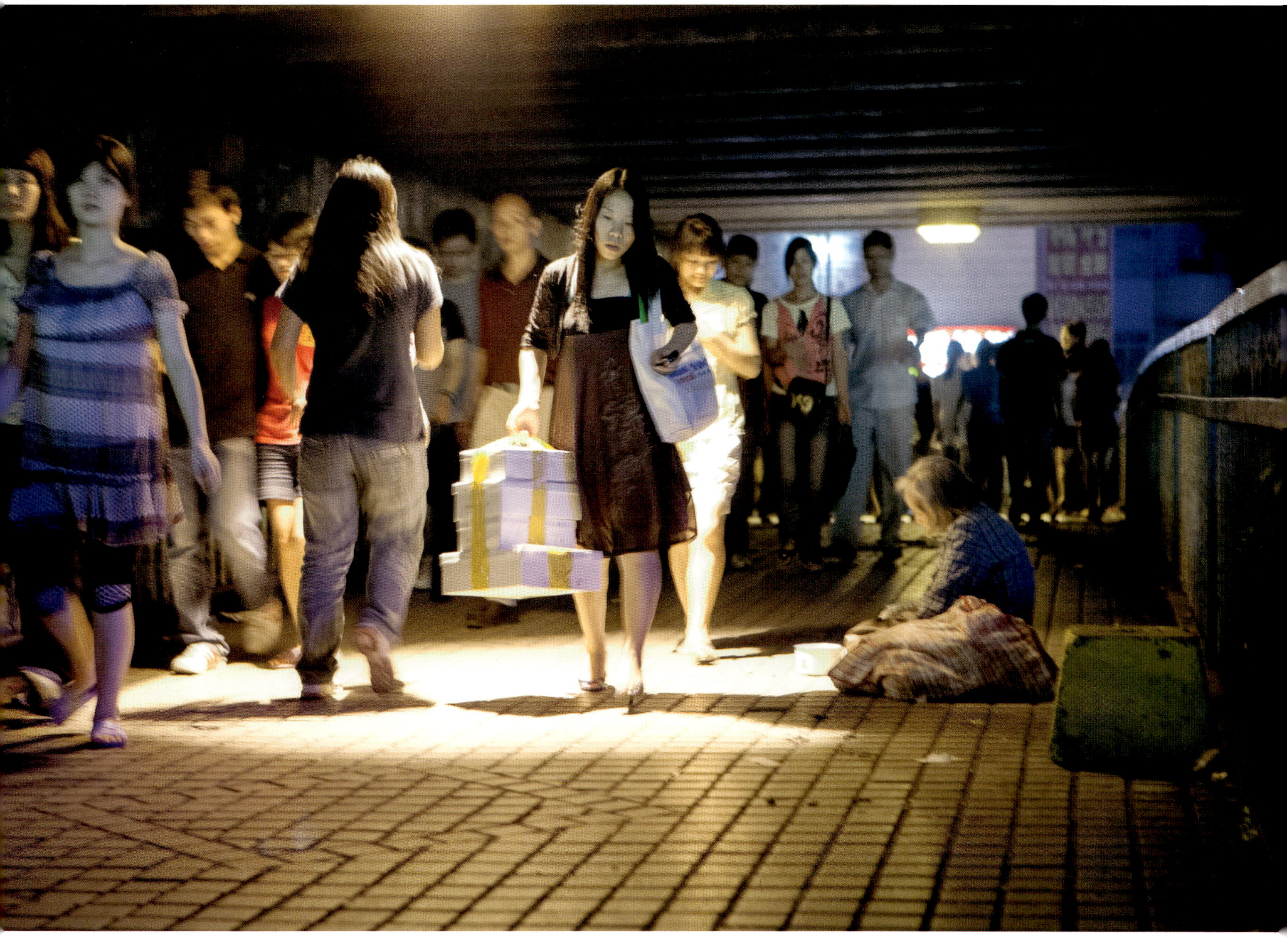

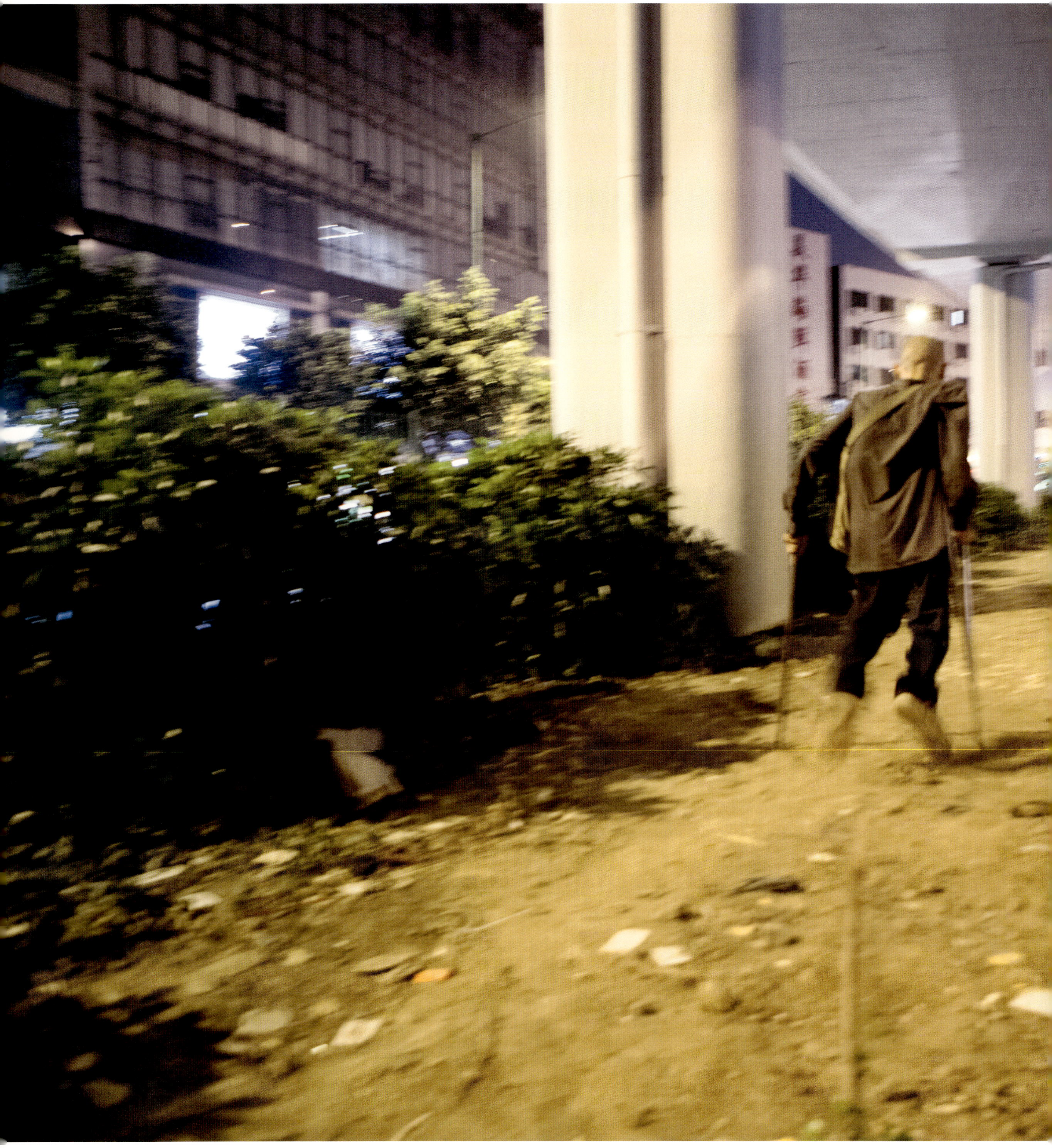

»Ich habe es 2 mal sogar fast geschafft, unter einem LKW nach Hong Kong zu kommen.«

»Twice, I almost made it to Hong Kong riding under a truck.«

Su Feng, 38

9

Backsteinfabrik, Ordos
Brick Factory, Ordos

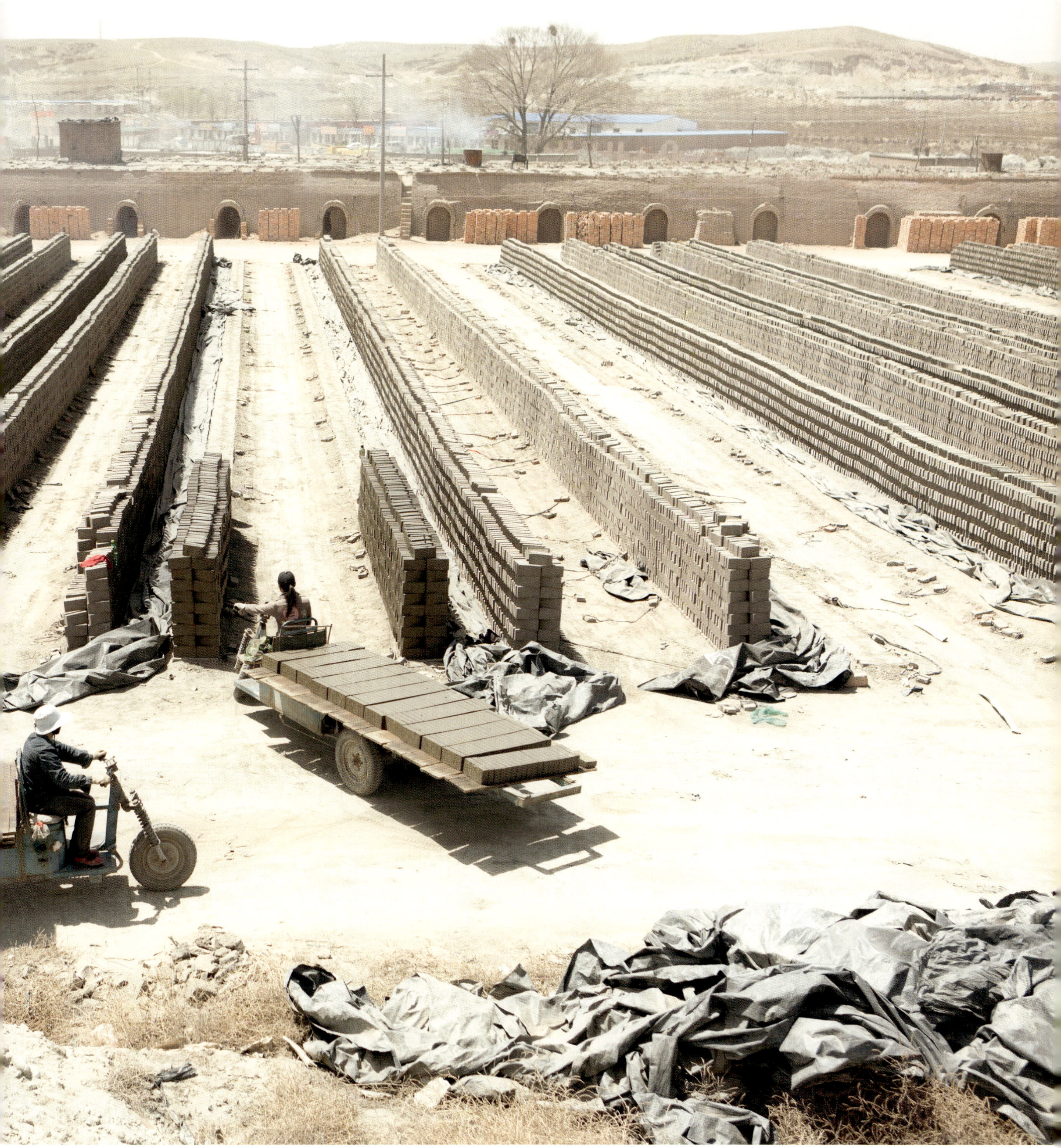

»Wo du auch hinschaust, nichts als Staub! Ich kenne keinen Arbeiter, der nicht sehnsüchtig davon träumt, hier endlich wegzukommen. Und doch sind zu Beginn der nächsten Saison dann fast alle wieder hier.«

»Everywhere you look, nothing but dust! I don't know one worker who is not desperately dreaming of leaving this place. But at the start of the next season, almost all of them will be back here.«

Ma Lin, 25

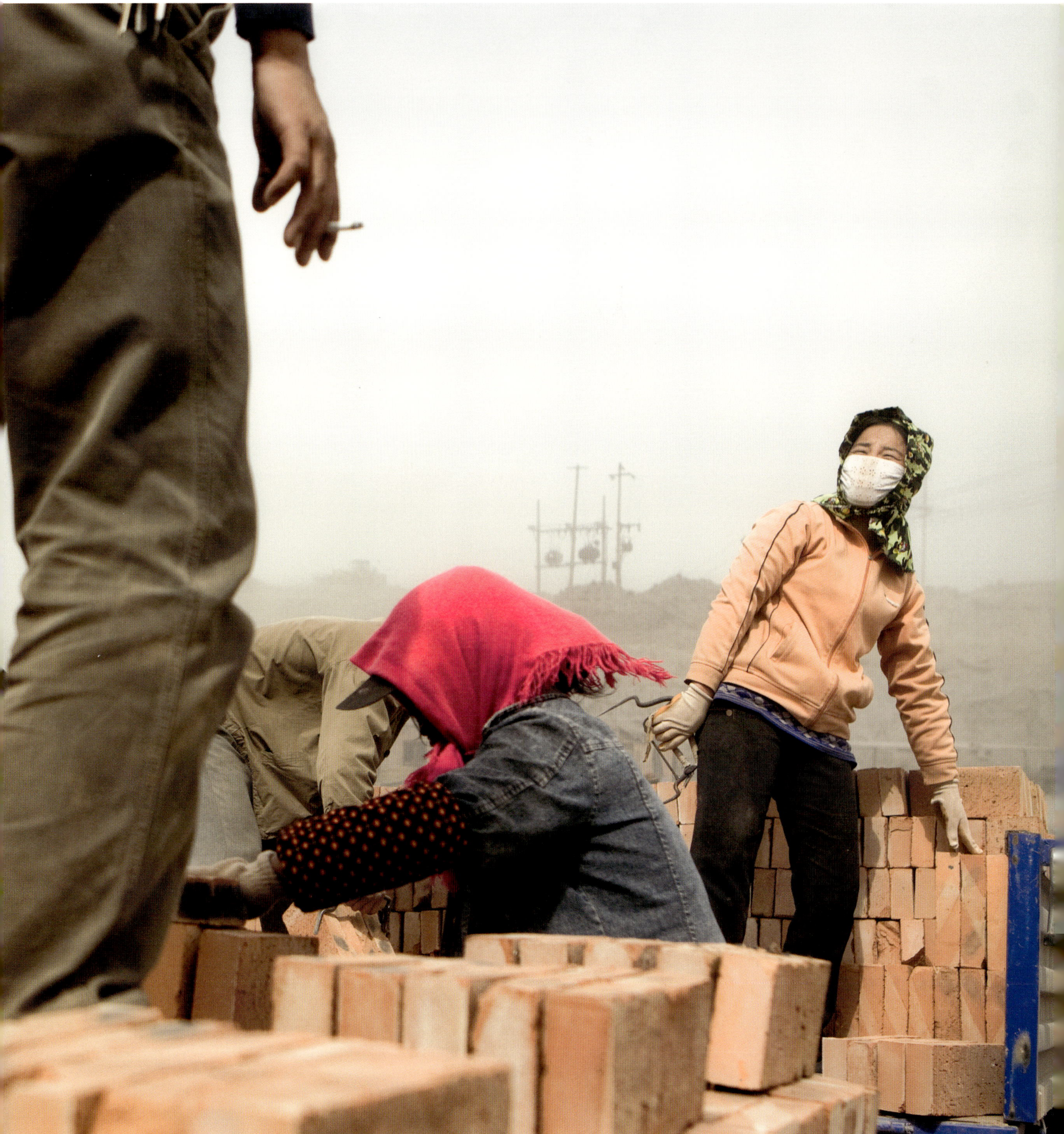

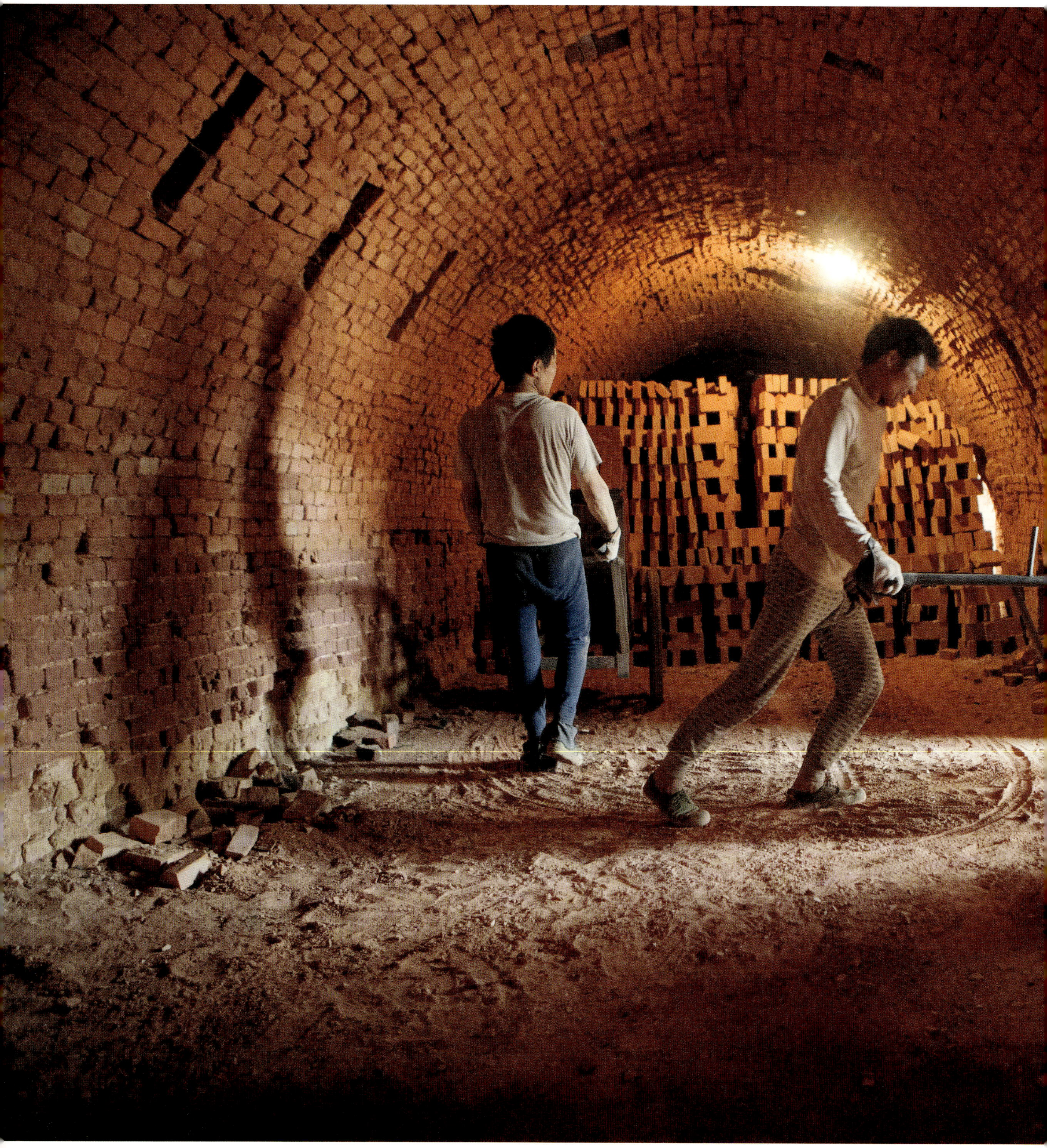

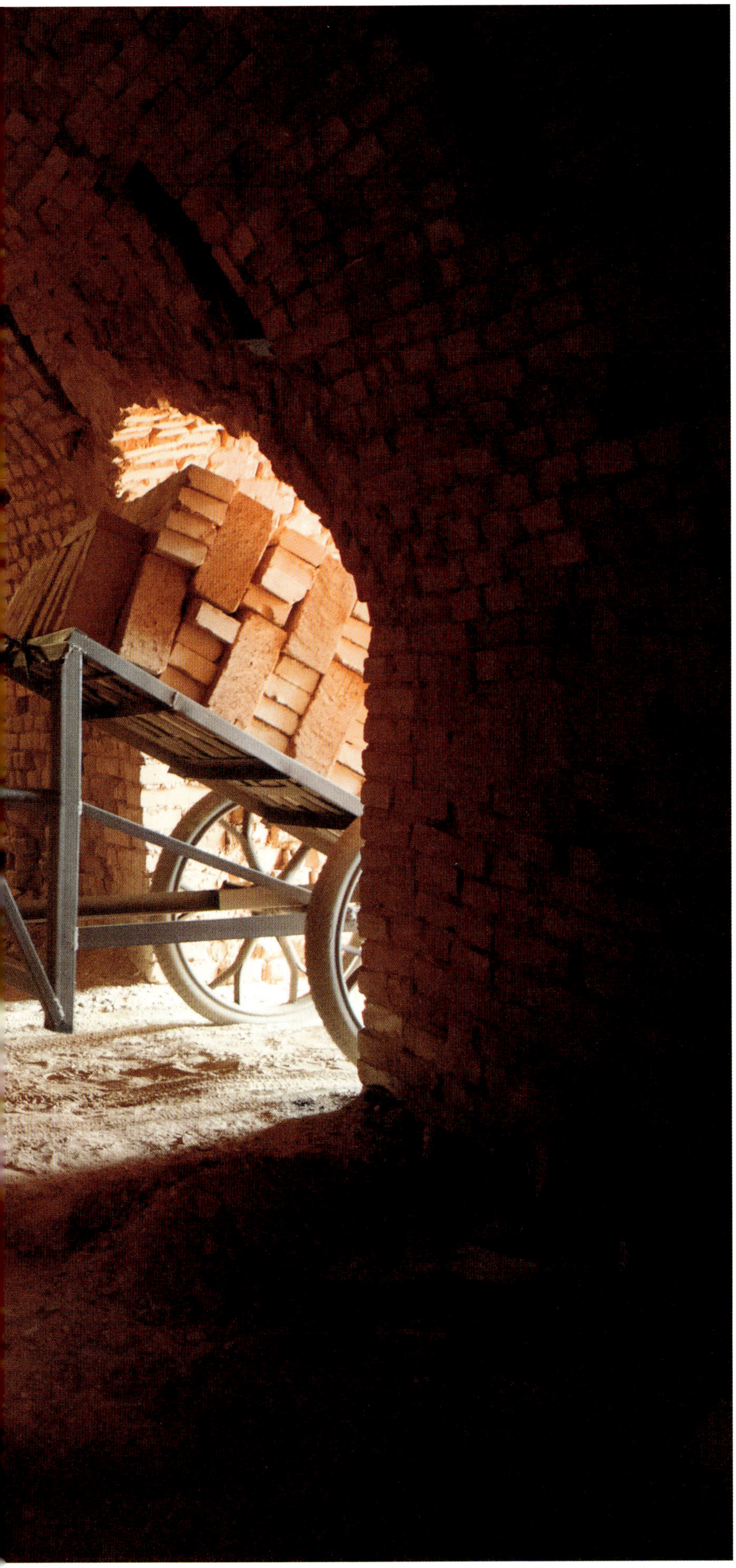

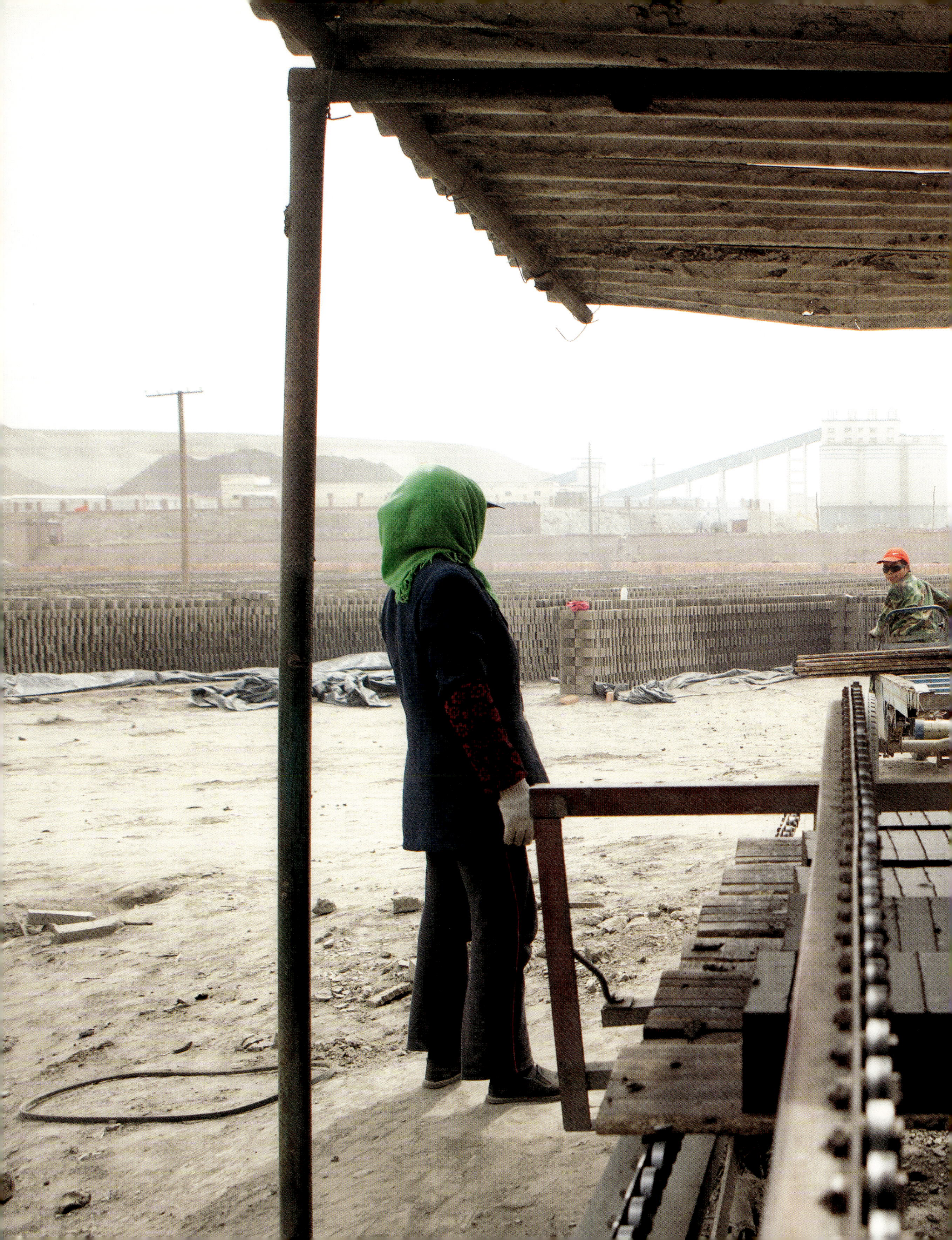

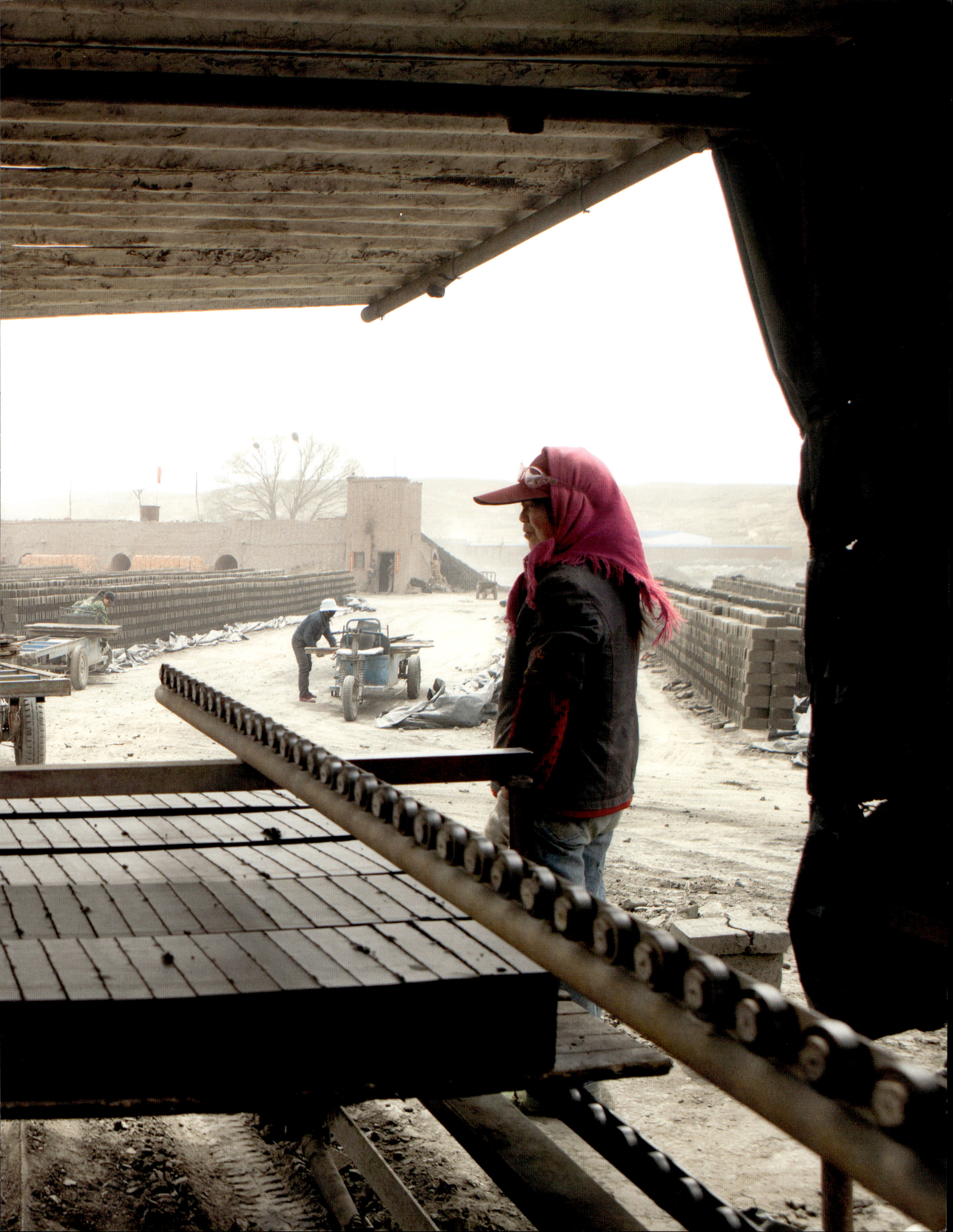

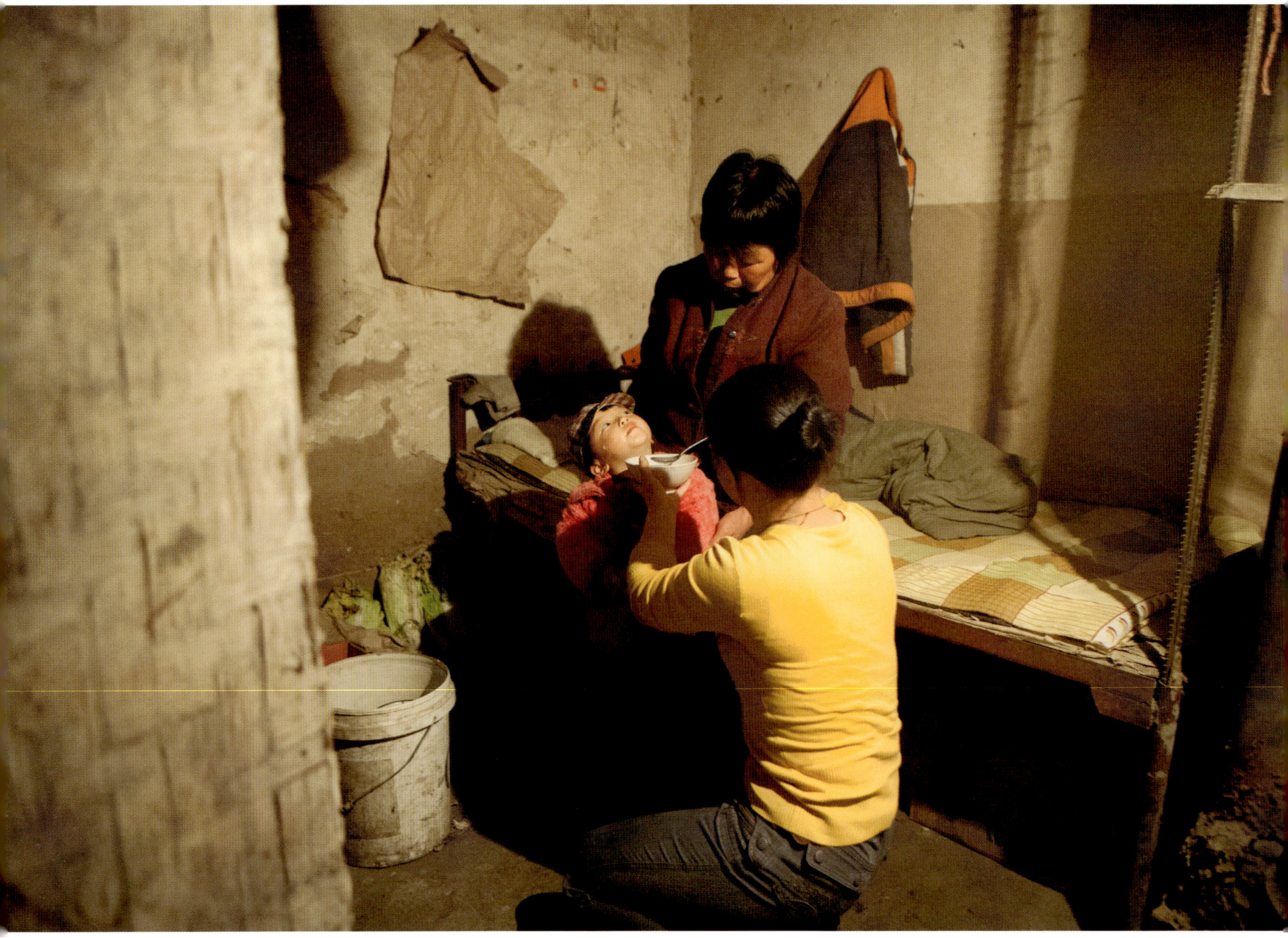

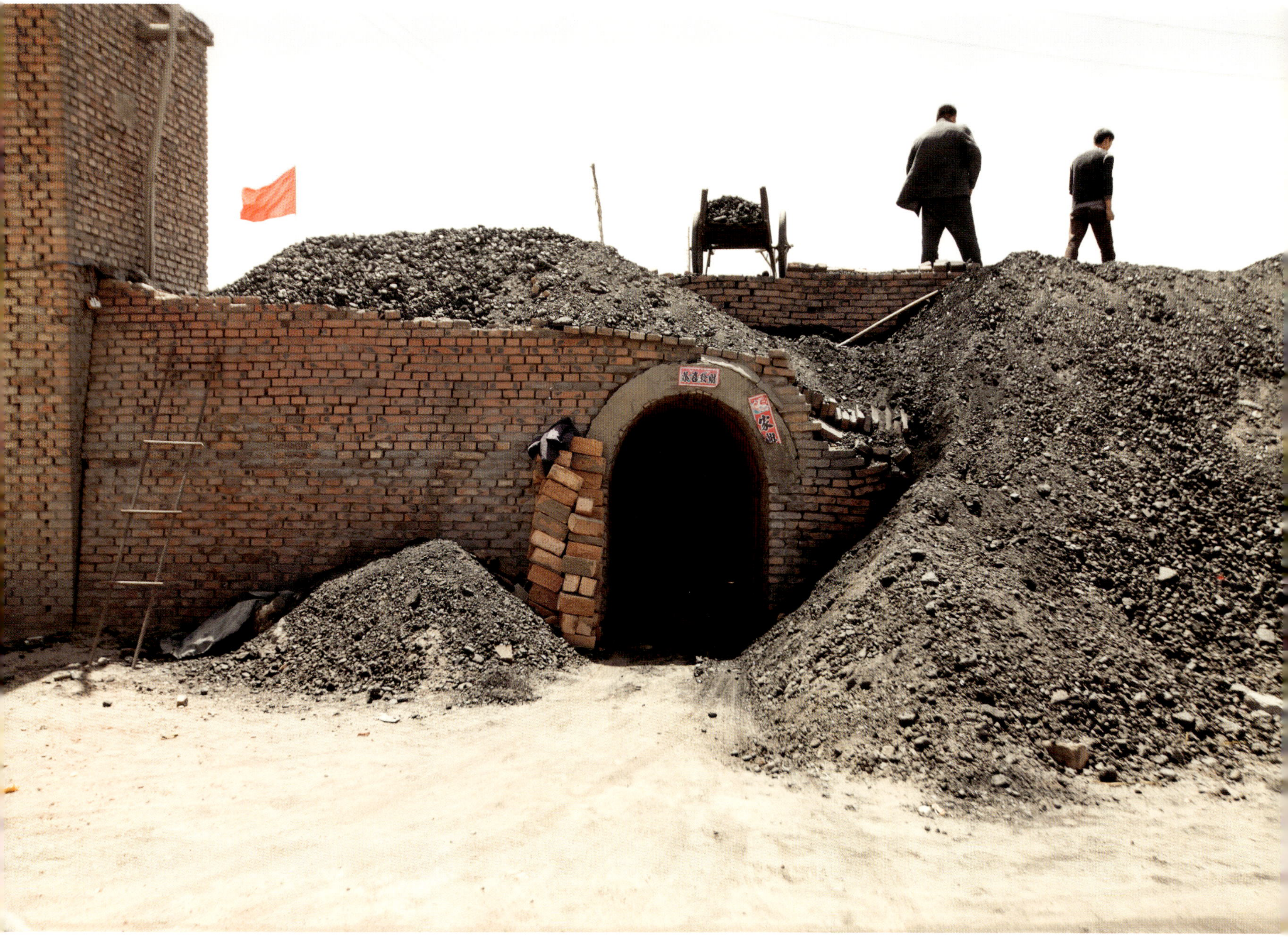

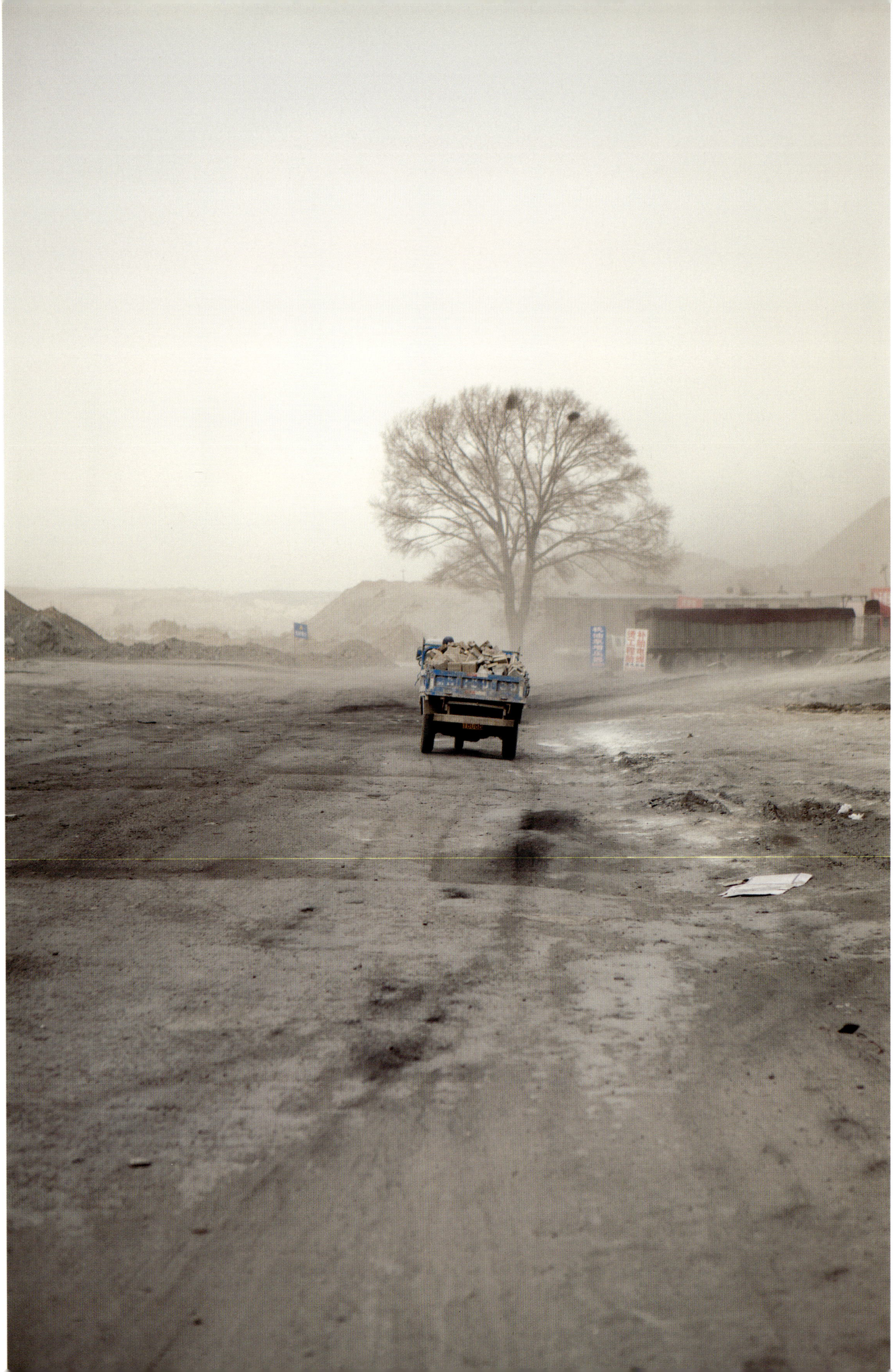

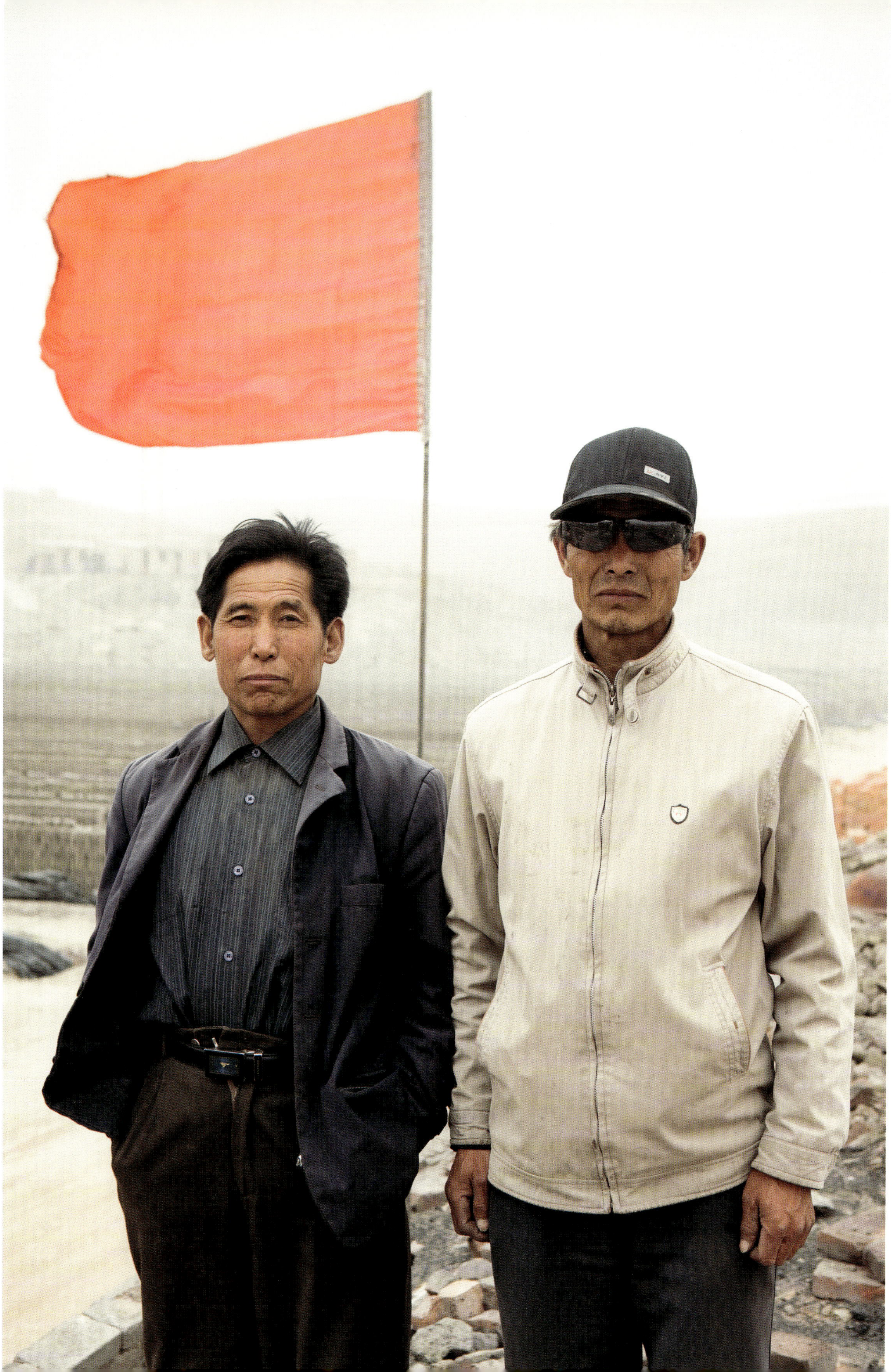

»Der Absatz von Backsteinen ist rückläufig.
Die Schamanen sollen helfen, Unfälle und Unglück
von der Anlage fernzuhalten – und den Verkauf
wieder in Gang zu bringen.«

»Brick sales are declining. This shaman is supposed
to help us keep accidents and misfortune away
from the plant – and make sales rise again.«

Wen Hui, 48

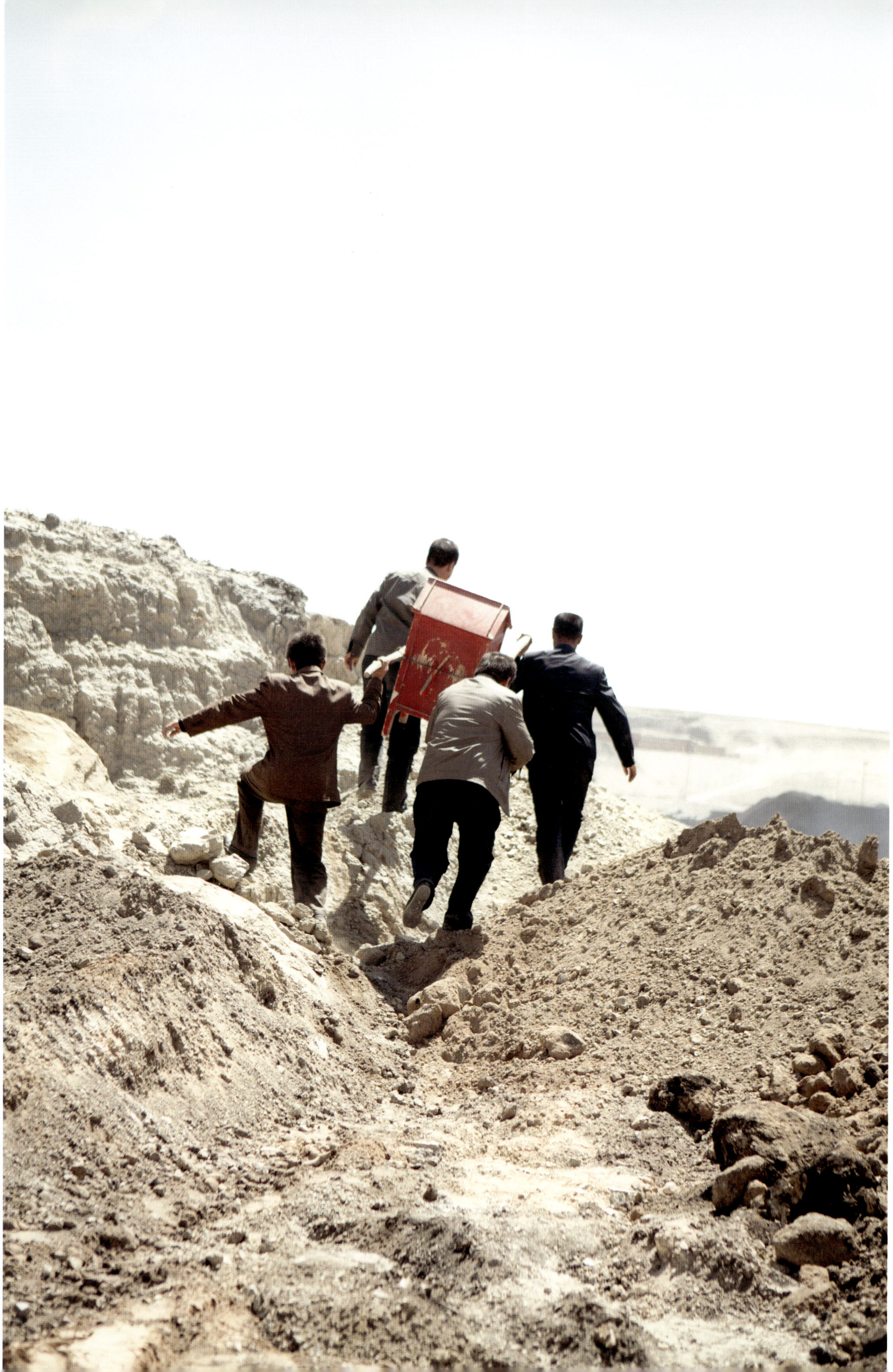

10

Han Chun, Wang Li

SchmucksteinschleiferIn, Haifeng
Gemstone Cutters, Haifeng

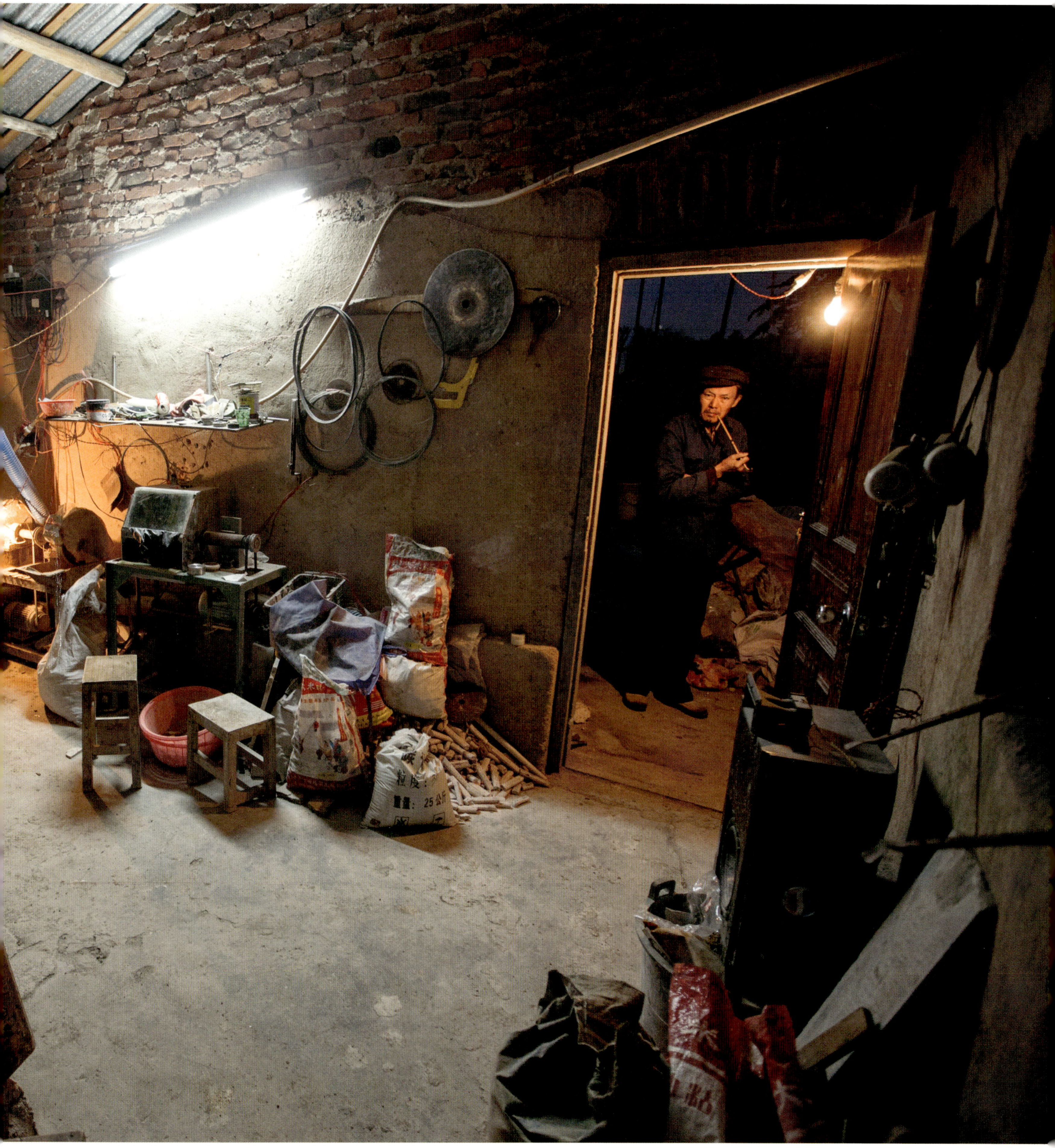
粒度:

»Nachdem meinem Mann gekündigt wurde, mussten wir uns selbstständig machen. Derzeit arbeiten wir hauptsächlich als Zulieferer großer Firmen.«

»When my husband was dismissed, we had to go into business for ourselves. Currently, we mainly work as suppliers for big companies.«

Wang Li, 36

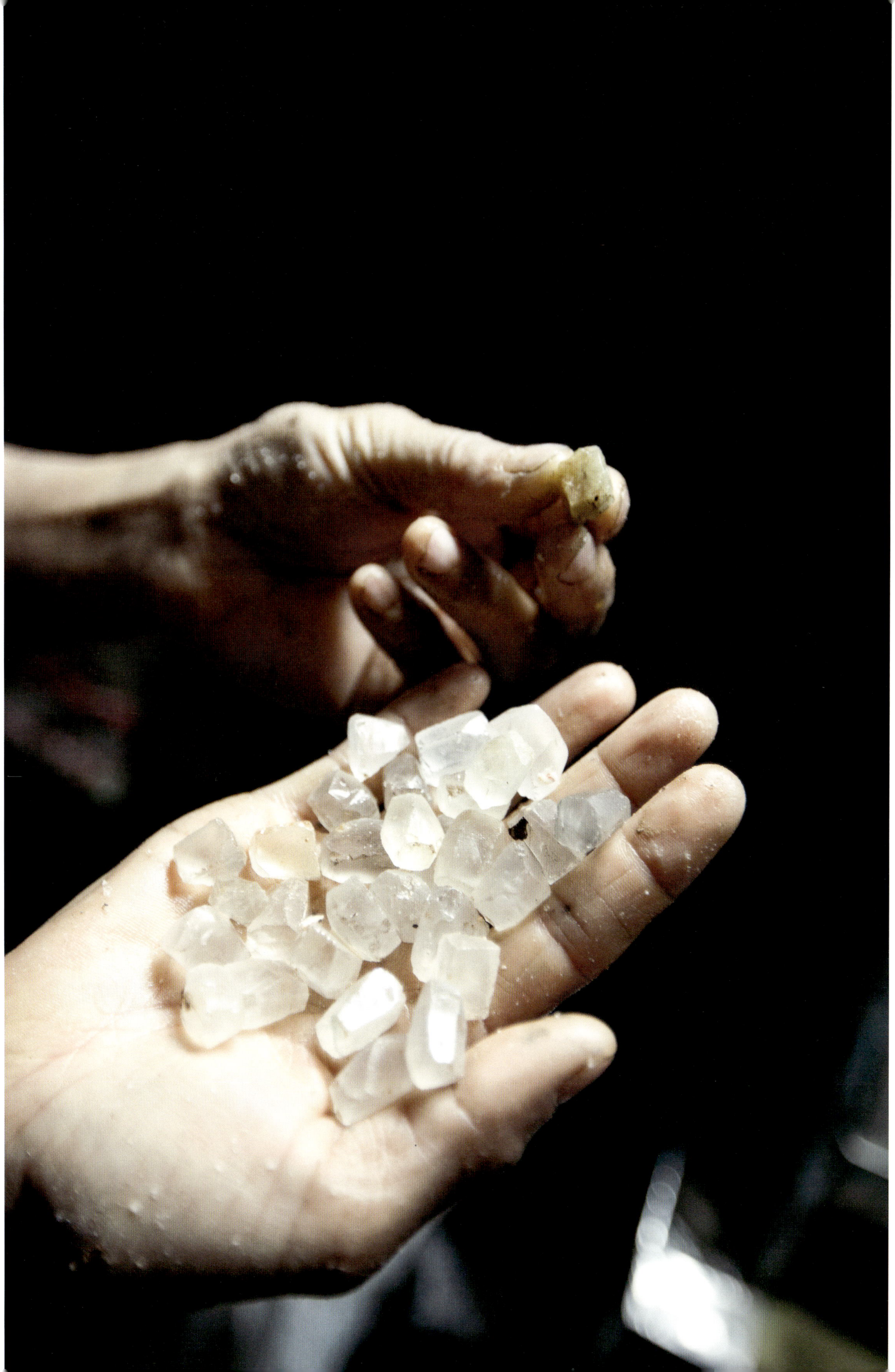

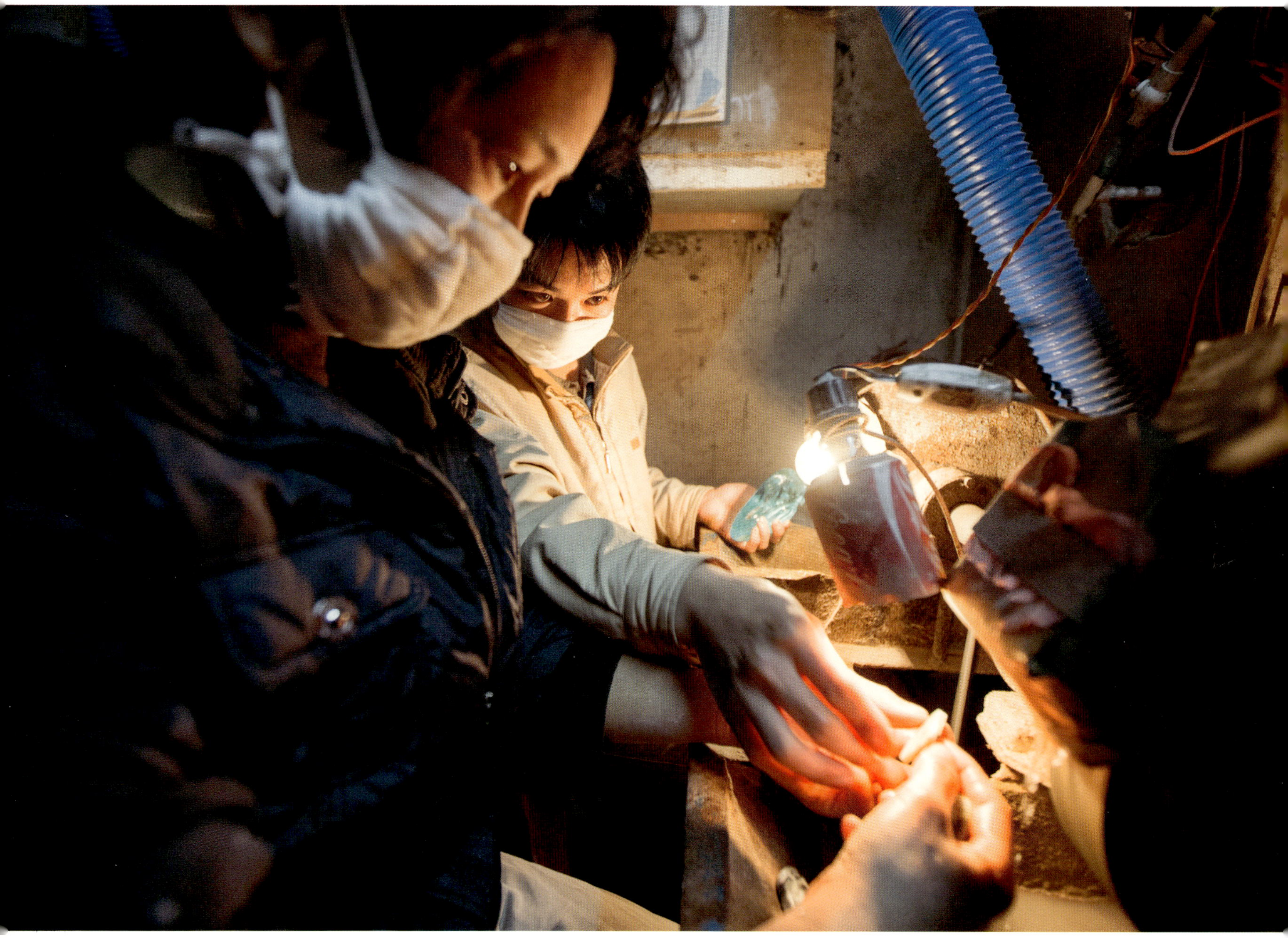

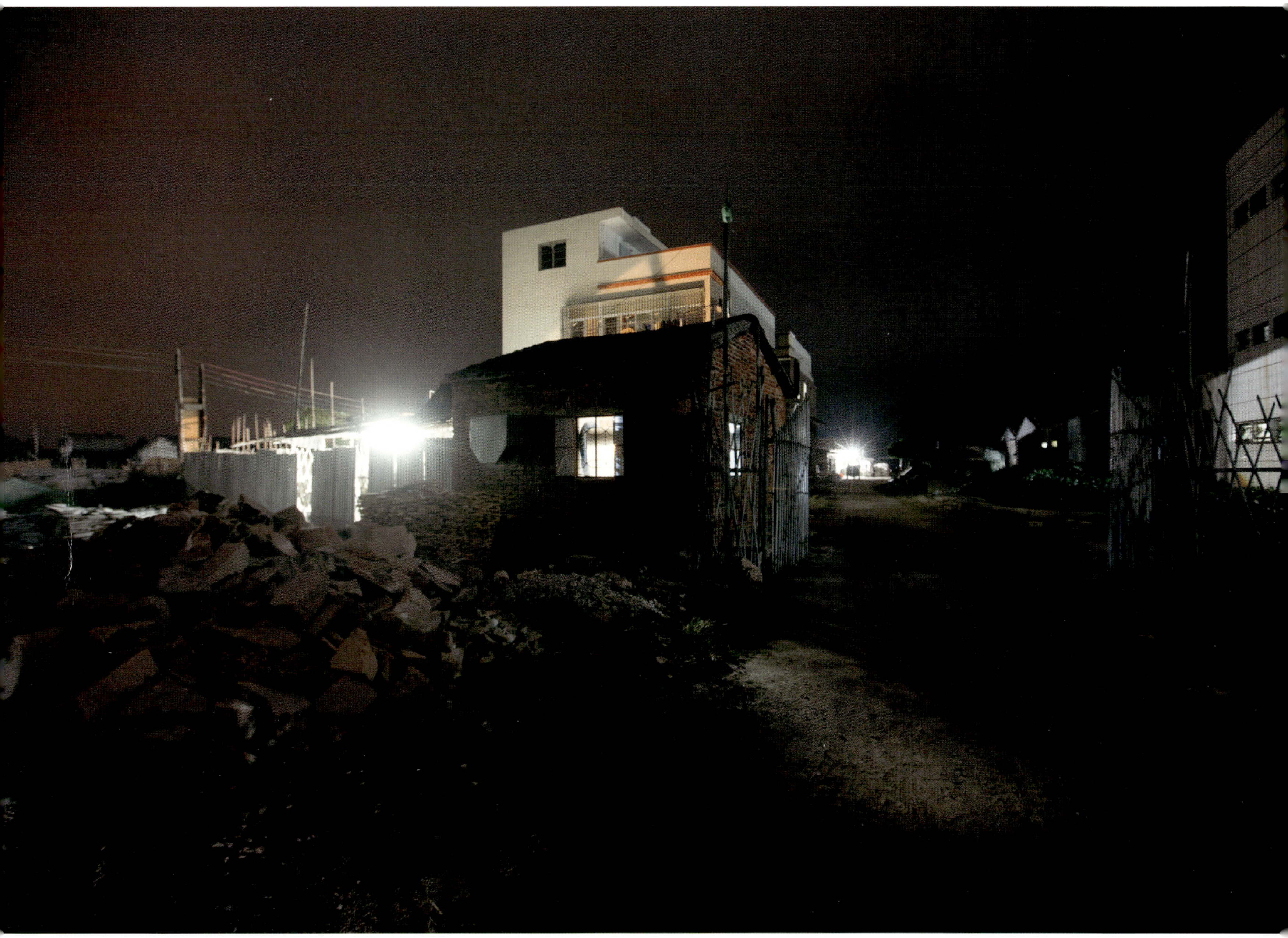

»Über Jahre hinweg hatte ich ohne Schutzvorrichtungen Steine zertrennt und geschliffen. Als bei mir Staublunge festgestellt wurde, wurde ich entlassen und sollte in mein Heimatdorf zurückkehren.«

»I had cut stones without protective gear or devices for many years. When I was diagnosed with silicosis, I was dismissed and was supposed to go back to my home village.«

Han Chun, 38

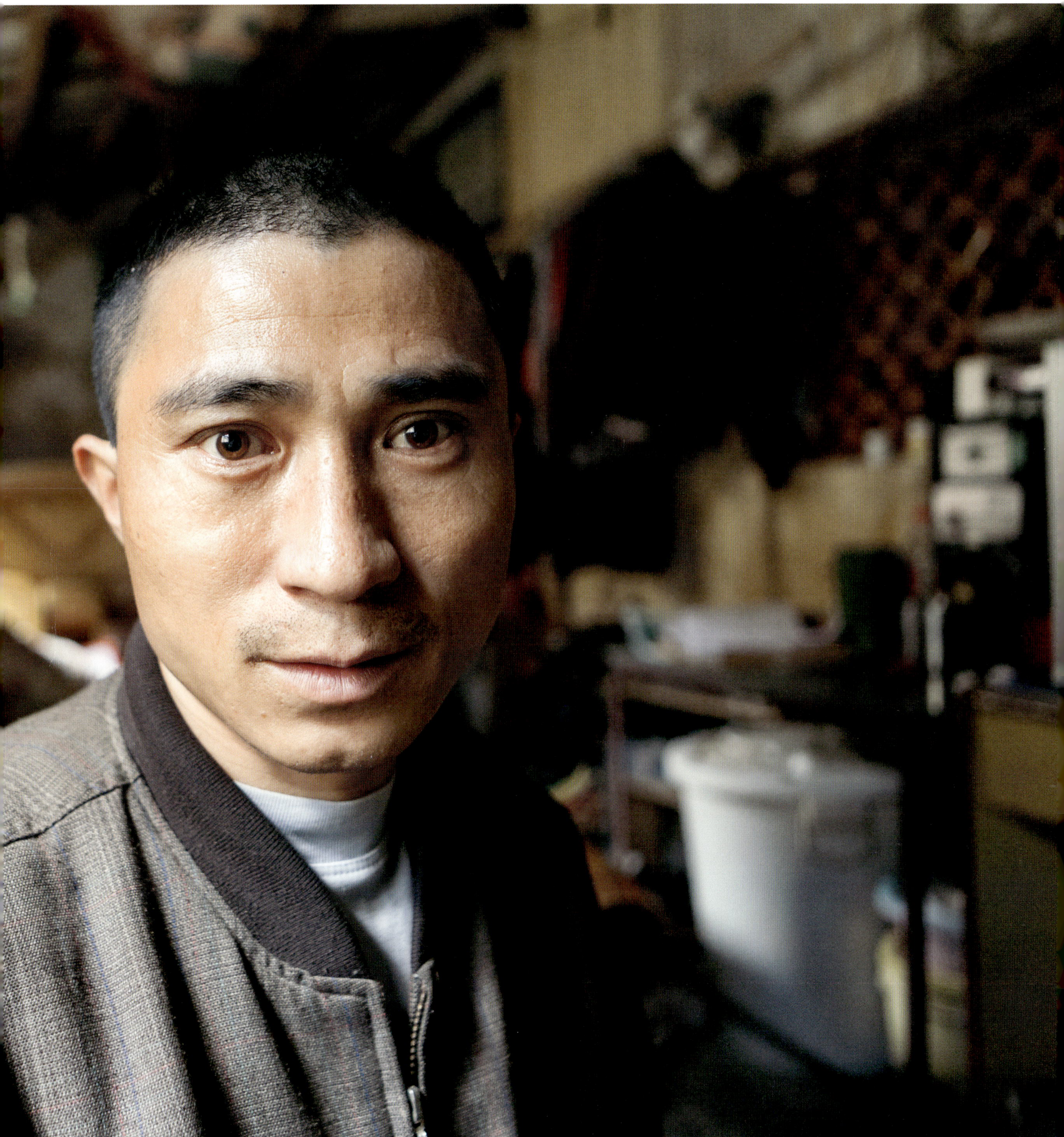

11

He Juan, Wen Feng

Kohlewäscherln, Fushun
Coal Washers, Fushun

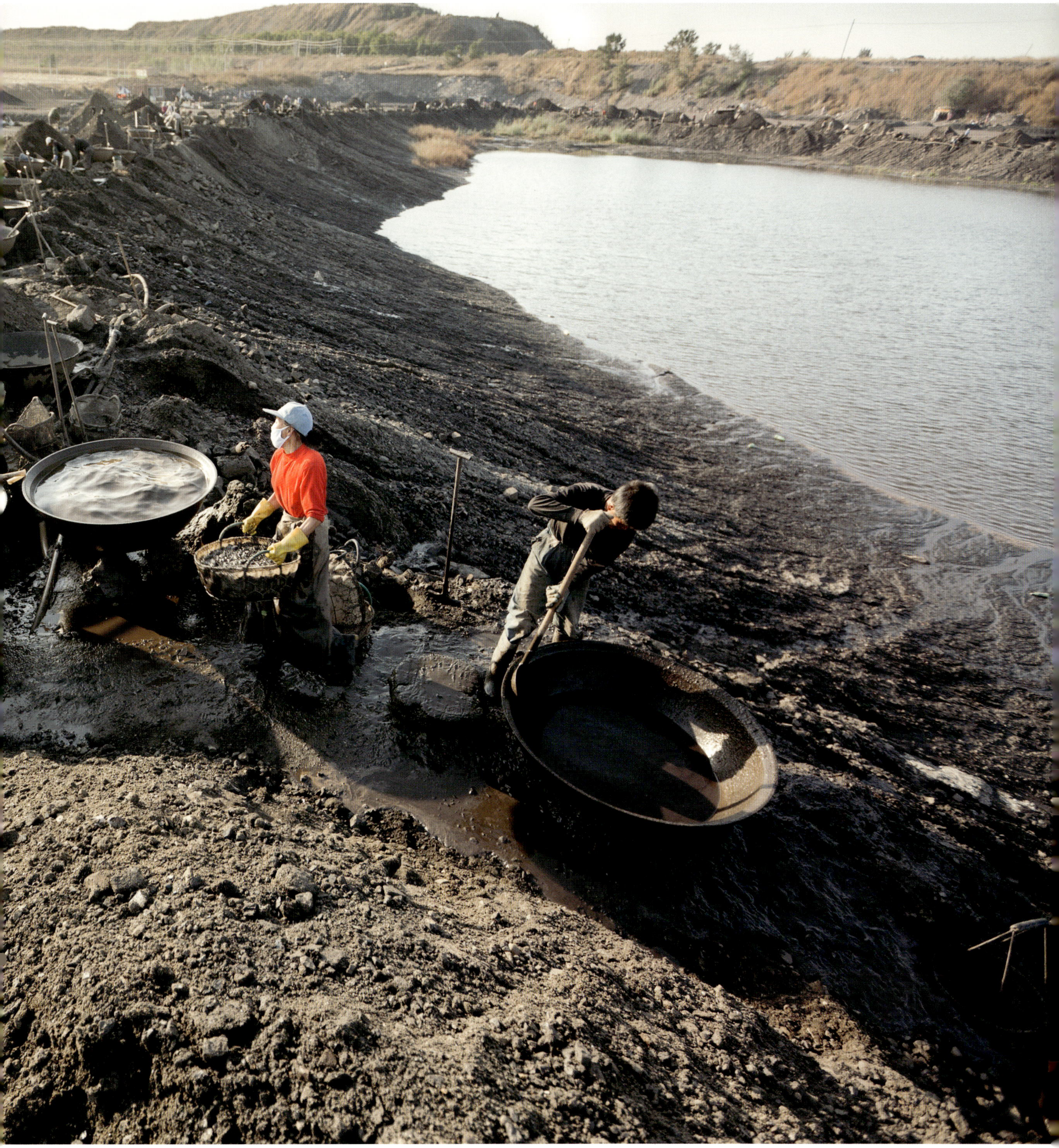

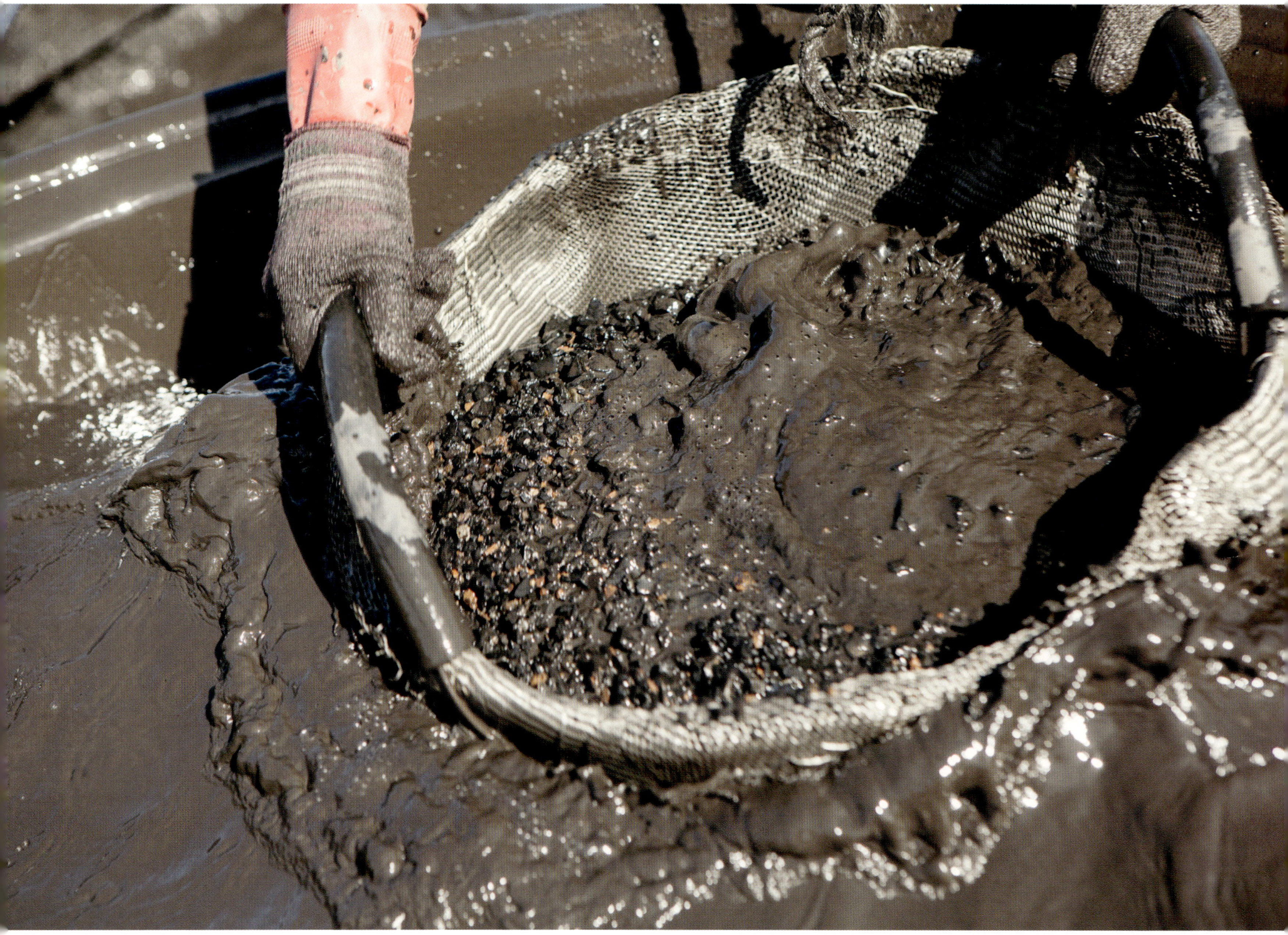

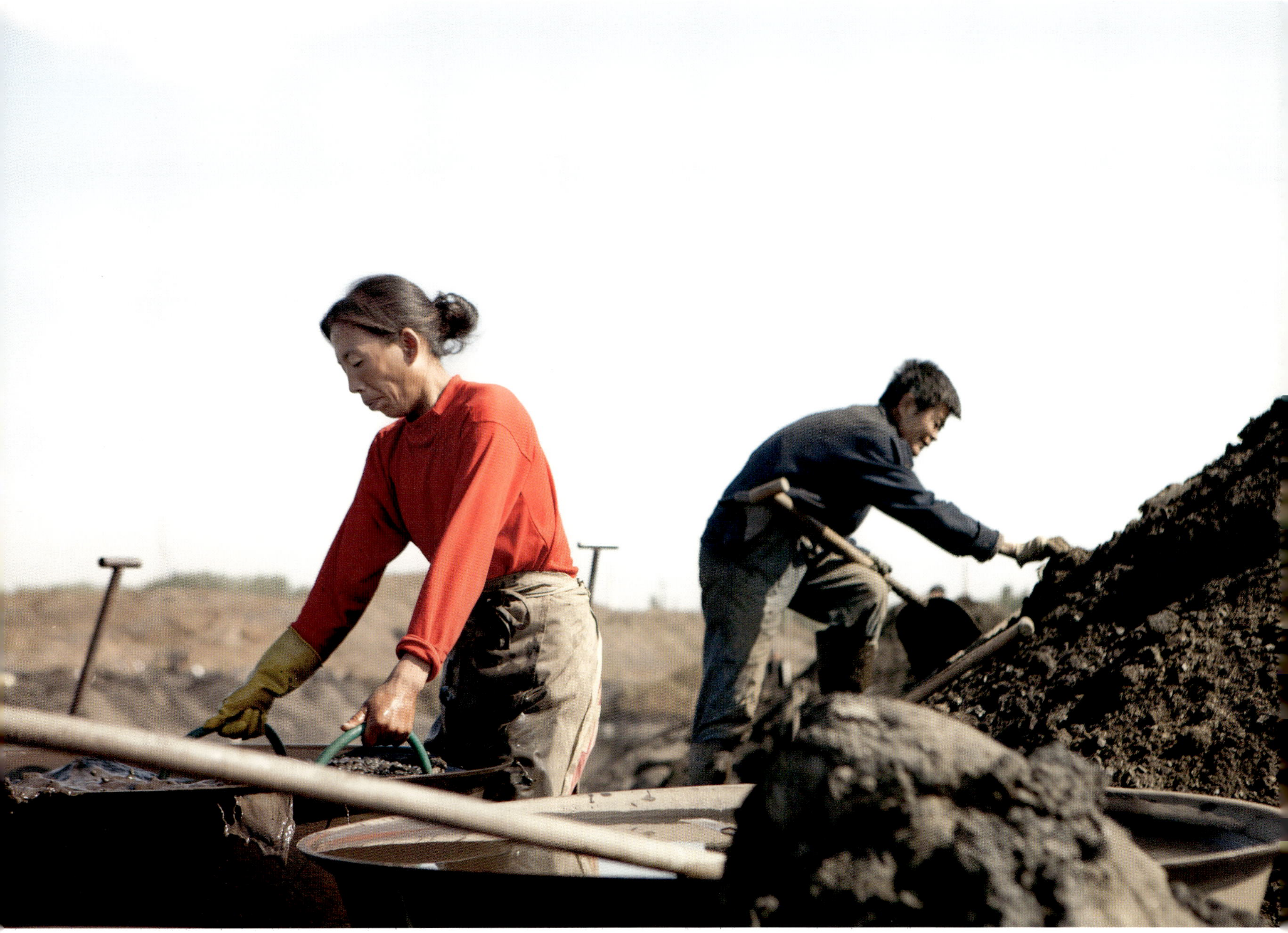

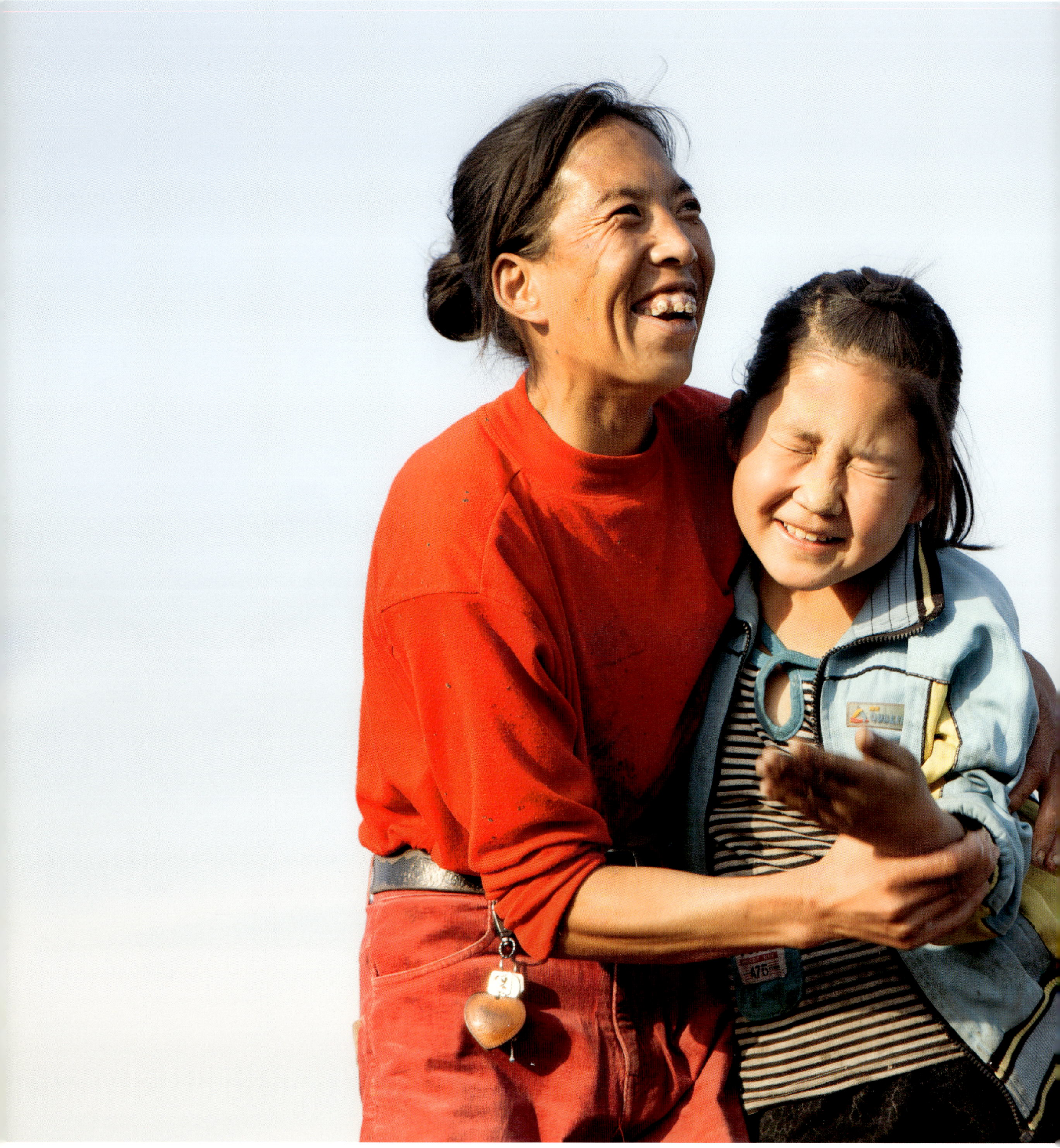

»Weil meine Tochter ihn nicht akzeptiert, hat mein neuer Mann sie vor die Tür gesetzt und ihr jeden weiteren Zutritt verboten. Jetzt lebt sie bei ihrem Großvater. So sehe ich sie nur, wenn sie uns auf der Arbeit besuchen kommt.«

»Because my daughter does not accept him, my new husband threw her out and banned her from entering the house. She now lives with her grandfather. So I only see her when she visits us at work.«

He Juan, 36

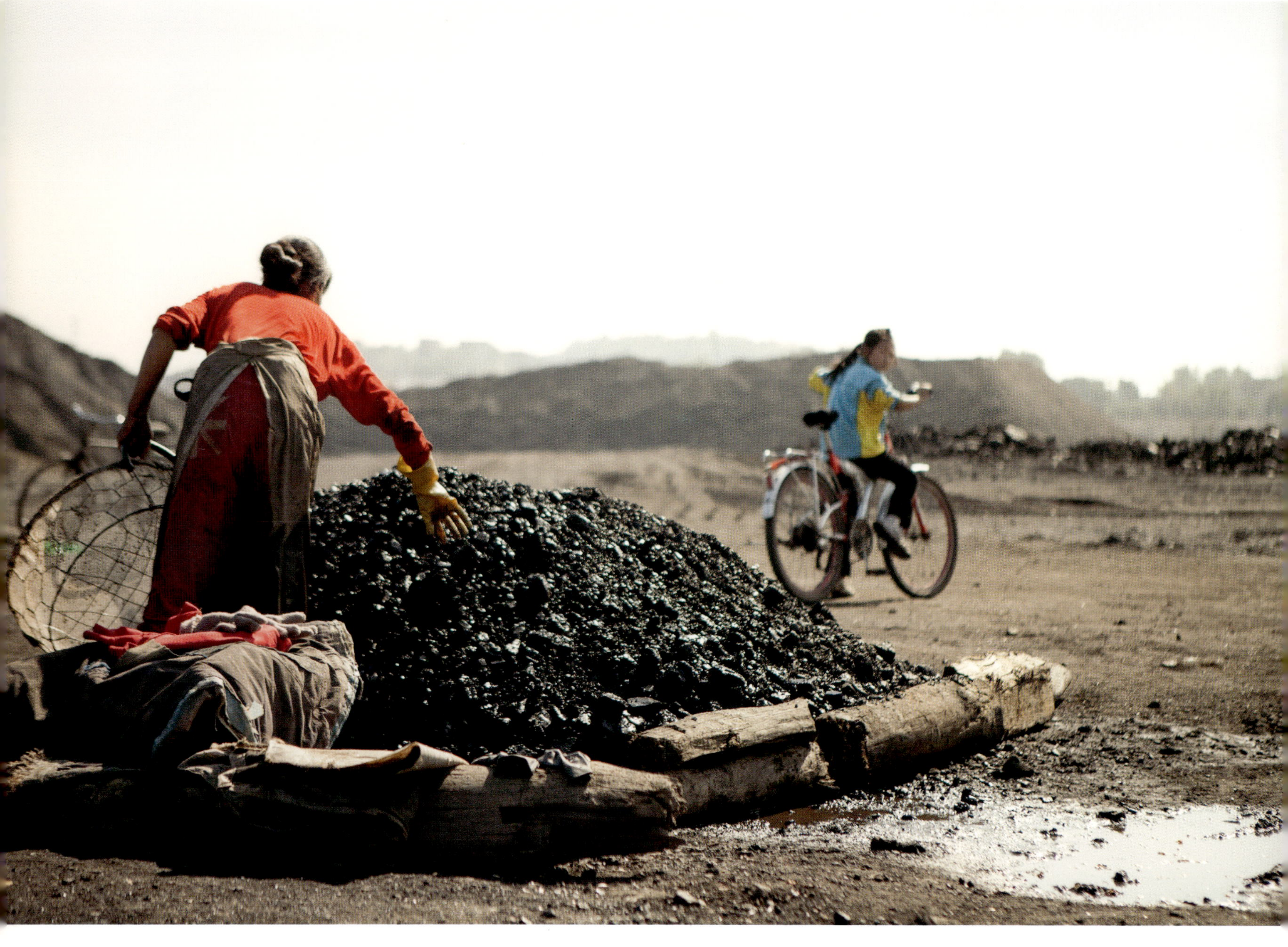

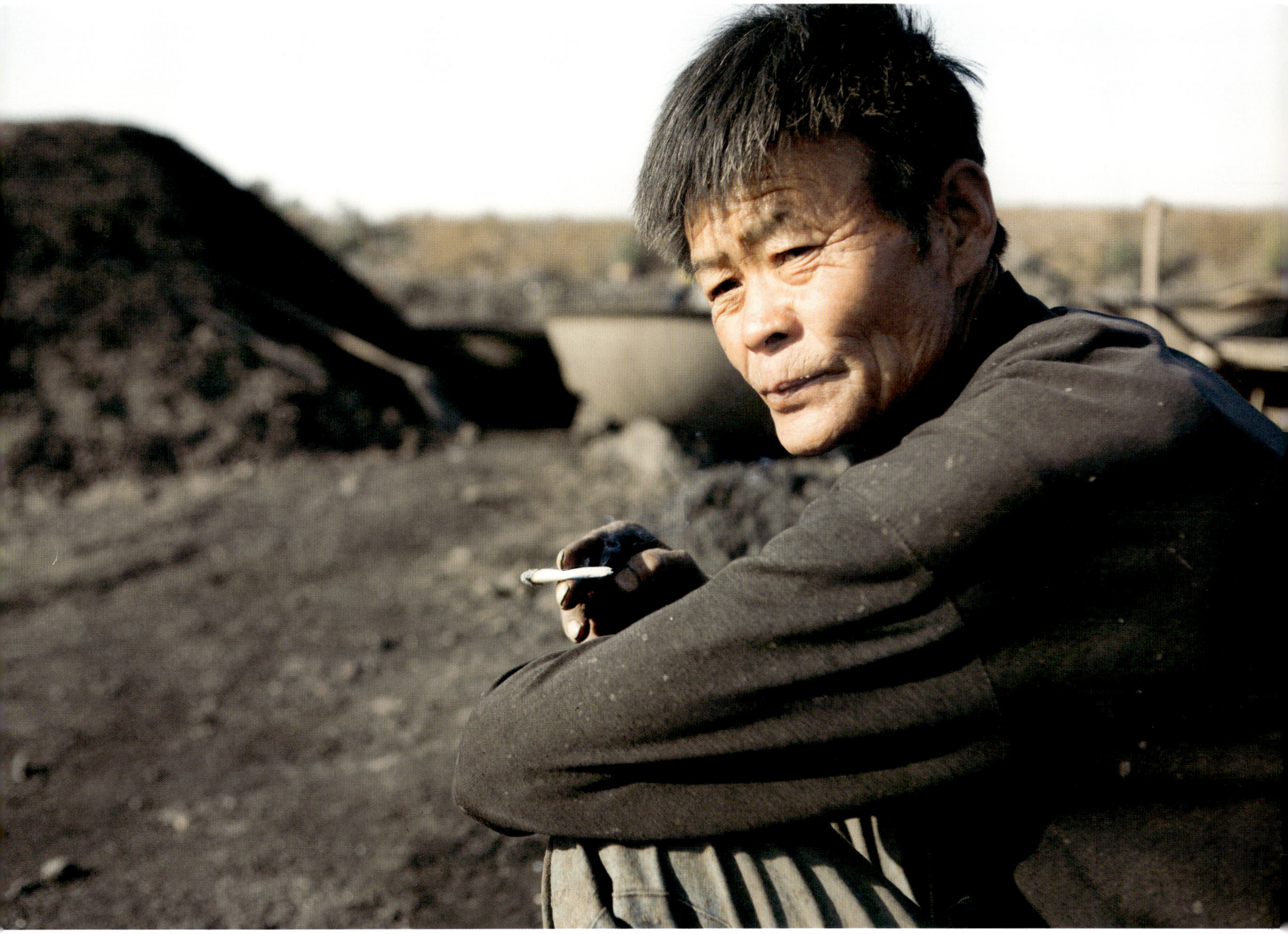

»Mein Sohn kümmert sich nur ungern um seine Tochter aus erster Ehe. Jetzt liegt es an mir, sie vor der Arbeit zur Schule zu bringen, für sie zu kochen und nach ihren Hausaufgaben zu schauen.«

»My son is unwilling to take care of his daughter from his first marriage. Now I'm the one who has to take her to school before work, to cook for her and help her with her homework.«

Wen Feng, 63

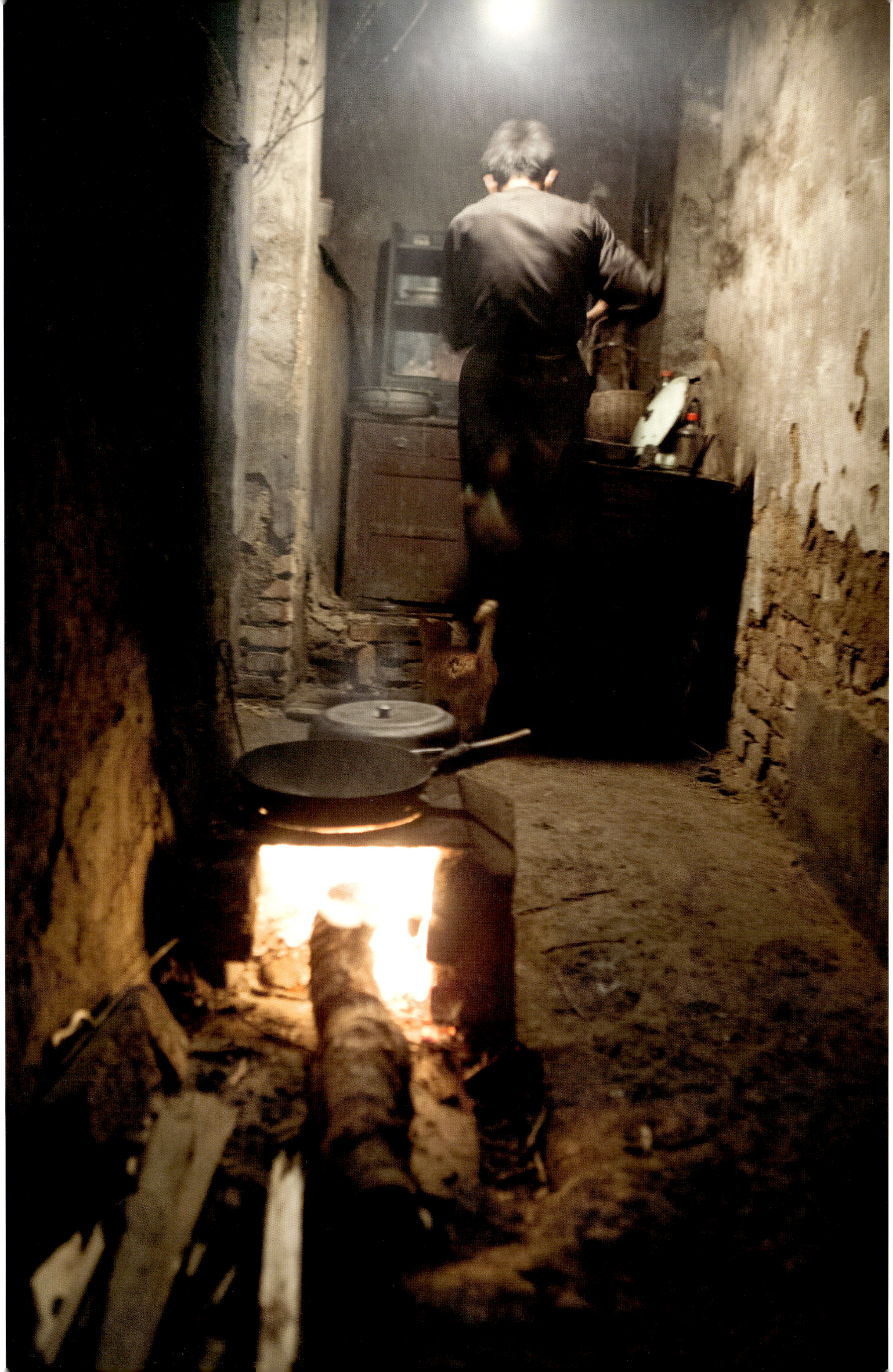

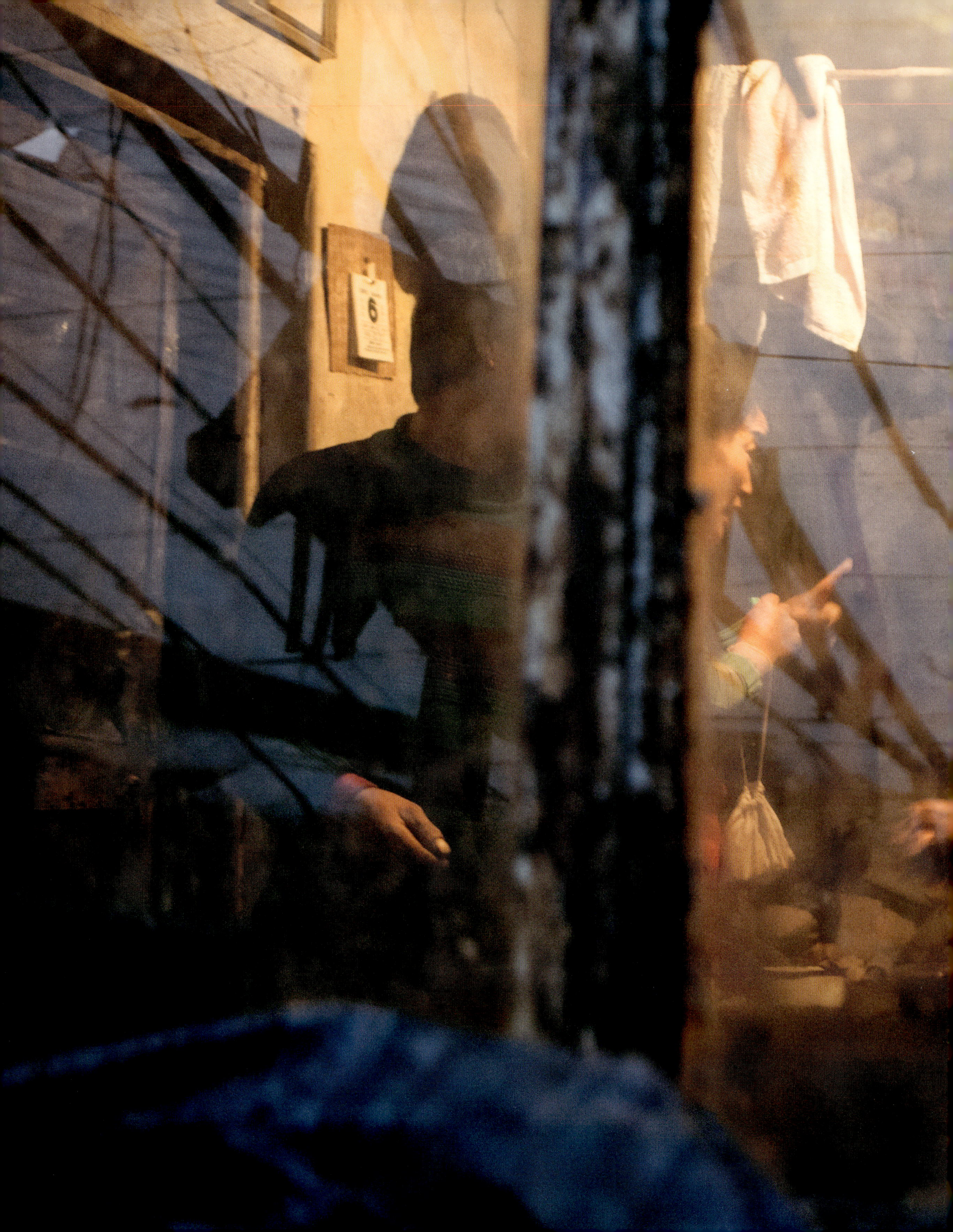
6

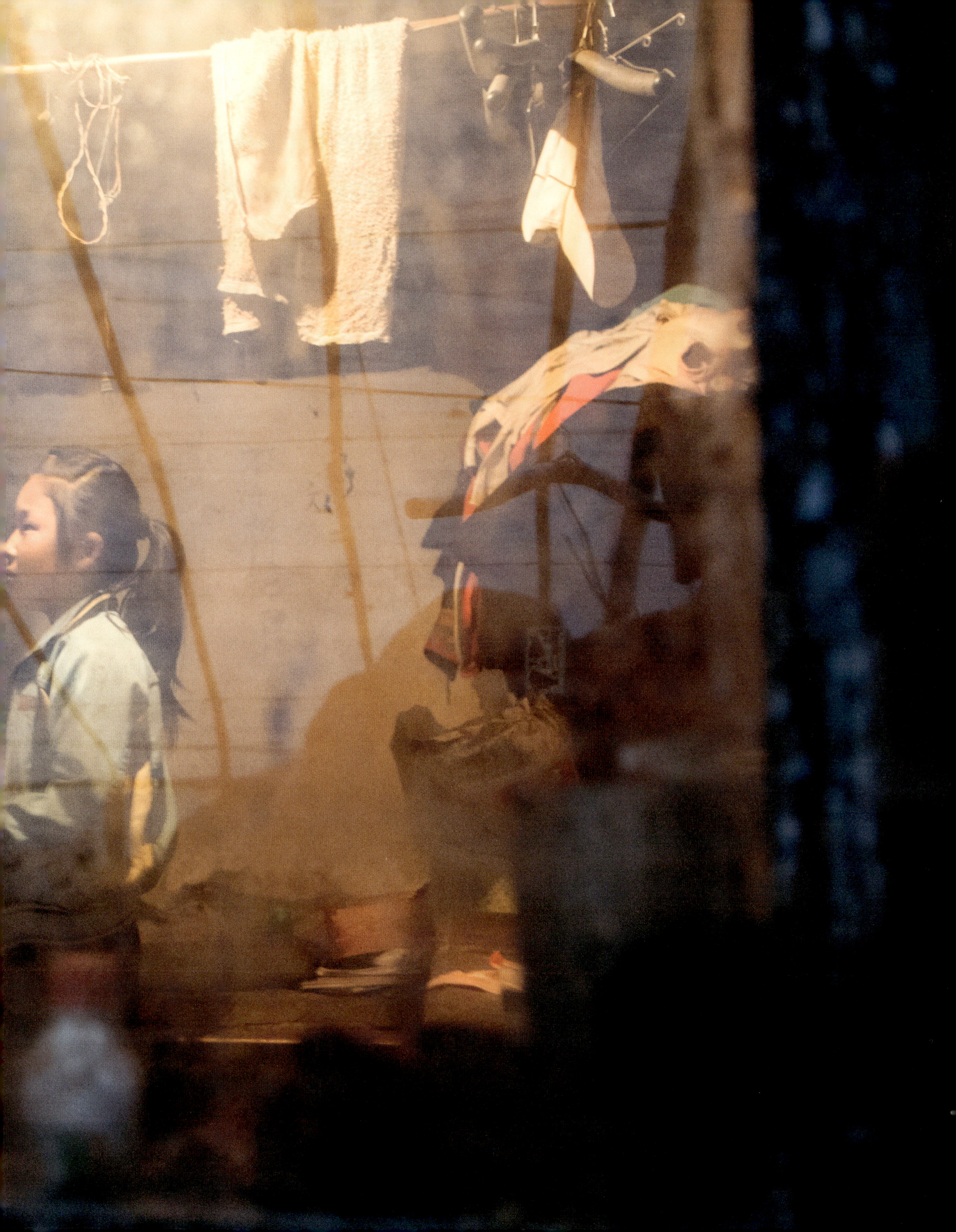

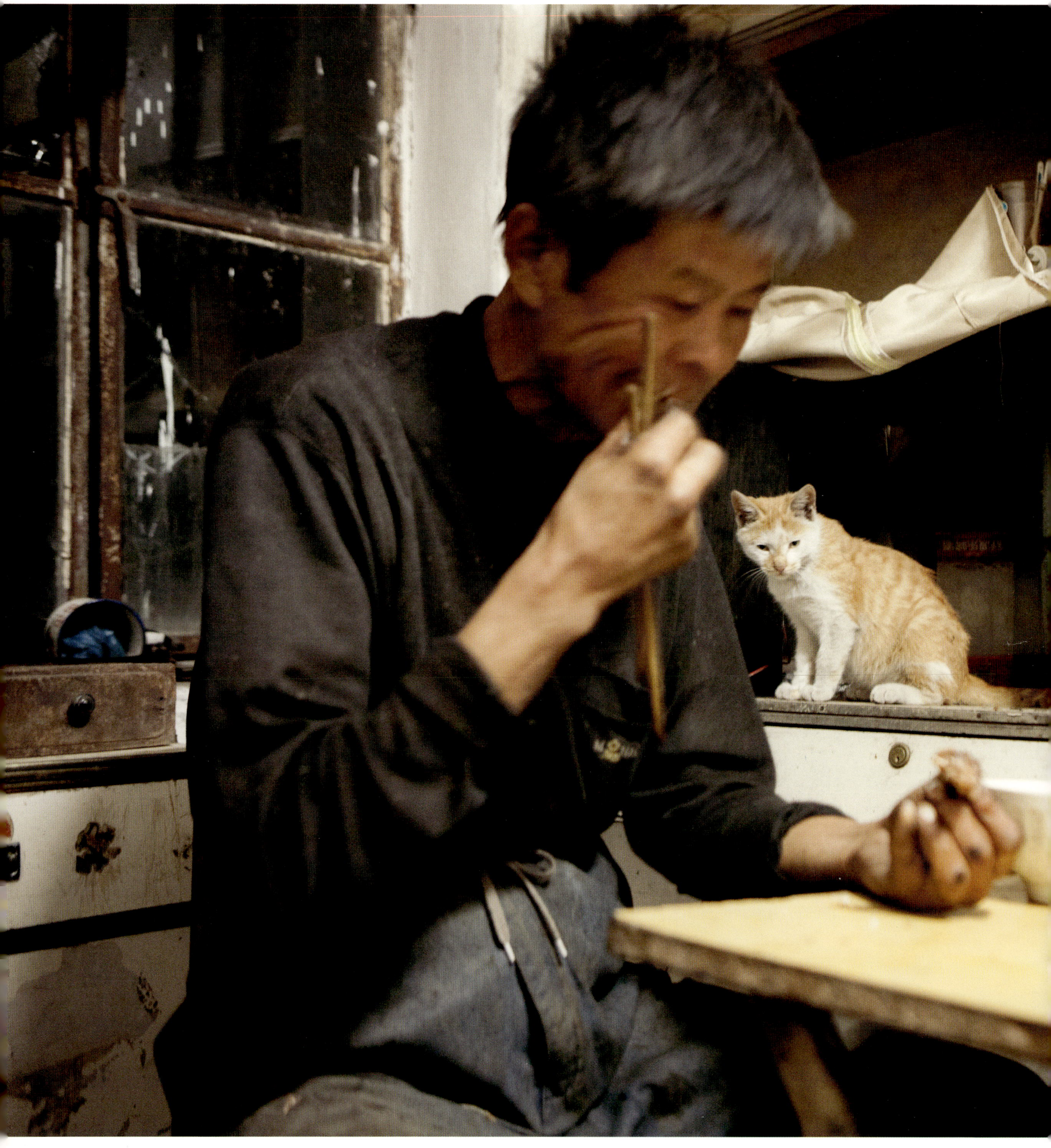

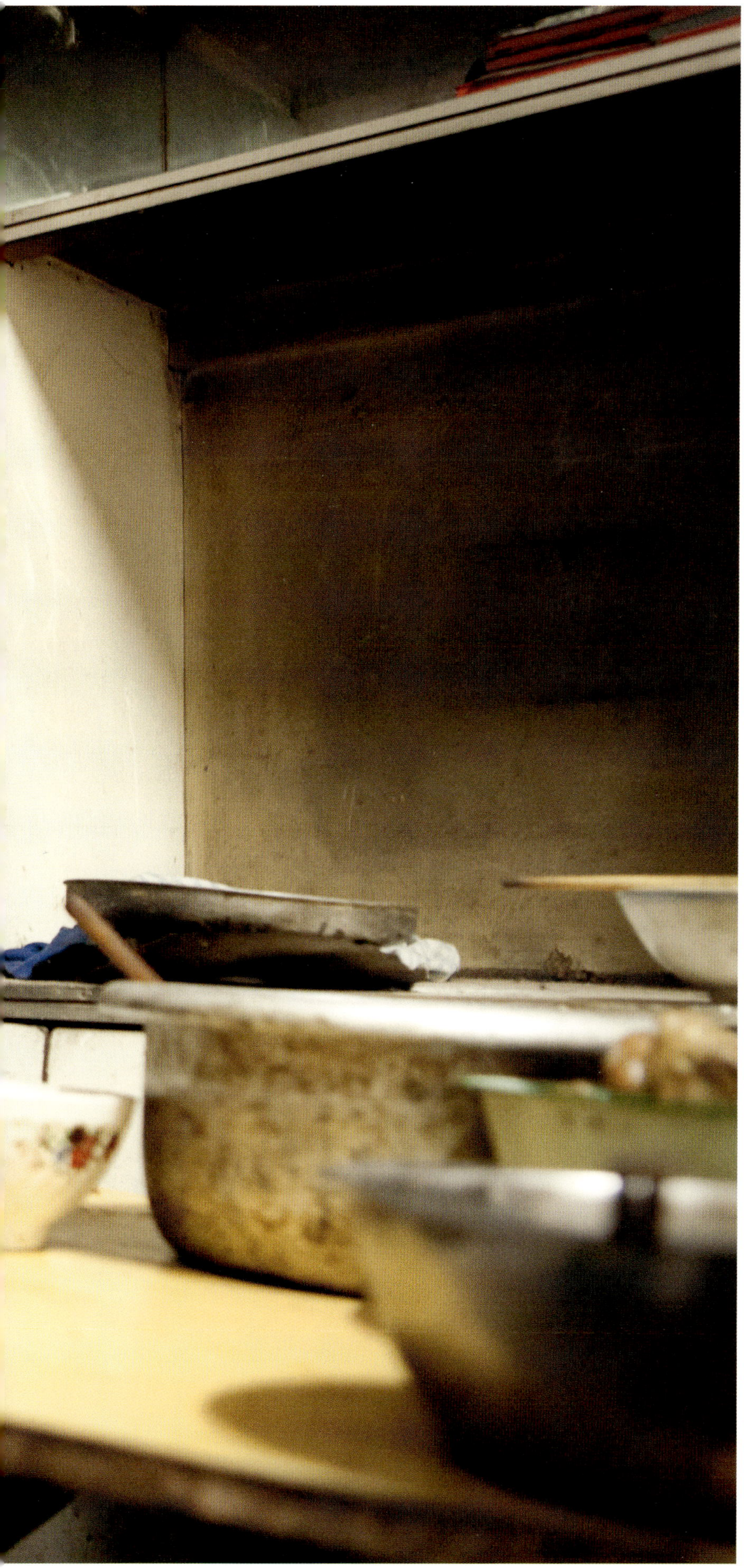

WanderarbeiterInnen in
der Volksrepublik China

Migrant Workers in the
People's Republic of China

Construction worker Wang Du has been defrauded of several monthly wages, garbage recycler Xu Fang dreams of traveling to Tibet, and gemstone cutter Han Chun is slowly dying of silicosis. Wang has helped erect high-rise buildings, Xu keeps the municipal waste disposal and Han the export industry running. China's roughly 200 million migrant workers have made the economic boom in the Middle Kingdom possible. Their stories are a testimony to the inequalities and contradictions of China's breakneck development. Many have paid a high price and only a few have achieved modest affluence. In search of a better life, they have left their rural homes and set off for the new industrial population centers. Frequently, they had hardly arrived when they found the courage, often under pressure, to move on and start from scratch somewhere else. To this day, they are fighting for recognition and their very own plans for happiness.

Moving on: China's economic development and its migrant workers

China's farmers first set out on their travels in the late 1970s. After the death of Mao Zedong in 1976, they turned their backs on the one-size-fits-all people's communes. Families again began to farm the land off their own bat and offered their products on markets they had organized themselves. The central government was left with no choice but to belatedly elevate all of this to national policy. With new market economy incentives, agricultural production boomed. But increasing mechanization made parts of the workforce redundant. More and more farmers were searching for alternative job and income opportunities.

Many of them found just that in the mushrooming rural industrial companies. Initially emerging from the people's communes, sometimes on behalf of villages or municipalities and with support from the government, resourceful families or individual farmers founded their own companies. They focused on the production of consumer goods such as textiles or toys, and later on electrical goods. Additionally, foreign investors began to build factories in the Special Economic Zones that had been set up for this purpose. The Chinese government wanted to attract capital as well as technology and boost the export industry. In return, Beijing offered investors financial concessions and cheap labor.

China's leadership chose the villages of Shenzhen and Zhuhai on account of their location on the borders to the booming big cities of Hong Kong and Macao. Due to their proximity to Taiwan, which was also prospering, the small towns of Shantou and Xiamen were declared Special Economic Zones as well. All four of these zones have developed into cities of over a million inhabitants and important centers of labor migration.

New working environments emerged in other Chinese cities as well, especially in the commercial and service industry. The government gradually also opened the latter to private activities. Small second-hand shops opened as well as hair salons, laundry shops, and hotels. Throughout

Land trieb Peking Infrastrukturprojekte voran. Bauleiter suchen Bauarbeiter, Restaurants Kellnerinnen und Köche, Haushalte Hilfskräfte.

Die städtische Dienst- und Infrastruktur, die ländlichen Industriebetriebe, die Werkbanken »Made in China«, – all dies gebe es ohne Chinas WanderarbeiterInnen nicht. Auch die leuchtend bunten Metropolen der Volksrepublik würden ohne sie zusammenbrechen: nach einem offiziellen Forschungsbericht des Staatsrats aus dem Jahr 2006 arbeiten 70 Prozent der WanderarbeiterInnen in den boomenden Küstenprovinzen Fujian, Gungdong, Zhejiang und Jiangsu oder in den Städten Peking und Shanghai. In Shenzhen, einer Metropole der Provinz Guandong an der Grenze zu Hongkong, gelten 12 der 14 Millionen Bewohner als WanderarbeiterInnen. Doch im Vergleich zu der städtischen Bevölkerung haben sie nur wenig von Chinas Boom profitiert. An ihren Arbeitsorten leben sie wie Bürger 2. Klasse. Schuld daran ist das »System Wanderarbeit«.

Das System Wanderarbeit

Die Krux ist das sogenannte Haushaltsregistrierungssystem (hukou zhidu). Um Verteilungskonflikten in den Städten vorzubeugen, ein staatliches Überwachungssystem aufzubauen und eine ausreichende Versorgung mit Grundnahrungsmitteln für die ehrgeizigen Industrialisierungsprogramme zu garantieren, führte die chinesische Regierung Anfang der 1960er Jahre das besagte Registrierungssystem ein. Bauern wurden mit einem »ländlichen Wohnsitz« registriert und bekamen als Lebensgarantie vom Staat ein Stück Land verpachtet. Für die Bevölkerung mit »städtischem Wohnsitz« richtete die Führung eine umfassende, nahezu kostenlose soziale Rundumversorgung ein: Zuteilung von Wohnraum, Arbeit, eines Kindergarten- und Schulplatzes. Stadtbewohner genossen kostenlose medizinische Versorgung, öffentlichen Transport und Freizeitaktivitäten. Und sie bekamen Lebensmittelmarken für den Zugang zu Grundnahrungsmitteln. Eine legale Land-Stadt Migration wurde somit unmöglich gemacht. Erst 1984 erlaubte die Zentralregierung den Bauern offiziell ihr Land zu verlassen, sprich dieses in die Obhut eines anderen zu geben. Als »Dienstleister und Kaufleute« – so die offizielle Bezeichnung für ihre potentiellen Arbeitsfelder – konnten sie sich in Gemeinden und Kreisstädten niederlassen. Eine Welle der Arbeitsmigration (dagongchao) erfasste die ländliche Gesellschaft. 1989 gab es nach offiziellen Angaben bereits 30 Millionen WanderarbeiterInnen, 1993 waren es 62 Millionen und 2006 wuchs die Zahl auf 131,8 Millionen an. Da die Behörden von einer temporären Arbeitsmigration ausgingen und die städtischen Ressourcen nicht belasten wollten, bekamen die WanderarbeiterInnen wenn überhaupt nur eine temporäre städtische Aufenthaltsgenehmigung. Sie behielten ihren ländlichen Wohnsitz. Dieser schloss sie aber von den Sozialleistungen an ihrem Arbeitsplatz aus.

the country, Beijing pushed infrastructure projects. Construction managers were hiring workers, restaurants waiters and chefs, households supporting staff.

Urban service industry and infrastructure, rural industrial firms, and »Made in China« workbenches – without China's migrant workers, there would be none of these. The brightly lit, colorful metropolises of the People's Republic would also face breakdown without them: According to an official 2006 research report by the State Council, 70 percent of migrant workers are found in the flourishing coastal provinces of Fujian, Guangdong, Zhejiang, and Jiangsu or in the cities of Beijing and Shanghai. In the city of Shenzhen, 12 out of 14 million inhabitants are considered to be migrant workers. But compared to the established urban population, they have profited little from China's economic boom. In the places they work, they live like second-class citizens. The blame rests with the »migratory labor system.«

The migratory labor system

The crux is the so-called household registration system (hukou zhidu). In order to guard against conflicts over distribution in the cities and build a state-run monitoring system that could guarantee sufficient supply of staple foods for its ambitious industrialization programs, the Chinese government introduced said registration system in the early 1960s. Farmers were registered at their »rural residence« and the government leased them a piece of land as a lifetime guarantee. The leadership provided the »urban residents« with comprehensive, almost free total social care: An allotment of housing space, work, a place in a kindergarten or school. City dwellers enjoyed free medical care, public transport, and leisure activities, and they received food stamps for access to staple foods. Consequently, it became impossible to legally migrate from the country to the cities. It was only in 1984 that the central government allowed farmers to officially leave their piece of land, which is to say, to entrust it to the care of someone else. As »service providers and business people« – these were the official terms for their potential areas of work – they could now settle in municipalities and district capitals. A wave of labor migration (dagongchao) went through rural populations. According to official figures, the number of migrant workers had already risen to 30 million in 1989. It climbed to 62 million in 1993, and to 131.8 million in 2006. Because the authorities assumed that they were dealing with a temporary labor migration and did not want to burden urban resources, migrant workers received temporary urban residence permits, if they received them at all. They kept their rural residences. But this made them ineligible for social benefits at their workplace.

Gegen Erniedrigung und Ausbeutung: WanderarbeiterInnen in Bewegung

Chinas Wissenschaftler streiten seit längerem darüber, ob der erstmals 1983 eingeführte Begriff für WanderarbeiterInnen, »Bauernarbeiter« (nongmingong) noch passend ist oder jemals passend war. Der Begriff ist diskriminierend, meint etwa der Publizist Xu Zongchou. Die in die Städte migrierten Bauern seien Arbeiter und sollten auch als solche behandelt werden, schreibt Xu in mehreren online veröffentlichten Aufsätzen.

Fakt ist, dass gerade in der Anfangszeit des chinesischen Kapitalismusrausches die WanderarbeiterInnen schonungslos ausgebeutet wurden. Denn Chinas kommunistische Partei hatte erkannt, nach dem Desaster der Kulturrevolution und der blutigen Niederschlagung der Demokratiebewegung 1989 brauchte sie eine neue Macht- und Legitimationsgrundlage. Mit Konsum und Wohlstand wollte Peking seine Bevölkerung politisch ruhig stellen. Das hieß Wachstum um jeden Preis. So kümmerte es lokale Arbeitsbüros und den gleichgeschalteten staatlichen Gewerkschaftsverband wenig, wenn Fabrikbesitzer und Firmenchefs WanderarbeiterInnen bis zu 20 Stunden am Stück schuften ließen. Sie zahlten ihnen Hungerlöhne und oftmals nach Wochen der Arbeit überhaupt nichts. Sicherheitsvorkehrungen oder Schutzkleidung bekamen sie nicht. Manche hielten dies nicht aus und verließen ihre Arbeitsstelle – natürlich ebenfalls ohne Lohn. Andere starben bei Fabrikbränden, Grubenunglücken oder durch Arbeitsunfälle. Wer konnte, ertrug die Schikanen mit dem Gedanken an die Eltern, die es zu Hause zu versorgen galt oder die Kinder, denen man eine bessere Zukunft ermöglichen wollte.

Doch dann setzen die WanderarbeiterInnen wieder etwas in Bewegung. Ende der 1990er Jahre erlebten sie wie tausende von entlassenen ArbeiterInnen städtischer Staatsunternehmen auf die Straße gingen. Und aus der vergleichsweise freien Sonderverwaltungszone Hongkong floss Expertise und Unterstützung von dortigen Arbeitsrechtsorganisationen nach China. Durch beide Erfahrungen inspiriert begannen auch die WanderarbeiterInnen sich zur Wehr zu setzen. Die anfänglichen Proteste waren kaum organisiert oder geplant. Doch fanden sich schnell hunderte, tausende von ArbeiterInnen zu Streiks, Blockaden von öffentlichen Straßen oder Demonstrationen zusammen. Sie forderten die Auszahlung einbehaltener Löhne, besseren Schutz am Arbeitsplatz oder Entschädigung für erlittene Unfälle oder Erkrankungen. Sie trugen ihre Fälle bis zu den Beschwerdebüros nach Peking. Chinas investigative Journalisten nahmen sich ihrer Geschichten an. Im Jahr 2003 wurde der Wanderarbeiter Sun Zhigang, Softwareingenieur bei einer IT-Firma, aufgrund nicht mitgeführter Ausweispapiere verhaftet. Kraft Gesetz mussten ihn die Polizisten in seine Heimat überführen. Doch Sun starb kurz darauf im Gefängnis – an Folter wie Journalisten bald herausfanden. Nach einem öffentlichen Aufschrei und einer konzertierten Medienkampagne gegen die Zentralregierung schaffte Peking sowohl die Zwangsrückführung als auch die Pflicht zur temporären Registrierung für WanderarbeiterInnen in Städten ab.

Against humiliation and exploitation: Migrant workers on the move

For some time now, China's scholars have been arguing about the question whether the Chinese term for migrant workers, »farm workers« (nongmingong), which was first introduced in 1983, is adequate, or if it ever was. The term is discriminating, journalist Xu Zongchou maintains. The farmers who have migrated to cities are workers and should be treated as such, Xu writes in several articles he has published online.

It is a fact that, especially in the early days of China's frenzied rush toward capitalism, migrant workers were mercilessly exploited. In the wake of the disaster of the Cultural Revolution and the bloody repression of the 1989 democracy movement, China's communist party had realized that it was in need of a new basis for its power and legitimacy. On the political level, Beijing aimed to placate its population through consumption and prosperity. It aimed for growth at all costs. Thus, factory owners and company bosses who had migrant laborers work 20-hour days were of little concern to local job offices and the state-controlled trade union federation, which functioned in lockstep with the government. They paid them a pittance or, often after weeks of work, nothing at all. There were no security measures or protective clothing. Some could not put up with this and left their job – again, without pay. Others died in factory fires and mining or work accidents. Those who could, endured the abuse and harassment because they were driven by the thought of the parents they needed to support or the children they wanted to have a better future.

But then, migrant workers began to stir. In the late 1990s, they saw thousands of workers dismissed by municipal state enterprises take to the streets. And from the comparatively free Special Administrative Region of Hong Kong, expertise and support flowed to Chinese labor law organizations. Inspired by both, migrant workers began to stand up for themselves, too. There was little organization or planning behind the initial protests. But soon hundreds and even thousands of workers joined in the strikes, blockades of public streets, and demonstrations. They demanded payment of withheld wages, better protections in the workplace, and compensation for accidents and illnesses. They took their cases all the way to the complaints offices in Beijing. China's investigative journalists told their stories. In 2003 migratory worker Sun Zhigang, a software engineer working with an IT company, was arrested for not carrying his identification papers with him. According to law, the police were supposed to return him to his place of origin. But Sun died in a prison a short time later – of torture, as journalists soon found out. In the wake of public outcry and a concerted media campaign against the central government, Beijing finally scrapped both forced repatriation and compulsory temporary registration for migrant workers in cities.

Machterhalt durch Modernisierung – die Rolle der kommunistischen Führung

Die kommunistische Führung hat erkannt, dass es die Interessen der WanderarbeiterInnen mit einbinden muss, um nicht größere soziale Unruhen zu provozieren. Diese könnten schnell ihre Macht gefährden. So hat sie die Lebens- und Arbeitsbedingungen der WanderarbeiterInnen sukzessive verbessert. 2003 – nach dem Skandal um den gestorbenen Sun Zhigang – bekamen die MigrantInnen die gleichen Rechte (u. a. in Bezug auf Mindestlohn oder Arbeitszeit) zuerkannt wie ArbeiterInnen mit städtischem Wohnsitz. Das 2008 in Kraft getretene Arbeitsvertragsgesetz sieht u. a. nur noch eine zweimalige Verlängerung von befristeten Arbeitsverträgen vor. Danach muss eine unbefristete Festanstellung erfolgen – auch für WanderarbeiterInnen. Laut dem seit Juli 2011 gültigen, lange diskutierten Gesetz zur sozialen Sicherung sollen alle chinesischen Bürger an dem bis dato nur für ArbeiterInnen mit städtischem Wohnsitz geltenden Versicherungssystemen (Arbeitsunfälle, Mutterschaftsregelung, Arbeitslosen-, Kranken- und Rentenversicherung) teilnehmen.

Die mustergültigen Gesetze werden in der Praxis allerdings nur unzureichend umgesetzt. 2011 sagte Peng Xuefeng, Delegierter des nationalen Volkskongresses, dass nur rund 43 Prozent der WanderarbeiterInnen mit einem Arbeitsvertrag eingestellt worden seien. Weniger als 30 Prozent nehmen an einer Kranken- oder Unfallversicherung teil. Laut offiziellen lokalen Umfragen aus den Jahr 2009 arbeiten die große Mehrheit von MigrantInnen in der Regel 26 Tage im Monat und 11 Stunden pro Tag. Peking schiebt die Schuld auf den Preis der Modernisierung und auf die Verfehlungen lokaler Kader und Bosse. Damit kann sie von ihrer eigenen politischen Verantwortung – u. a. anhaltendes Verbot von unabhängigen gewerkschaftlichen Vertretungen – ablenken. Und auch wenn linke Intellektuelle in China die Allianz zwischen Macht und Kapital ankreiden – wobei sie nationalistisch meist primär die ausländischen Unternehmer kritisieren – stellt Chinas Führung das neoliberale System nicht in Frage. Und das System Wanderarbeit mit seinen Diskriminierungsmechanismen hat, wenn auch in abgeschwächter Form, weiterhin Bestand. Zwar ist es in vielen Städten mittlerweile möglich einen urbanen Wohnsitz zu erwerben. Voraussetzung dafür ist u. a. der Besitz einer Eigentumswohnung. Ein Großteil der WanderarbeiterInnen kann sich dies nicht leisten. Schon außerhalb der Fabrikwohnheime ein eigenes Zimmer oder gar eine Wohnung zu mieten, ist für viele finanziell unmöglich. Ohne Wohnsitz dürfen ihre Kinder keine städtischen Schulen besuchen. Und ihre Krankenversicherung – sofern sie eine haben – gilt meist nur an ihrem Heimatort. Sie leben zwischen den Welten – nicht mehr Bauern, aber auch (noch) nicht Städter.

Staying in power through modernization – the role of communist leadership

The communist leadership has realized that it needs to take the interests of migrant workers seriously, so as not to provoke widespread social unrest. These could otherwise quickly jeopardize their power. Thus, the living and working conditions of migrant workers have gradually improved. In 2003 – in the wake of the scandal surrounding the death of Sun Zhigang – migrants were granted the same rights (with regard to minimum wages or working hours, among others) as workers with an urban residence. The employment contract law, effective since 2008, allows for only two consecutive renewals of fixed-term work contracts. After that, a permanent contract must be issued – to migrant workers, as well. According to the much-discussed law on social security, which came into effect in July 2011, all Chinese citizens will have access to the insurance system (work accidents, maternity regulation, unemployment as well as health insurance, and pension scheme), which previously had only covered workers with urban residences.

But in real life, these perfect laws are only partially implemented. In 2011, Peng Xuefeng, a delegate to the National People's Congress, issued a statement saying that only some 43 percent of migrant workers had been employed with a work contract. Less than 30 percent had health or accident insurance. According to official local surveys from 2009, as a rule, the majority of migrants worked 26 days a month and 11 hours a day. Beijing says this is a price that is paid for modernization and blames the misconduct of local cadres and bosses. This is aimed at distracting attention from its own political responsibilities – which is to say, the continuing ban on independent unionized representation, among others. And even though left-leaning intellectuals in China criticize the alliance between power and capital – which, as patriots, they usually frame as pertaining to foreign entrepreneurs – China's leadership never questions the neoliberal system. And the migratory labor system with its mechanisms of discrimination continues to exist, albeit in a mitigated form. Even though it has now become possible to acquire an urban residence in many cities – ownership of an apartment is a prerequisite – the majority of migrant workers cannot afford one. Even renting a room of their own or an apartment outside the factory rooming houses is financially out of reach for many. Without a city residence, their children cannot attend schools. And their health insurance – if they have any, that is – is only valid in their place of origin. They live between two worlds – no longer as farmers, but also not (yet) as urbanites.

Wir wollen leben wie die Städter – Chinas zweite Generation der WanderarbeiterInnen

Die 2. Generation der chinesischen WanderarbeiterInnen, die in den 1980ern geboren wurde und meist Kinder von WanderarbeiterInnen sind, will sich damit nicht abfinden. Sie haben den Großteil ihrer Kindheit und Jugend in städtischen Regionen verbracht. Sie haben eine höhere Schulbildung – wenn auch auf dem Land und nicht in den Städten – als ihre Eltern. Sie wissen nicht was ein Bauer macht und wollen auch nicht als solcher arbeiten. Sie sehen wie gleichaltrige städtische Jugendliche leben und wollen genauso leben. Durch Handys und Internet sind sie ständig und überall miteinander vernetzt. Die jungen WanderarbeiterInnen sind selbstbewusst und kennen ihre Rechte.

So entwickeln ihre Proteste eine neue Dynamik und neue Ziele. Ende Mai 2011 protestierten Hunderte von ArbeiterInnen in der Zulieferproduktionsfabrik Nanhai Honda in der südchinesischen Stadt Foshan. Sie demonstrierten für die Wahl eigener Repräsentanten in den staatlichen Gewerkschaftsbund und eine 35-prozentige Lohnsteigerung. Sie hatten größtenteils Erfolg. Auf der Plattform des chinesischen Webunternehmens Tencent (QQ) richteten sie eine Diskussionsgruppe »Einheit heißt Stärke« ein. Trotz Internetzensur fand in den Diskussionsgruppen ein Austausch über den neusten Stand der Dinge, aber auch über Strategien und Schwierigkeiten statt. In den nächsten zwei Monaten legten sieben verschiedene Honda-Zulieferbetriebe in ganz China ihre Arbeit nieder. Ihre Forderungen: bessere Löhne, mehr Sozialleistungen, Mitbestimmung bei der Gestaltung des Schichtsystems und die Wahl eigener Gewerkschaftsvertreter.

Solche Proteste zeigen: Chinas junge WanderarbeiterInnen sind mehr denn je in Bewegung. Sie sind angekommen in der städtischen Lebenswelt. Nun wollen sie sich dort eine eigene Zukunft aufbauen. Sie wissen, dass ihnen die demographische Entwicklung aufgrund der chinesischen Ein-Kind-Politik in die Hände spielt. In vielen Ballungszentren Chinas zeichnet sich ein Arbeitskräftemangel ab. Wenn Peking nicht bald auf das neue Selbstbewusstsein der WanderarbeiterInnen reagiert, denn wird aus den einstmals anarchischen und vereinzelt Kämpfenden eine zunehmend gefährliche politische Kraft.

Kristin Kupfer

We want to live like city-dwellers – China's second generation of migrant workers

The second generation of Chinese migrant workers, which was born in the 1980s, mostly as children to migrant workers, do not want to reconcile themselves with their fate. They spent most of their childhood and youth in urban regions. Their education is superior to that of their parents. They have no idea what a farmer does and don't want to work as one. Seeing urban youth of the same age, they want to live like them. Via cell phones and the Internet, they are connected with each other at any time and place. These young migrant workers are self-confident and know their rights.

Thus, their protests developed new dynamics and new goals. In late May of 2011, hundreds of workers joined protests against the supply company Nanhai Honda in the southern Chinese city of Foshan. They demonstrated for the right to elect their own representatives to the state-run federation of labor unions and a 35 percent wage increase. They were largely successful. Using a platform provided by Chinese web company Tencent (QQ), they set up a discussion group called »Unity Means Strength.« In spite of Internet censorship, an exchange about the current state of affairs as well as strategies and problems took place through these discussions groups. Over the following two months, workers at seven more of Honda's supplier companies across China went on strike. They demanded higher wages, expanded social benefits, worker participation in the organization of the shift system, and the election of union representatives.

Such protests show that China's young migrant workers are, more than ever, moving on. They have arrived in urban environments. Now, this is where they want to build a future for themselves. They know that, due to China's one-child policy, demographic developments play into their hands. In many of China's population centers, a manpower shortage is looming. If Beijing does not react to the new self-assurance of migrant workers soon, the anarchic and isolated fighters of days past will form an increasingly dangerous political force.

Kristin Kupfer

Baustellen, Verschiedene Orte

Essensdämpfe erfüllen die feuchten Kellerräume. Hier unten, unter dem Fundament des künftigen Hochhauses, das sie über sich errichten, findet das soziale Leben der chinesischen Bauarbeiter auf dicht gedrängtem Raum statt. Konzentriert auf ihr Essen sitzen viele der Wanderarbeiter zurückgezogen auf doppelstöckigen Pritschenbetten. Andere haben angefangen, sich zu waschen oder lassen sich von Kollegen die Haare schneiden. Danach werden sie versuchen auf ihren kargen Betten Schlaf zu finden. Diese sind nur durch trocknende Wäsche auf Wäscheleinen von dem Nachbarbett abgegrenzt. Manche der Männer stellen auch Pappkartons auf, um zwischen den eng aufgestellten Etagenbetten etwas Privatsphäre zu schaffen.

Auf chinesische Arbeitsmigranten bin ich zum ersten Mal 2005 auf einer Baustelle in der russischen Kleinstadt Blagoweschensk nahe des Grenzflusses Amur getroffen. Die Eindrücke dort werden für mich schließlich zum Ausgangspunkt mehrer Reisen durch die Volksrepublik in den Jahren 2005 bis 2011. Ich möchte mehr vom Leben chinesischer Wanderarbeiter und Wanderarbeiterinnen in ihrem Herkunftsland erfahren. Sie sind dort Teil einer umfassenden Arbeitsmigration, welche die gesamte Gesellschaft durchdringt. Einige ihrer Wege möchte ich nachzeichnen.

In dem Kellerraum auf der russischen Amurseite treffe ich etwas zurückgezogen von der Hauptgruppe auf Wang Du (42) aus der an Russland grenzenden Provinz Heilongjiang. Er erzählt, dass er zuletzt 2003 um seinen Lohn betrogen wurde. Wang war einem Subunternehmer aus seiner Heimatregion gefolgt. Diesen Anwerbern fällt es in Zeiten des Booms und knapper Arbeitskräfte zu, in ihren Heimatregionen neue Arbeiter zu rekrutieren. Der Mann hatte Wang das Blaue vom Himmel versprochen, aber mehr als Essensgutscheine bekam Wang nie zu sehen. Er und seine drei Kollegen aus der gleichen Kleinstadt wurden immer wieder auf das Ende des Jahres vertröstet, bis der Subunternehmer schließlich nicht mehr aufzufinden war. Es hieß, er hätte seinen Auftrag auf der Baustelle verloren. Aber was hätte Wang schon unternehmen können, etwa zur Polizei gehen? Einen Arbeitsvertrag, um sein Beschäftigungsverhältnis nachzuweisen, hatte er ja nicht. Alles wird mündlich ausgemacht in der Baubranche und damit ist am Ende niemand mehr zu belangen.

Dieses Jahr versucht Wang es noch einmal auf einer Baustelle. Einen anderen Job hat er nicht finden können. Ein Freund hatte ihm von einer staatlichen Agentur erzählt, die Arbeitskräfte auch nach Russland vermittelt. Wang hofft, dass er sich diesmal auf die Auszahlung seines Lohnes am Ende des Jahres verlassen kann.

Ich treffe Xu Lin (18) aus der nicht weit entfernten Großstadt Harbin an der Essensausgabe und begleite ihn zu seinem Platz auf den Pritschenbetten. Es ist sein erster Einsatz auf einer Baustelle. Xu träumt davon, ein neues Land kennen zu lernen. Bisher hat er es aber nicht einmal geschafft, die mit einer Mauer von der Umwelt abgeschirmte Baustelle zu verlassen. Zu enorm ist der Arbeitsdruck, oft haben sie Tag und Nacht zu arbeiten. Mit der Begründung »Termindruck« lässt der Kolonnenführer kaum

Construction Sites, Various Places

The smell of food and cooking fumes fill the damp basement rooms. Here, in the cramped quarters beneath the foundations of a future high-rise building, the social life of Chinese construction workers unfolds. Sitting on plank bunk beds and appearing withdrawn, many migrant workers are focusing their attention on eating. Others are washing themselves or having their hair cut by colleagues, before they will try to get some sleep on their austere beds. They are separated only by full clotheslines. Some have partitioned the narrow space between their bunk beds with arrangements of cardboard boxes, so as to create some privacy.

I first came into contact with Chinese migrant workers in 2005 on a building site in the small Russian town of Blagoveshchensk near the Amur River, which forms the border between Russia and China. The impression this left on me formed the point of departure for several journeys through the People's Republic between 2005 and 2011. I wanted to learn more about the lives of Chinese migrant workers caught up in a massive labor migration that has permeated all of society. I wanted to trace some of their paths.

In a basement room on the Russian shore of the Amur River I met Wang Du (42), who kept somewhat of a distance to the main group and hailed from the province of Heilongjiang, which borders on Russia. He recalled that he was last defrauded of his pay in 2003. Wang had followed a subcontractor from his home region who hired new workers in boom times when labor was in short supply. The man had promised Wang a pie in the sky, and all he ever got were food vouchers. He and three of his colleagues, who also hailed from his hometown, were repeatedly put off until the end of the year. Finally, the subcontractor vanished into thin air. He was told he had lost his job on the site. But what could Wang have done, go to the police? He didn't have a work contract or any other evidence of his employment. All of these jobs in the construction industry are based on verbal agreements, so that ultimately no one is legally responsible.

This year, Wang is giving it another try on a construction site because he hasn't found any other job. A friend told him about a state-run agency, which places workers with companies in Russia. Wang is hopeful that this time around, he can count on being paid his salary at the end of the year.

I meet Xu Lin (18), who hails from the nearby big city of Harbi, at the serving counter and accompany him to his plank bed. It's the first time he has worked on a construction site. Xu dreams of getting to know a new country. So far, however, he hasn't even managed to leave the construction site, which is separated from the world outside by a wall. There is enormous pressure to work, often day and night. Due to this »pressure to meet deadlines,« the gang leader hardly allows them to take breaks at all. He asks me whether it's hard to come to Germany.

New workers have arrived. They were dropped off at the site by a minibus at night and led to the damp basement rooms. Like almost all of them, Zhao Guihua (34) is

eine Pause gelten. Ob es schwierig sei, nach Deutschland zu kommen, will er von mir wissen.

Eine neue Gruppe von Arbeitern trifft ein. Sie sind in der Nacht mit dem Kleinbus auf der Baustelle abgesetzt worden und werden nun zu den feuchten Kellerräumlichkeiten geführt. Einer von ihnen ist Zhao Guihua (34), wie fast alle aus der Provinz Heilongjiang. Die Schuhfabrik, in der Zhao gearbeitet hatte, war privatisiert worden. Restrukturierung unrentabler Staatsbetriebe, lautete die offizielle Politik. Die neuen alten Manager hatten Zhao wie viele Andere fristlos und ohne Entschädigung entlassen. So kam er auf der Suche nach Arbeit nach Russland.

Mit den 1500 Yuan (ca. 177 Euro), die er hier pro Monat verdienen soll, ist er nicht unzufrieden. Nur über die Unterbringung, die er dicht gedrängt mit seinen Kollegen die nächsten Wochen und Monate wird teilen müssen, regt er sich auf. »Das ist doch wie in einem Hühnerstall hier!«, schimpft Zhao.

Textilfabrik, Nanjing

Zielsicher führt He Qing (19) die Passtücke eines künftigen Mantels unter der ratternden Nähmaschine durch, bevor sie die Stücke ohne aufzuschauen auf einen Haufen wirft. Sie ist Ende 2010 aus der Provinz Shandong in die Textilfabrik nach Nanjing gekommen. Hier fertigen die rund 900 Mitarbeiterinnen jeden Monat 60–80.000 Kleidungsstücke, vorrangig für den europäischen wie auch japanischen Markt. Über einen Grundlohn hinaus wird ihr Einkommen nach Stückzahlen berechnet. Mit ihrem inzwischen erreichten Arbeitstempo kommt He auf einen durchschnittlichen Lohn von 2500 Yuan (ca. 295 Euro) im Monat.

Sie kommuniziert mit ihren Kolleginnen über laute Zwischenrufe. Ihre genähten Stoffhaufen trägt sie selbst zu denjenigen, die sie weiterverarbeiten. Dabei lachen alle viel. Erst gegen Abend wird die Stimmung deutlich angespannter und es verbleibt einzig das Dröhnen und Rattern der Maschinen in den großen Fabriksälen. Das Schichtende um 21 Uhr rückt näher und jede versucht noch die eigenen Stückzahlziele zu erreichen.

An einem der wenigen arbeitsfreien Tage gelingt es mir, He auch außerhalb der Fabrik zu treffen. Die junge Näherin ist gut aufgelegt und hat später noch eine Verabredung mit Freunden zum Rollerskaten. Die Frage nach ihren beruflichen Plänen, ob sie mit ihrem relativ guten Einkommen in der Firma bleiben wolle, beantwortet sie mit einem klaren »Nein«. Selbstbewusst sagt He, sie sei noch jung und wolle sich in anderen Fabriken umschauen.

Ihr Erzählen kommt ins Stocken, als es um das Verhältnis zu ihren Eltern geht. Diese hätten sich immer nur um den Bruder gekümmert und sie der Großmutter zur Erziehung überlassen. »Selbst wenn ich krank wurde, haben sie nicht nach mir geschaut«, sagt He. Dafür geht es jetzt, wenn sie zu Hause anruft, immer nur ums Geld. »Sie behandeln mich wie eine Geld-Druckmaschine«, so die junge Frau.

Anders geht es Yan Zhen (19). Seine Eltern arbeiten noch und sind nicht auf seine Unterstützung angewiesen. Er legt nicht nur Geld zurück, sondern gibt es auch gerne

from the province of Heilongjiang. The shoe factory where Zhao had worked was privatized. Officially, it was called a restructuring of unprofitable government enterprises. The new managers fired Zhao and many others without notice and compensation. This is how his search for work led him to Russia.

He is happy with the monthly 1500 yuan (approx. 177 euros) he will earn here. Still, he complains about the crowded and cramped accommodation he is going to share with his colleagues over the next weeks and months. »This place is like a henhouse,« Zhao protests.

Textile Factory, Nanjing

With a sure hand, He Qing (19) feeds pieces of a future coat through the clattering sewing machine, before throwing them onto a pile without looking up. In late 2010, she came to Nanjing from the province of Shandong to work in the textile factory. Here, some 900 employees produce 60–80,000 pieces of clothing every month, primarily for European and Japanese markets. In addition to a fixed basic wage, she is paid a piece rate based on output. The pace she is working at by now will get He an average salary of 2500 yuan (approx. 295 euros) per month.

She intermittently communicates with her colleagues by shouting above the din. She carries the sewed fabrics over to others for further processing. They laugh a lot. Towards the evening, though, the atmosphere gets tenser and the only sound left is the rumble and clatter of machines. They are approaching the end of their shift at 9 p.m. and all of them make a last-ditch effort to reach the quantities they have set as their goal.

On one of her few days off, I manage to meet He outside of the factory. The young seamstress is in good spirits and will later meet up with friends to go roller-skating. Asked whether she intends to stay with the company given the comparatively good income it pays her, she answers with a resounding »No.« Self-confidently, He says that she is still young and intends to explore her options in other factories.

When she touches on her relationship with her parents, she begins to falter. All through her childhood, they only looked after her brother, while she was raised by her grandmother. »They didn't even take care of me when I got sick,« He remembers. And when she calls home now, all they ever talk about is money. »They treat me like a money-printing machine,« He said.

Yan Zhen's (19) situation is different. His parents still work and do not have to rely on his support. He not only saves some of his money, but also spends it when he goes shopping with his girlfriend. Like many of his colleagues, Yan has been involved in labor disputes. At his last factory, workers had gone on strike to protest poor working con-

beim Shopping mit seiner Freundin aus. Wie viele seiner Kollegen blickt auch Yan auf Arbeitskampf-Erfahrungen zurück. In seiner letzten Fabrik hatte die Mehrzahl der Arbeiter und Arbeiterinnen aufgrund schlechter Bedingungen zunächst ihre Tätigkeit niedergelegt. Nachdem der Fabrikleiter ihre Kompensationsforderungen nicht erfüllte, verließen sie schließlich das Unternehmen. In Zeiten des wirtschaftlichen Aufschwungs suchen die Firmen oft händeringend nach neuen Arbeitskräften. So war es für Yan und die anderen nicht schwer, einen neuen und sogar besser bezahlten Arbeitsplatz zu finden.

Allerdings stößt das von den Arbeitern und Arbeiterinnen zu Zeiten des Booms erstrittene höhere Lohnniveau an seine Grenzen. Auch die Nanjinger Textilfabrik liegt in einer Hochlohnregion. Deshalb diskutiert die Firmenleitung eine Verlagerung der Produktion in den noch weniger entwickelten Westen Chinas. Bei einem fortschreitenden Ausbau der Infrastruktur wird ein Umzug in Landesteile mit niedrigerem Lohnniveau immer interessanter. Möglicherweise ist der Westen Chinas aber auch nur ein Zwischenschritt in Richtung Vietnam oder Kambodscha – Länder, in denen das Lohnniveau noch niedriger ist als in China.

Spielzeugfabrik, Shenzhen

Ich bin gespannt, als mir Zhang Quanshou, einer der größten Leiharbeitshändler Chinas, endlich gegenübersteht. Vormals selbst Wanderarbeiter hatte ihn seine Karriere über die Eröffnung eines Restaurants und einer Spielzeugfabrik in die Leiharbeitsbranche geführt. Diese Branche trifft die Bedürfnisse vieler Arbeitgeber. Zahlreiche Firmen können zu Spitzenzeiten der Produktion nicht mehr genügend Arbeitskräfte finden. Darüber hinaus haben diese inzwischen nicht nur ein verbessertes Bewusstsein ihrer rechtlichen Lage, sondern mit dem 2009 in Kraft gesetzten Arbeitsvertragsrecht auch eine verbesserte rechtliche Position. Dies begrenzt die Zahl wiederholter befristeter Einstellungen. Um auch weiterhin über eine extrem flexible Belegschaft verfügen zu können, greifen viele Unternehmer auf Leiharbeit zurück. So hat sich die Zahl der von Zhang Quanshou entliehenen Arbeitskräfte von nur wenigen Dutzend auf inzwischen fast 20.000 erhöht.

Nach einem Geschäftsessen nimmt er mich mit in eine Spielzeugfabrik, deren Gesamtbelegschaft von ca. 2000 Arbeiter und Arbeiterinnen er fast ausschließlich stellt. Dort müssen nach Ende der Spätschicht gegen 22 Uhr sämtliche seiner ArbeiterInnen in Formation antreten. Sie haben Leibesübungen zu verrichten und auch seiner über einstündigen Rede zu lauschen. Deren Kern ist, sich als WanderarbeiterInnen an ihm und seinem Erfolg ein Beispiel zu nehmen – wer fleißig ist, kann es auch zu etwas bringen, so Zhang. Er bezeichnet sich selbst als »Kommandeur« und seine ArbeiterInnen als »Familie«. Eine Sozial- und Krankenversicherung gibt es für seine Belegschaft nicht. Dafür nimmt er am Ende der nächtlichen Versammlung Krankmeldungen persönlich entgegen und entscheidet darüber, inwieweit er die Behandlungskosten direkt übernimmt.

Er rekrutiert seine Belegschaft ausschließlich aus der Provinz Henan, aus der er selbst stammt. Es ist eine der

ditions. When the factory manager refused to meet their demands, they left the company. In times of economic upswing, companies often urgently and desperately search for additional manpower. Thus, it wasn't hard for Yan and the others to find new and better-paid jobs.

There are, however, limits to the higher wage levels workers fight for and win during boom times. The Nanjing textile factory is located in a high-wage region, which is why the company's management is considering moving production to a less developed area in Western China. Relocation to the low-wage parts of the country is becoming more attractive because infrastructure is improving in these areas. It is conceivable that Western China could serve as an interim solution before factories are moved to Vietnam or Cambodia – where wage levels are even lower.

Toy Factory, Shenzhen

My expectations are high when I finally stand face to face with Zhang Quanshou, one of China's leading temporary work agents. A former migratory laborer himself, he went on to open a restaurant as well as a toy factory. His career then led him into the temporary work industry, which caters to the needs of numerous employers. Many companies are unable to find sufficient manpower during peak production times. By now, China's workers have not only developed a better understanding of their legal situation; the labor contract legislation that came into effect in 2009 has also improved their legal position. New employees may be given no more than two consecutive fixed-term employment contracts. In order to be able to continue to rely on an extremely flexible workforce, many businesses resort to temporary workers. Thus, the number of Zhang Quanshou's temporary laborers has risen from a few dozen to almost 20,000.

Following a business lunch, he takes me to a toy factory whose entire workforce of about two thousand he almost exclusively supplies. After the late shift has ended at about 10 p.m., all his workers are required to fall into formation, go through a physical exercise session, and listen to his over one-hour speech. Its core message is that migrant workers should take him and his success as an example – if you work hard, you can make it, says Zhang. He calls himself the »commander« and his workers »family.« There is no social security or health insurance for his workforce. Instead, he personally accepts sick notes at the end of the nocturnal gathering and decides, to what extent he will directly foot the bill for medical treatment.

He recruits his workers exclusively from his home province of Henan. It is one of China's poorest provinces. To this day, many Chinese look down on its population. In earlier days, being from Henan was reason enough to not get a job. Zhang, on the other hand, offers his workers a

ärmsten Provinzen Chinas. Bis heute schauen viele Chinesen auf deren Bewohner hinab. Früher konnte die Angabe von Henan als Herkunftsprovinz ausreichen, um eine Arbeitsstelle nicht zu bekommen. Umgekehrt bietet Zhang seinen Arbeiterinnen und Arbeitern eine Prämie, wenn sie Bekannte aus derselben Provinz anwerben. 300 Yuan (ca. 35 Euro) bietet er für die Anwerbung einer weiblichen und 250 (ca. 23 Euro) für die einer männlichen Arbeitskraft.

Im Wohnheim der Fabrik treffe ich Tan Yaru (20). Der Rhythmus des Fließbandes lässt während der Schichten kaum Zeit für ein Gespräch. Sie arbeitet je nach den Anforderungen neun bis elf Stunden täglich an den Montagebändern der Spielzeugfabrik oder auch in der ohne gesonderte Abzugsvorrichtungen stark nach Lösungsmitteln riechenden Lackiererei. Tan beschwert sich, dass sie seit zwei Monaten keinen einzigen freien Tag mehr hatte.

Tan gibt an, bis heute keinen Arbeitsvertrag bekommen zu haben und für die gleiche Arbeit als »Anfängerin« nur 1300 Yuan (ca. 153 Euro) anstatt der regulären 1500 Yuan (ca. 177 Euro) pro Monat zu verdienen. Um ihren Anfängerinnen-Status los zu werden und um ihre Kaution bei Austritt aus der Leiharbeitsfirma zurück erhalten zu können, muss Tan mindestens drei Jahre dort gearbeitet haben. Auch darf sie während des traditionellen Neujahrsfestes der Arbeit nur einen Monat fernbleiben. Das ist ihr aber, wie sie sagt, nicht immer gelungen. Auch wenn Tan ihre Kolleginnen aus der gleichen Provinz vermissen wird, will sie sich doch noch nach anderen Arbeitsplätzen umschauen und weitere Erfahrungen sammeln.

Wir treffen auf ihre Zimmerkollegin Li Meiju (18), die nach einem vorzeitigen Schulabbruch zunächst in einem Schönheitssalon arbeitete. Durch den Eintritt in die Leiharbeitsfirma hat sich ihr Einkommen spürbar verbessert. Li, die ihre Mitbewohnerinnen noch zu einem Besuch in eine Karaoke-Bar überreden kann, ist mit ihrem Einkommen zufrieden und träumt davon, einmal ihren eigenen Schönheitssalon zu eröffnen.

Unter der Mehrheit besonders der unerfahrenen ArbeiterInnen stiftet die kollektive Herkunft ein Gemeinschaftsgefühl, das über die Härten des Arbeitsalltages hinwegtrösten kann. Die Umkehrung der negativen in eine positive Diskriminierung der Arbeiterinnen aus Henan hilft bei der Akzeptanz des Geschäftsmodells von Kommando und quasi-familiärer Zusammengehörigkeit.

Bettler, Guangzhou

Sie fallen mir vom vorüber fahrenden Bus aus ins Auge – die Obdachlosen, die sich auf dem begrünten Mittelstreifen einer Hauptverkehrsstraße in Guangzhou niedergelassen haben. Dort, unter der Brücke einer über sie hinweg führenden Stadtautobahn gegen Regen geschützt, treffen sich mehrheitlich die, die die Mühle Wanderarbeit bereits durchlaufen haben und als unverwertbar herausgefallen sind. Es sind Menschen aus allen Teilen des Landes, die es in die südchinesische Metropole verschlagen hat. Die, die inzwischen zu alt sind, um noch eine Chance auf dem Wanderarbeitsmarkt zu haben; die, die von ihren ehemaligen Chefs um das ihnen zustehende Gehalt und oft auch

premium for the recruitment of relatives from their province, which amounts to 300 yuan (approx. 35 euros) for a female and 250 (approx. 23 euros) for a male worker.

At the factory rooming house I meet Tan Yaru (20). The rhythm of the assembly line hardly leaves any time for a conversation during shifts. Depending on demand, she works between nine and eleven-hour days at the assembly line or at the toy factory's paint shop, where a strong smell of solvents is in the air because it lacks special fume collection devices. Tan complains that she hasn't had a single day off for two months.

She maintains that, to this day, she has not received a work contract and, as a »beginner,« is paid only a monthly 1300 yuan (approx. 153 euros) for the same work that normally earns workers 1500 yuan (approx. 177 euros). In order to shake off her rookie-status and to be refunded the security she has deposited upon leaving the temporary employment agency, Tan must work there for a minimum of three years. Furthermore, during the traditional New Year celebrations, she is only allowed to take one month off from work. That is something she has not always been able to comply with. Although Tan will miss her colleagues, she will stay on the lookout for new jobs and try to gain further experience.

We meet her roommate Li Meiju (18) who, after dropping out of school, first worked at a beauty parlor. Joining the temporary employment agency has noticeably improved her income. Li, who is able to persuade her roommate to join her at a karaoke bar, is satisfied with her income and dreams of one day opening her own beauty parlor.

With the majority of inexperienced workers, their collective origin gives rise to a sense of community, which can help them get over the hardships of everyday work. The reversal of negative into positive discrimination of Henan workers leads to the acceptance of a business model with military-style command and a sense of quasi family and belonging.

Beggars, Guangzhou

They caught my eye when I rode by on a bus – homeless people who have settled down on the green median strip of a main thoroughfare in Guangzhou. Safe from rain under the bridge of a city highway, this is mostly a meeting place for people who have already been through the wringer of migratory labor and were discarded as unserviceable. People from all around the country end up in this southern China metropolis. Those too old to stand a chance on the job market; those whose former bosses defrauded them of salaries and often identification papers; those who got into trouble with the authorities as well as some who no longer saw any point in getting taken on by a

um die Ausweispapiere gebracht wurden; die, die mit den Behörden in Konflikt gerieten oder auch solche, die gar keine Lust mehr haben, sich für 80–90 Euro pro Monat bei einer Sicherheits- oder Reinigungsfirma zu verdingen. Im tropischen Klima Guangzhous kann man gut draußen leben und sich die Kosten für eine Wohnung sparen. So lässt sich selbst nur durch tägliches Flaschensammeln ein Auskommen finden. Hier auf dem Mittelstreifen scheint sich das Leben mit Kartenspielen aushalten zu lassen. Ob Tag oder Nacht, scheinbar immer findet sich eine Gruppe zu einem Spiel bereit.

Nicht zuletzt haben hier auch diejenigen einen Platz gefunden, die auf Grund von Behinderung gar keine Chance haben, ihre Arbeitskraft überhaupt zu Markte zu tragen. Etwas abseits von der Hauptgruppe wohnt Su Feng (38), ein behinderter Obdachloser. Seit seinem zweiten Lebensjahr kann er eines seiner Beine wegen einer Kinderlähmungserkrankung nicht mehr bewegen. Seine Eltern, Bauern in der Provinz Sichuan, konnten nur schwer für ihn aufkommen. Deshalb verließ er mit 16 das Elterhaus und verdient seither mit Betteln oder zeitweilig auch mit Glücksspiel sein Geld. Mit Krücke und Stock unterwegs reist er auf der Suche nach aussichtsreichen Plätzen zum Betteln im ganzen Land umher. Guangzhou und Shenzhen gefallen ihm besonders gut. Hier herrschen auch im Winter günstige klimatische Verhältnisse. Außerdem seien in wohlhabenden Städten Menschen großzügiger gegenüber Bettlern, sagt Su.

Die Liste seiner bereits bereisten Provinzen ist beeindruckend. Wenn auch aus unterschiedlichen Gründen unterwegs, begegnen wir uns doch als Reisende. Das ist wahrscheinlich auch der Grund warum er sich mir gegenüber öffnet. Früher, sagt er, war es noch einfach, schwarz mit der Eisenbahn zu fahren. Da konnte man sich noch einfach auf der Toilette oder unter einem Tisch verstecken. Jetzt müsse er sich ein Kurzzielticket kaufen, um dann damit die Fahrt über das Ziel hinaus fortsetzen zu können.

Oder aber noch besser: Su kennt die Praxis der Bahn, Wanderarbeiter ohne Arbeit und temporäre Registrierung laut Gesetz verpflichtend und kostenlos aus den Städten in ihre Heimatorte zurück zu transportieren. Dabei informiert sich Su vorher über das Ziel seiner Wahl genau, um es hinterher besser als seinen Heimatort ausgeben zu können. Zwei Mal hat er es unter einem LKW auch schon probiert, bis nach Hongkong zu kommen. Beide Male ist er bei der Grenzkontrolle leider entdeckt und festgenommen worden. Nach ein paar Tagen wurde er aber jeweils wieder auf freien Fuß gesetzt. Auf die Frage, warum er denn nach Hongkong wollte, antwortet er mit einem Lächeln – »nur so zum Spaß!«

security or cleaning company for 80–90 euros a month. In the tropical Guangzhou climate, one can live outside and save the money an apartment would cost. Thus, collecting bottles can make them enough money to live on. Here on the median strip, life seems to be about playing cards. Day or night, it appears there will always be a group ready for a game.

This is where people whose physical disabilities leave them with no chance to compete on the job market have found a place. A little away from the main group, lives Su Feng (38), a physically challenged homeless man. Ever since he was two, he has been unable to move one of his legs due to a polio infection. His parents were farmers in the province of Sichuan and barely able to support him. That led him to leave his parents' house at 16 and make his money from panhandling or, on occasion, gambling. Traveling with his crutch and cane, he has roamed the whole country in search of the most promising places for beggars. He particularly likes Guangzhou and Shenzhen. Climatic conditions are favorable here, even in winter. What's more, people in affluent cities are more generous to beggars, says Su.

The list of provinces he has traveled is impressive. Even though we are on entirely different journeys, we still meet as travelers. That is probably the reason why he opens up to me. In the past, he says, fare dodging on trains was easy. One could hide in a toilet or under a table. Now he has to buy a short haul ticket, in order to continue his ride beyond the ticket destination.

Or, even better: Su knows about the railroad's policy to transport, free of charge, unemployed migratory laborers without temporary registration from the cities back to their home towns or villages, as required by law. He gathers detailed information about the destination of his choice, so as to better be able to pass it off as his hometown.

Su has tried twice to hitch a ride to Hong Kong under a truck. In both cases, he was discovered by border controls and arrested. He was released after one day. Asked why he wanted to go to Hong Kong, he answers with a smile – »just for fun!«

Fensterputzer, Peking

Zhang Wei (39) arbeitet als Fensterputzer im Pekinger Finanzdistrikt. Dabei wird mir jedes Mal ganz flau, wenn ich zuschaue, wie er vom Hochhausdach aus rückwärts über die Dachkante hinaus auf einem schmalen Holzbrett Platz nimmt. Alles hängt dabei von seinem Gleichgewichtssinn und dem Halt der Seile ab. Jeder der Fensterputzer ist darauf bedacht, sein Seil an einem möglichst festen

Window cleaners, Beijing

Zhang Wei (39) works as a window cleaner in Beijing's financial district. It makes my stomach turn to watch him descend backwards over the edge of the roof of a high-rise building and take his seat on a narrow wooden board. All he can rely on is his sense of balance and the support of the ropes he is suspended from. It is of great concern to every window cleaner to tie his ropes

Ankerpunkt zu verknoten. Dann ist es soweit – mit einem am Sitzbrett befestigtem Eimer voll Reinigungsflüssigkeit lassen sich Zhang und seine Kollegen in Abständen von etwa vier Metern nebeneinander an der Außenseite des Hochhauses herab. An den langen vertäuten Seilen pendelnd putzen sie dabei mit einem Schwamm und Wischer in der Hand die Glasfassaden.

In dem Zimmer, das er sich mit einem Kollegen aus seinem Herkunftsdorf teilt, fängt Zhang an, über die wilde Zeit zwischen 1990 und 2010 zu berichten. Als ob er es selbst nicht mehr glauben kann, unterstreicht er manche seiner Erzählungen mit wiederholtem Kopfschütteln. Im Alter von 20 Jahren hatte Zhang sein Heimatdorf in der Provinz Hubei auf der Suche nach Arbeit verlassen. Wo hatte er nicht überall schon gearbeitet: im Straßenbau, in Steinbrüchen, beim Ziehen von Zäunen mit Gefangenen zusammen, im Kraftwerksbau, in Eisen- und Kohleminen, in einer Nudelfabrik, einer Backsteinfabrik und auf einer Baustelle, auf der sie ihm bis heute einen Monatslohn schuldig geblieben sind. Oft schuftete er nur wenige Monate, wie in der Eisenmine in der nördlichen Provinz Hebei. Dort gab es keine Zuständigkeiten und Regeln, außer der, dass du jemanden kennen musst, um überhaupt dort arbeiten zu können. Es war wie auf einem großen Schwarzmarkt, sagt Zhang, die Leute kamen und gingen. 200–300 Yuan (ca. 23–35 Euro) den Monat, mehr war nicht drin. Zu wenig für einen so gefährlichen Job, wie er und seine Freunde entschieden.

Aus Zhangs Erinnerungen springt eine gemeinsame Zugfahrt in die Provinz Henan hervor. Er und seine Freunde waren auf dem Weg in eine Kohlemine, wo man angeblich gutes Geld verdienen konnte. Leider reichten die verbliebenen Mittel nur noch für fünf anstatt der benötigten sieben Bahnfahrkarten. Kaum waren die fünf eingestiegen, reichten sie zwei der Fahrkarten durch das Fenster nach draußen an die Freunde weiter. Bei dem Gedränge auf dem Bahnsteig war das keine sonderliche Herausforderung. So konnten die Freunde die Einstiegskontrolle ungehindert passieren.

Auf der folgenden Fahrt scheinen sich die fünf mageren Pfannkuchen besonders tief in Zhangs Gedächtnis eingegraben zu haben. Sie mussten für den Hunger der ganzen Gruppe während der über zehn Stunden langen Bahnfahrt herhalten. Einer der Freunde wurde aber schließlich doch ohne Fahrschein aufgegriffen und musste in der Stadt Handan, noch in der Provinz Hebei den Zug verlassen. Von ihm heißt es, er würde noch heute dort in einer Mine arbeiten.

Zhang beschreibt sich als streitbereit zu jener Zeit. Wiederholt berichtet er vom Kampf um knappes Essen. Und einmal, so erinnert er sich, ist er dem Boss der Backsteinfabrik mit zwei Messern zu Leibe gerückt. Der Boss wollte sie vor die Tür setzen. Wohl deshalb haben er und seine Freunde beim Verlassen der Firma schließlich auch ihren Lohn ausgezahlt bekommen. Andere Arbeiter sind leer ausgegangen.

Seit etwa fünf Jahren arbeitet Zhang nun als Fensterputzer. Er kennt die Regeln des Geschäfts und weiß was er tun muss, um nicht um seinen Lohn zu bangen. Zhang hat samt der vier Monate, in denen wegen extremer Tem-

to a firm anchor. After that, they are all set – with a bucket full of cleaning liquid attached to their board, Zhang and his colleagues lower themselves down the facade of a high-rise at intervals of fifteen feet. Sponge and wiper in hand, dangling from long ropes fixed to the top of the building, they clean its glass facades.

In the room that he shares with a colleague from his home village, Zhang begins to tell me about the wild 1990s and the first decade of the 2000s. As if he could hardly believe it himself, he repeatedly shakes his head as his story unfolds. At the age of 20, Zhang left his home village in the province of Hubei in search of work. He has been to so many places, working in road construction and quarries, building fences together with prison inmates or power stations, doing stints in iron and coal mines, noodle and brick factories, as well as on a building site, where they still owe him one month's salary. Often, he would slave on for a few months only, for instance in an iron mine in the northern province of Hebei. It was a place where there were no responsibilities or rules, except the one that you had to know someone to be able to work there in the first place. It was like a big black market, Zhang continues, people came and went. 200–300 yuan (approx. 23–35 euros) per month, that's the best it got. Not enough for such a dangerous job, as he and his friends thought.

One story about a train ride to the province of Henan stands out in Zhang's memory. He and his friends were on their way to a coal mine, where, it was said, wages were high. Unfortunately, the money they had left bought them only five instead of the seven train tickets they needed. As soon as five of them had boarded the train, they reached through the windows to pass two of their tickets on to their friends outside. The commotion on the platform was such that this was not a big challenge. Thus, their friends were easily able to pass the ticket check.

The mere five pancakes they shared during the entire ten-hour train ride are indelibly etched into Zhang's memory. That was all the group had to supress their hunger. In the end, however, one of them was caught without a ticket and had to get off in the city of Handan, still in the province of Hebei. From what they have heard, he has been working in a mine there ever since.

Zhang describes himself as always ready for a fight. He repeatedly recounts scuffles about scarce food. And at one point, he remembers, he threatened the boss of a brick factory with two knives. The boss wanted to kick them out. That was the only reason he and his friends finally got their pay when they left the company. Other workers came away empty-handed.

Zhang has been working as a window cleaner for five years. He knows the rules of his trade and knows what it takes to not have to worry about getting his pay. Including the four months in which cleaning is impossible due to extreme summer and winter temperatures, Zhang earns an average monthly income of approx. 4000 yuan (approx. 470 euros). Not without pride, he notes that they sometimes earn more than the »white collars« on the other side of the windows.

peraturen im Sommer wie im Winter nicht geputzt wird, ein monatliches Durchschnittseinkommen von ca. 4000 Yuan (ca. 470 Euro). Nicht ohne Stolz merkt er an, dass sie sogar manchmal besser verdienen als die »Weißkragen« auf der anderen Seite der Fenster.

Mit 40 Jahren, so heißt es, geht die Arbeit eines Fensterputzers zu Ende. Dann lässt die Konzentrationsfähigkeit nach und der Job wird zu gefährlich. Zhang hat noch ein Jahr. Wenn er dann die Schulden für sein neu gebautes Haus abgezahlt hat, will er nach Hause zu seiner Familie zurückzukehren. Zhang hat sein Ziel erreicht: eine finanzielle Basis für seine Großfamilie. Da Zhang und seine Frau keinen städtischen Wohnsitz haben, kann ihr Sohn nicht die Pekinger Schulen besuchen. Diese sind den Kinder von Städtern vorbehalten. Zu Hause möchte Zhang als Taxifahrer arbeiten. Er hat schon den Führerschein gemacht.

Backsteinfabrik, Ordos

Der Wind pfeift scharf und nichts ist vor dem feinen Staub der Steppe wirklich sicher. Die Arbeiterinnen und Arbeiter der Backsteinfabrik in der Inneren Mongolei im Norden Chinas versuchen sich durch Kappen, Mundschutz und Brillen soweit wie möglich vor dem Staub zu schützen.

In der Saison von April bis Oktober, in der im rauhen Klima der Inneren Mongolei ein Arbeiten überhaupt möglich ist, stellen rund 70 Arbeiterinnen und Arbeiter hier jeden Tag um die 120.000 Backsteine her. Dabei wird der mehr als 12-stündige Arbeitstag nur durch eine Stunde Mittagspause unterbrochen. Nach dem Formen und Beschneiden der Rohmasse werden die Backsteine fünf bis sechs Tage zum Trocknen an die frische Luft gelegt. Danach werden sie abhängig von der verbliebenen Feuchtigkeit und der Hitze des Feuers drei bis vier Stunden gebrannt.

Die ArbeiterInnen verdienen je nach Tätigkeit durchschnittlich zwischen 1500 und 3000 Yuan (ca. 177 und 354 Euro) monatlich. Auch wenn die Arbeit hier sehr anstrengend ist, sind die Einkommen doch höher als in den bergigen Gegenden der Provinz Sichuan, aus denen die meisten von ihnen stammen. Was sie vereint, ist der Traum diesen Flecken staubiger Erde möglichst schnell wieder zu verlassen. Und doch ist klar, dass sich die meisten von ihnen zu Beginn der nächsten Saison wieder hier treffen werden. Sie werden eine weitere Periode, nur kärglich durch einen Mundschutz vor dem Einatmen der feinen Staubpartikel geschützt, Tag für Tag dem tonhaltigen Lehmboden Backsteine abringen.

Ma Lin (25) und ihre Schwiegereltern gewähren mir Eintritt in ihre gemauerte Unterkunft auf dem Firmengelände und Zuflucht vor dem Staub. Ma ist nach Abbruch der Schule vor fünf Jahren in die Backsteinfabrik nach Ordos gekommen. Hier hat sie auch ihren Mann kennen gelernt, der als Bulldozer-Fahrer in der gleichen Fabrik arbeitet. Ihr Kind ist jetzt zwei Jahre alt und sie arbeitet als Trägerin auf Abruf. Sobald ein Kunde auf das Fabrikgelände gefahren kommt, wird Ma gerufen, um mit anderen TrägerInnen den LKW zu beladen. Nach jedem Einsatz schmerzen sie Rücken wie Arme. Gerne würde sie nur

They say that at the age of 40 the work life of a window cleaner has reached his end. That's when their ability to concentrate wanes and their job becomes too dangerous. Zhang has one year left. After paying off the debt on his newly built house, he wants to return home to his family. Zhang has achieved his goal: A financial basis for his extended family. As Zhang and his wife have no permanent address in the city, their son cannot attend schools in Beijing. Only the children of urban dwellers are accepted there. At home, Zhang wants to work as a taxi driver. He already has a driver's license.

Brick factory, Ordos

A sharp wind is whistling across the steppe, whose fine dust permeates everything. The workers at this brick factory in Northern China use caps, face masks, and glasses to protect themselves from it as much as possible.

In the rough climate of Inner Mongolia, it is only possible to work from April through October. During these months, some 70 laborers produce 120,000 bricks here every day. Only a one-hour lunch break interrupts their over twelve-hour workday. After the loam is molded and cut into shape, the bricks are laid out to dry in the open air for five to six days. Subsequently, they are fired between three and four hours, depending on their wetness and the heat of the fire.

Based on the jobs they perform, workers take home an average monthly wage of between 1500 and 3000 yuan (approx. 177 to 354 euros). While working here is tough, incomes are higher than in the mountainous regions of the Sichuan province where most of them come from. What unites them is the desire to leave this patch of dusty earth again as quickly as possible. Nevertheless, it is clear that most of them will be back here at the start of the next season. Day after day, month after month, they will again wrest bricks from the clayey loam soil, poorly protected by face masks.

Lin Lin (25) and her parents-in-law allow me to visit their lodgings on the company premises. After dropping out of school five years ago, Lin took a job at the brick factory in Ordos City. That is where she met her husband, who works as a bulldozer operator at the same factory. Her child is two years old now and she works as an on-call carrier. As soon as a customer drives onto the factory premises, Lin is called to load the truck together with other carriers. Her back and arms hurt every time the job is done. She would love to only work as a mother and housewife. In the end, however, she needs every single yuan she can make so that she and her family can leave Ordos City behind forever.

One of the three owners of the brickworks also comes from the province of Sichuan. His yearly salary

noch als Mutter und Hausfrau arbeiten. Doch letztlich wird jeder Yuan gebraucht, damit sie und ihre Familie Ordos sobald wie möglich für immer den Rücken kehren können.

Auch einer der drei Besitzer der Ziegelei kommt aus der Provinz Sichuan. Sein Verdienst beträgt um die 300.000 Yuan (ca. 35.400 Euro) pro Jahr. Er beschwert sich, dass das Geschäft nicht sehr gut läuft – nächstes Jahr wolle er nach Sichuan zurückkehren. Es gebe inzwischen einfach zu viele Backsteinfabriken. Außerdem würden heutzutage doch immer mehr Häuser aus Beton gebaut.

Er will dieses staubige Stück Erde verlassen. Da trifft sich sein Traum mit dem seiner Arbeiter und Arbeiterinnen. Auch wenn er ihn am Ende als erster realisieren werden kann. Erst einmal will der Besitzer es aber doch mit einem Schamanen versuchen. Der soll mit einem Ritual Unglück und Misserfolg von dem Platz fernhalten und helfen, den Umsatz wieder zum Laufen zu bringen.

amounts to 300.000 yuan (approx. 35.400 euros) per year. He complains that business is slack – next year he wants to return to Sichuan. There are too many brick factories now, he adds. And more and more houses are built of concrete these days.
He, too, wants to leave this dusty piece of land. In this way, he dreams the same dream as his workers. For now, however, the owner wants to try his luck with a shaman. He is supposed to perform a ritual to keep misfortune and failure away from this place and make sales rise again.

Hostess, Dongguan

Mit vibrierender Stimme scheint der Gast des Karaoke-Klubs in der südlichen Stadt Dongguan all seine Sentimentalität ins Mikrophon schütten zu wollen. Der Abend ist fortgeschritten und Wang Xiuxiu (21) füllt mit einem ihm zugeworfenen frechen Lachen zum wiederholten Male sein Glas. Eine ihrer Kolleginnen prostet einem Unternehmer bereits auf seinem Schoß sitzend zu. Heute betreuen Wang und drei ihrer Kolleginnen eine größere Gruppe, die den Abschluss eines Geschäftes in einem Karaoke-Klub feiert. Wang und ihre Kolleginnen stehen aber auch einzelnen Kunden in den kleineren Räumen des Klubs zur Seite.

Wang hatte es bei ihrem geschiedenen Vater und seiner neuen Frau nicht mehr ausgehalten und ist vor drei Jahren von zu Hause abgehauen. Ihr Vater war gewöhnlich auf Geschäftsreisen und ihre Stiefmutter verbrachte ihre Zeit am liebsten in Kasinos in Macao. Wang hatte zwar einiges an Geld mitgehen lassen, aber das ist längst verbraucht. Nein, sagt sie, ihre Familie weiß nicht, wo sie gerade steckt. Nachdem sie sich schon in verschiedenen Landesteilen nach einer Zukunft für sich umgeschaut hatte, arbeitet sie aktuell in Dongguan als Hostess in einem Karaoke-Klub. Sie kümmert sich um die Animation, d. h. die Unterhaltung und die Anregung der Kunden zum Trinken. Ob sie auch auf sexuelle Wünsche der Gäste eingeht, bleibt jeder Hostess selbst überlassen.

Prostitution ist in der Volksrepublik nach wie vor illegal. Und um ihre weit verbreitete Gegenwart nicht allzu sichtbar werden zu lassen, findet sie zum großen Teil im Schatten von Institutionen wie Massagesalons, Hotels und Karaoke-Klubs statt.

Wang weist allzu plumpe Begehrlichkeiten ihrer Kunden mit Bestimmtheit zurück. Sie bevorzugt das nächtliche Spiel von Zuwendung und Abstand bewahren, sie will die Bestimmende bleiben und sich doch auch verlieren können. Schwankend zwischen unverbindlichem Spaßhaben-Wollen und der Suche nach dem »richtigen« Mann. Sie sagt, wenn sie eines Tages heiraten wird, dann will sie sich ihren Mann wenigstens selbst ausgesucht haben. Wang lebt in den Tag und in die Nacht hinein. Mit Offen-

Hostess, Dongguan

With a trembling voice, the patron at a karaoke club in the southern city of Dongguan seems intent on pouring all his sentimentality into the microphone. The evening is well advanced and it's not for the first time that Wang Xiuxiu (21) refills a glass with a cheeky smile. One of her colleagues says cheers to a businessman whose lap she is already sitting on. Today, Wang and three of her colleagues attend to a larger group that is celebrating the conclusion of a business deal in this karaoke club. Wang and her colleagues also offer their services to individual clients in the club's smaller rooms.

Wang couldn't take life with her divorced father and his new wife anymore and ran away from home three years ago. Most of the time, her father was away on business trips and her stepmother preferred to spend her time in the casinos of Macao. Even though Wang walked off with a fair amount of money, it has long been spent. No, she says, her family doesn't know her whereabouts. After trying to find a future for herself in different parts of the country, she now works as a hostess in a Dongguan karaoke club. She encourages guests to drink and entertains them. Whether or not she also caters to guests' sexual desires is a decision each hostess makes for herself.

In the People's Republic, prostitution is still illegal. And in order to keep its widespread presence from becoming too visible, it mostly takes place in the shadow of establishments such as massage parlors, hotels, and karaoke clubs.

Wang firmly dismisses overly forward advances from her clients. She takes part in the night-time game of opening up while keeping a distance, of staying in control while still being able too lose herself, of searching for both casual, noncommittal fun and the »right« man. She says that if she marries one day, she will at least have chosen her husband herself. Wang lives for the day and the night. She is open to sharing some of her time and story with me. The half-life of the presents she receives from her admirers, such as a large white teddy bear that she carries through the night, is short. She is currently living in rooms she shares with colleagues or in cheap hotels.

heit lässt sie mich daran teilhaben. Die Halbwertszeit der Geschenke ihrer Verehrer, wie den großen weißen Teddy, den sie durch die Nacht trägt, ist kurz. Derzeit wohnt sie in Zimmern, die sie mit Kolleginnen teilt oder auch in billigen Hotels.

Aber im Gegensatz zu vielen ihrer Kolleginnen, von denen erwartet wird, dass sie Geld nach Hause schicken, um ihre Familien zu versorgen, schaut Wang nicht vor allem nach Männern mit viel Geld. Sie weiß aus Erfahrung, je reicher der Typ, desto schwieriger ist es, sein Herz zu gewinnen.

But unlike many of her colleagues, who are expected to send money home to support their families, Wang is not only looking for men with lots of money. She knows from experience, the richer a guy is, the harder it is to win his heart.

Müllrecyclerin, Peking

Beim Durchstreifen der Recyclinghöfe an der Peripherie Pekings stoße ich an einer Behausung vor Bergen aufgetürmter Plastikflaschen auf Xu Fang (24). Entgegen den verhärmten Blicken anderer Bewohner treffe ich bei Xu auf Neugier und Aufgeschlossenheit.

Sie ist erst vor kurzem mit ihrem Mann aus der südlichen Stadt Guangzhou hierher gekommen. Die beiden haben sich in einer dortigen Elektronikfabrik kennen gelernt. Jetzt lebte Xu mit ihm, den beiden gemeinsamen Kindern, den Schwiegereltern und anderen Familien dicht gedrängt in einer Unterkunft aus Holzbrettern, Plastikplanen und einem Wellblechdach. Diese ist um die beidseitig aufgestellten Doppelstockbetten gebaut. Auf den Betten ist ein Rest an Privatheit nur durch das Zuziehen eines Vorhangs zu erreichen. Trotzdem ist Xus Stimmung vom Optimismus des Aufbruchs gekennzeichnet. Es gehe ihr hier auf den Müllsammelplätzen besser als in den Fabriken zuvor. Hier kann sie sich bei vergleichbarem Einkommen ihre Arbeitszeit viel freier einteilen. Trotzdem schwingt eine Portion Wehmut in ihrer Stimme mit, als sie auf ihre Jugend zu sprechen kommt. Diese hat sie mit ihrem Mann zusammen in Guangzhou verbracht. Jetzt zeugt nur noch ein Tatoo von diesem Kapitel ihrer gemeinsamen Geschichte. Aber schließlich sei es jetzt auch an der Zeit, an ihre Zukunft und die ihrer Kinder zu denken und Erspartes zurückzulegen, so Xu.

Immer in der Hoffnung auf eine Verbesserung der Verdienstmöglichkeiten ziehen sie und ihr Mann von einer Sammelstelle für PET-Flaschen zur nächsten. An der dritten Sammelstelle treten sie schließlich in einen Streik. Der Verwandte, der sie dort eingestellt hatte, hat ihnen und den anderen dort arbeitenden Familien seit einem Vierteljahr keinen Lohn mehr gezahlt. Obwohl ihr Arbeitgeber auch Streikbrecher einsetzt, mit denen sie aneinander geraten, harren sie und andere Kollegen dort solange aus, bis er sie schließlich auszahlt. Ob sie nicht Angst vor einem gewaltsamen Übergriff des Arbeitgebers gehabt hätten? Nein, wir waren schlicht mehr als er und seine Streikbrecher, sagt Xu. Zudem seien Arbeitsniederlegungen auch in Guangzhou schon nichts Außergewöhnliches mehr gewesen.

Je öfter sie im Folgenden ohne große Verbesserungen zu erreichen ihren Arbeitsplatz wechseln und je weiter sie die Umzüge in die Außenbezirke Pekings verschlagen, desto mehr geht auch Xus Traum vom Aufbruch verloren. Inzwischen ist ihre Unterkunft zwischen Bergen von Recyclingflaschen oft schon mehr als eine Stunde zu Fuß von

Garbage Recyclers, Beijing

Strolling through the recycling centers on the outskirts of Beijing, I come across a shack in front of huge piles of plastic bottles and meet Xu Fang (24). In contrast to the careworn gaze of the others that live here, Xu exudes curiosity and openness.

She has recently come here with her husband from the southern city of Guangzhou. The two met at an electronics factory there. Their impromptu abode is built around two bunk beds at either side and consists of wooden boards, plastic sheeting, and a corrugated-iron roof. Xu shares it with her husband, their two children, parents-in-law, as well as other families. The only form of privacy available here is the one they create by drawing curtains shut in front of the beds. Nevertheless, Xu's mood is one of optimism and living towards a better future. The garbage collection points, she says, have made her life better than factories ever did. She is achieving a comparable income but has more flexibility to make her own hours. Still, there is a melancholy tone in her voice when she begins to talk about her youth, which she spent with her husband in Guangzhou. The only token left from this chapter of their life together is a tattoo. But ultimately, Xu says, now is the time to think of their future and children and put aside savings.

Always in hope of better income opportunities, she and her husband move from one PET bottle collection point to the next. At the third collection point, where I have met her, they are about to go on strike. For a quarter of a year, the relative who employed them there has failed to pay them and the other families working there any wages.

Even though their employer is using strikebreakers they have clashed with, she and her colleagues will hold out until he finally pays them their wages. Weren't they afraid that their employer would resort to force and violence? No, we outnumber him and his strikebreakers, says Xu. What's more, she has already gained experience with walkouts during her time in Guangzhou.

Every time she changes jobs without achieving great improvements and the farther these moves bring her into the outskirts of Beijing, the more Xu's dream of making it fade. By now, the shack she occupies between mountains of recycling bottles is more than a one-hour walk from the nearest shopping possibilities. Due to the hopelessness of her situation, her past and background gain importance for Xu, who hails from the larger Wuhan area, a central Chinese city of over a million inhabitants. Wouldn't she have had better opportunities there?

der nächstgelegenen Einkaufsmöglichkeit entfernt. Aufgrund der Trostlosigkeit ihrer Situation gewinnt für Xu ihre Vergangenheit und Herkunft aus dem Einzugsgebiet der zentralchinesischen Millionenstadt Wuhan zunehmend an Bedeutung. Hätte sie dort nicht noch andere Möglichkeiten gehabt?

Ihr Traum, den eigenen Herkunftsort und auch den ihres Mannes in der Nachbarprovinz Hunan zu besuchen, scheitert im Herbst 2010 jedoch an der chinesischen Gesetzgebung. War sie doch mit 18 zum ersten Mal schwanger geworden und hatte so ihren Mann vor Erreichen des dafür vorgeschriebenen Mindestalters von 20 Jahren geheiratet. Auch ihr Mann war bei ihrer Heirat noch keine 22 Jahre alt, wie es das Gesetz vorschreibt. Insofern hatten sie im Folgenden weder ihre Ehe noch die Geburt ihrer Kinder offiziell registrieren lassen können. Das wurde aber auch erst relevant, als ihre Tochter das Schuleintrittsalter von sechs Jahren erreichte. Sowohl für einen geregelten Schulbesuch als auch für die Absicherung durch eine Krankenkasse ist die Anmeldung im Herkunftsort der Eltern väterlicherseits Vorschrift. Für die nachträgliche Legalisierung ihrer Ehe und Registrierung ihrer Kinder war jetzt eine Strafzahlung erforderlich. Die dafür übliche Summe von 5000 Yuan (ca. 590 Euro) hatten sie bei der zuständigen örtlichen Behörde auch schon gezahlt. Nur verkompliziert eine anstehende Volkszählung in der Provinz Hunan die Situation, so dass die Behörde plötzlich von der erfolgten Zahlung nichts mehr wissen will und sich jetzt querstellt.

Und so weigert sich Xu, die geplante Reise anzutreten. Sie fürchtet wegen zweier illegaler Geburten dort in eine Klinik eingewiesen und zwangssterilisiert zu werden. Dies soll auch anderen Frauen in einer vergleichbaren Situation passiert sein. Es ist erst Großvater Luo, der in den folgenden Monaten die zugespitzte Situation in Hunan auf seine Art zu lösen versteht. Es gelingt ihm, einen alten Schulfreund in der örtlichen Verwaltung ausfindig zu machen. Mit Hilfe einiger Geschenke sind nun sowohl Xus Ehe als auch ihre Kinder behördlich registriert.

Vor der jetzt geplanten Reise zum traditionellen Neujahrsfest 2011 zu Xus Eltern brechen alte Wunden wieder auf. Nein, bricht es aus Xu heraus, ihr Vater habe ihr trotz Bettelns und Streitens nie den Besuch einer weiterführenden Schule zugestanden. Das durfte erst ihr jüngerer Bruder. Mit 16 Jahren hat Xu es dann zu Hause nicht mehr ausgehalten. Sie wollte frei sein und trat 2001 ihren ersten Job in einer Elektronikfabrik in Guangzhou an.

Ihr Vater hatte sich mit dem Fortgehen seiner Tochter in die entfernte Großstadt nie abgefunden. Bei ihrer ersten Rückkehr aus Anlass des Neujahrsfestes wollte er sie nicht mehr gehen lassen und versuchte ihre Abreise schließlich durch ein Einsperren im Zimmer zu verhindern. Sie sollte doch einen Mann aus der Umgebung heiraten und sich eine Zukunft im Dorf aufbauen. Dabei hatte der Vater aber offensichtlich die Entschlusskraft seiner Tochter unterschätzt. Sie ließ sich nicht von ihrem eigenen Weg abbringen.

Tatsächlich besuchen Xu, ihr Mann und die Kinder ihre Familie wie geplant Anfang des Jahres 2011. Trotz einer erfolgten Wiederannäherung bleibt während ihres ganzen

Due to Chinese laws, her dream of visiting her hometown and her husband in the neighboring province of Hunan fell apart in the fall of 2010. She was 18 when she became pregnant for the first time and, thus, married her husband before reaching the required minimum age of 20. Her husband, too, had not turned 22 when he tied the knot with her, as required by law. As a result, she was unable to have either her marriage or the birth of her children officially registered. That only became relevant when her daughter turned six and reached school age. Applications for both regular school enrollment and health insurance coverage must be filed with authorities in the paternal parents' place of origin. Furthermore, she was required to pay a fine for the belated legalization of her marriage and registration of her children. They had paid 5000 yuan (approx. 590 euros), the sum commonly levied for such an offence, to the respective local authority. However, an upcoming census in the province of Hunan made the situation complicated again, because the authority now suddenly refused to acknowledge the payment and made difficulties.

Thus, Xu refused to take the planned trip. Due to her two illegal births, she feared being sent to a clinic and subjected to forced sterilization. Allegedly, this has happened to other women in similar situations. In the following months, it turned out that only grandfather Luo was able to find a solution of his own to the Hunan situation that had come to a crisis. He was able to find an old friend from school in the local administration. With the help of some gifts, both Xu's marriage and her children are now registered with the authorities.

As the next trip to Xu's parents for the traditional New Year celebration 2011 draws near, old scars cloud the fond memories of her former home. No, Xu bursts out, her father never allowed her to attend a secondary school, despite pleading and arguments. That privilege was reserved for her younger brother. At 16, Xu couldn't take it anymore at home. She wanted to be independent and got her first job at an electronics factory in Guangzhou in 2011.

Her father has never come to terms with the fact that his daughter left for a far away big city. When she first returned to visit for the Chinese New Year celebration, he tried to keep her from leaving by locking her into a room. She was supposed to marry a man from the area and build a future in the village. Her father, however, had underestimated his daughter's determination. She wouldn't let anyone shake her resolve.

In early 2011, Xu, her husband, and their children finally visited her family as planned. Despite efforts to mend ties, father and daughter kept their distance during their entire stay and their relationship remains palpably strained.

Following their return to the Chinese capital, Xu and her husband took over the PET bottle collection center in the sparsely populated no-mans-land as subcontractors. Separating plastic bottles from their brand names with a cutter, Xu shares her thoughts about her future. To all appearances, her dreams are coming true. They are the same as those of millions of migrant workers. She thinks about her children's education and building a house of their own in the remote village her husband grew up in. Stopping to

Aufenthaltes über die Distanz zum Vater spürbar und ihr Verhältnis reserviert.

Nach ihrer Rückkehr in die chinesische Hauptstadt übernehmen Xu und ihr Mann den PET-Flaschen-Sammelplatz im dünn besiedelten Niemandsland als Subunternehmer. Plastikflaschen mit einem Cutter von ihren Markennamen befreiend, denkt Xu über ihre Zukunft nach. Sie scheint angekommen zu sein und sich in die sie erwartende Zukunft eingefügt zu haben. Dabei träumt sie den Traum von Millionen von WanderarbeiterInnen, denkt an die Ausbildung der Kinder und an das zu errichtende eigene Haus im abgelegenen Dorf des Ehemannes. Dann hält sie inne und schaut von den Plastikflaschen auf. Sie würde gerne einmal nach Tibet reisen, um das Grasland zu sehen und den Potala Palast zu besuchen. Beide hätte sie schon öfters im Fernsehen gesehen.

Müllsammler, Peking

Der Strom der an- und abfahrenden Dreiräder zu dem Schrottplatz reißt nicht ab. Stetig treffen neue, teils hoch bepackte Räder ein, die sich zu dem auf ihre Fundstücke spezialisierten Abfallhändler drängen. Hier treffe ich auf Li Chen (33) und Zhou Dong (40). Die beiden Männer kommen mit Möbelstücken, die bei einem Holzhändler nur wenig Beachtung und ein entsprechend geringes Entgelt finden.

Beide stammen aus demselben Dorf in der Provinz Henan, einer der ärmsten in China, und sind nach Peking aufgebrochen, um sich dort Arbeit zu suchen. Ihre Felder sind zu klein, um den Familien mit der Landwirtschaft eine Perspektive bieten zu können. Wie viele andere Wanderarbeiter ohne Ausbildung haben sie keine andere Möglichkeit gefunden als sich in der Müllentsorgung selbstständig zu machen. Ein Heer von Dreiradfahrern durchstreift täglich die Straßen der Stadt auf der Suche nach Wiederverwertbarem. Die Ergebnisse ihrer Sammlungen bringen sie dann zu den Schrottplätzen, von wo aus die Gegenstände dann auf die an der Peripherie gelegenen Recyclinghöfe transportiert werden.

Li und Zhou sind Teil dieses Stroms täglicher Müllentsorgung und -verwertung. Jeden Morgen bringen sie den Hausmüll eines Wohngebietes gegen ein Entgelt zu einer Sammelstelle. Dazu wurden sie von dem Nachbarschaftskommitee, dem niedrigsten Verwaltungsorgan auf städtischer Ebene, autorisiert. Danach sammeln auch sie recyclebaren Müll. Neben ihrem von einem Elektrohilfsmotor angetriebenen Dreirad sind dabei Knowhow und soziale Kontakte ihr wichtigstes Kapital. So helfen sie Händlern beim Entpacken neu angelieferter Ware, um anschließend die Verpackungsmaterialien mitnehmen zu können.

Li, seine Frau und seine zwei Töchter wohnen in einem gemieteten, knapp 15 Quadratmeter großen Backsteinhaus in einer Siedlung, deren Ausscheidungen und Abfallgerüche untrennbar mit ihr verbunden scheinen. Zhou teilt sich das Nachbarhaus mit einem anderen Arbeiter aus der gleichen Provinz. Trotz niedrigen Lebensstandards reichen die Einkünfte nicht immer, um ihre Lebenshaltungskosten zu decken. So nehmen Li und Zhou jede Gelegenheit wahr, weitere Ressourcen zu erschließen. Gerade durch-

work for a moment, she looks up from the plastic bottles. She'd love to travel to Tibet to see the grassland and visit the Potala Palace. She has seen both of these on TV.

Garbage Collectors, Beijing

The steady stream of arriving and departing tricycles never stops at the scrapyard and its dealers. Some of the incoming cyclists are packing huge loads. This is where I meet Li Chen (33) and Zhou Dong (40). The two men are bringing in pieces of furniture, which elicit little interest from the timber dealer and earn them only a small amount.

Both grew up in the same village in the province of Henan, one of the poorest in China. They set out for Beijing in search of work, their fields being too small to offer families viable economic prospects. Like so many other migratory laborers without education, they were left with no other option than to start their own garbage collection enterprise. Every day, an army of tricyclists scours the city's streets for reusable items and materials. They bring their spoils to the scrapyards, where they are transported to recycling centers on the outskirts of town.

Li and Zhou are part of this endless stream of daily refuse disposal and recycling. Subject to payment, they ferry the household waste of a residential area to a collection point every morning. They are authorized to do so by a residents' committee, the lowest administrative body on the municipal level. Next, they collect the recyclable waste. Aside from their electric motor-assisted tricycles, know-how and social contacts are their most valuable assets in this process. For instance, they help retailers unpack newly delivered goods in order to collect the packaging material.

Li, his wife, and his two daughters rent a 160 square foot brick house in a shantytown where the smell of waste and sewage permeates everything. Zhou shares the neighboring house with another worker from the same province. Despite low living standards, their earnings are not always sufficient to cover daily expenses. Thus, Li and Zhou seize on every opportunity to tap additional resources. Presently, they are scouring the nearby shantytown of Bajia in northwestern Beijing, which is slated for demolition. Other garbage collectors are already combing its demolition sites for metal scraps and have collected and stacked up undamaged bricks they plan to resell. Li and Zhou are looking for residents still selling furniture from their houses, which have been deliberately rendered

streifen sie die nahe gelegene und zum Abbruch freigegebene Siedlung Bajia im Nordwesten Pekings. Dort werden die Abrisshalden bereits von anderen Müllsammlern nach Metallresten durchwühlt bzw. unbeschädigte Backsteine zum Weiterverkauf zu Stapeln aufgeschichtet. Li und Zhou suchen nach Bewohnern, die noch die Möbel ihrer schon unbewohnbar gemachten Häuser verkaufen. Sie erwerben etliche davon, um sie wiederum auf einer Müllsammelstelle weiterverkaufen zu können. Es ist meist schon nachts, wenn die beiden mit ihrem Dreirad zum letzten Mal einen der Schrottplätze ansteuern, um für ihre Fundstücke einen Käufer zu finden.

uninhabitable. They acquire a number of pieces in order to resell them at a collection point. On most days, it is already dark when the two bring their last load to the scrapyard in search of a buyer for their finds.

Schmucksteinschleifer und -schleiferin, Haifeng

Das Heulen der Schleifmaschine erfüllt die abgelegene Werkstadt im Niemandsland nahe der südlichen Stadt Haifeng. Nur eine Verbindungsstraße durchzieht die öde Gegend. Unter dem Schutz von Staubmasken werden nachts noch Jade- und andere Schmucksteine einer ersten Bearbeitung unterzogen. Han Chun (38) war Mitte der 1990er Jahre auf der Suche nach Arbeit mit seiner Frau aus der Provinz Sichuan nach Guangdong gekommen. Er war froh, in der hier konzentrierten Schmuck- und Edelsteinverarbeitung einen Job gefunden zu haben.

Dabei zersägte und schliff Han die Steine gewöhnlich 12 Stunden am Tag ohne jegliche Abzugsanlagen oder Staubschutzvorrichtungen. Und selbst wenn er oder seine Kollegen nach einfachen Staubschutzmasken verlangten, blieben ihre Bitten ungehört. Als sie Atemprobleme bekamen, wurden manche von ihnen gegen Tuberkulose, andere gegen Hepatitis behandelt, entlassen und in ihre Herkunftsorte zurückgeschickt. Viele starben dort, ohne überhaupt von dem Grund ihrer Erkrankung erfahren zu haben. Silikose ist eine Staublungenerkrankung, die nicht heilbar ist und die in mehreren Stadien bis zum Tode führt. Nach Schätzungen der Hongkonger Nichtregierungsorganisation Labour Action China, die Staublungenopfer in ihrem Kampf um Entschädigung unterstützt, sind allein in der Provinz Guangdong rund 200.000 Personen an Silikose erkrankt.

Han Chun hat beschlossen mit drei weiteren erkrankten Kollegen zu bleiben und um sein Recht auf Entschädigung zu kämpfen. Dabei haben sie sich auf eine Odyssee durch verschiedene Institutionen begeben, von der nicht klar ist, ob sie vor ihrem Tod überhaupt noch zu einem Ergebnis führen wird. Es bedarf langwieriger Behördengänge ehe überhaupt der Rechtsweg über zwei Instanzen beschritten werden darf. Aber selbst ein positiver Gerichtsentscheid ist noch keine Garantie auf eine Entschädigung. Namensänderungen der Firmen und Umzüge in andere Verwaltungsdistrikte sind in der Auseinandersetzung um Entschädigungszahlungen keine Ausnahmen. Dann beginnt der über Jahre dauernde, vorgezeichnete Weg durch die Institutionen auf's Neue.

Ungeachtet von Hans Plänen wie auch seines labilen Gesundheitszustandes sind aber auch die Kosten für den Lebensunterhalt der Familie weiterhin zu bestreiten. Und diese sind in der Zwischenzeit wegen der Behandlungen und Arzneimittel noch deutlich gestiegen. So hat sich Han

Gemstone Cutters, Haifeng

The whine of a grinding machine fills the remote workshop in the no-man's-land near the southern city of Haifeng. Only a link road runs through this desolate area. At night and with dust protection masks, jade and other gemstones are subjected to the first stage of processing. In the mid-1990s, Han Chun's (38) search for work led him and his wife from the province of Sichuan to Guangdong. He was happy to have found a job in the jewelry and gemstone processing industry that is concentrated here.

Han usually cuts stones 12 hours a day without any exhauster or dust protection devices whatsoever. When he or his colleagues wanted simple dust protection masks, their request fell on deaf ears. When they developed respiratory problems, some were treated for tuberculosis, others for hepatitis. In the end, they were dismissed and sent back to their places of origin. Many died without knowing the reason behind their illness. Silicosis is an incurable lung disease, which, after progressing through several stages, leads to certain death. According to estimates by Hong Kong-based NGO Labor Action China, which supports victims of pneumoconiosis in their fight for compensation, some 200,000 people are suffering from silicosis in the province of Guangdong alone.

Han Chun and three colleagues, who also suffer from the disease, decided to stay and fight for their right to compensation. They have embarked on an odyssey through various institutions and authorities, and it's not even clear whether it will yield results before they die. Lengthy visits to the authorities are required even before legal action can be taken and the case eventually proceeds through two courts. But even a positive court decision is no guarantee that damages will be paid. Changes of company names and relocations to other administrative districts are no exception when claims for compensatory damages are filed. Then, it's back to square one for the required path through the institutions, which can take years.

Han's plans and his unstable health notwithstanding, the family's living costs must, of course, still be met. And they have risen sharply due to his treatment and medication. Consequently, after his dismissal, Han started his own workshop, one that is part of a widespread shadow economy. The large majority of Haifeng's 3000 gemstone industry companies are not registered as businesses to avoid taxes and licensing fees. Nonetheless, the numer-

nach seiner Kündigung selbstständig gemacht und ist zum Bestandteil der weit verbreiteten Schattenökonomie geworden. Die große Mehrheit der allein in Haifeng angesiedelten 3000 Betriebe der Schmuckstein Industrie haben sich nicht als Gewerbe registriert, um Steuern und Lizenzgebühren zu sparen. Dabei sind die zahllosen Familienbetriebe, die schwarz produzieren, keineswegs nur das Gegenstück zu den großen Weltmarktfabriken. Vielmehr sind die kleinen Betriebe als Zulieferer oft auch fest mit eingeplanter Bestandteil der Ökonomie der Global Player. Verbunden über eine Kette von Zulieferern werden oft gerade die besonders gefährlichen Produktionsschritte in die »Scheinselbstständigkeit« von Familienbetrieben ausgelagert.

So systemtragend die Schattenwirtschaft auf der einen Seite auch ist, so sehr ist sie doch auch mit Illegalität und Ausgrenzung verknüpft. Ein anstehendes Sportereignis von regionaler Bedeutung genügt, um die lokalen Behörden zu einer Serie von Razzien zu veranlassen. Das führt zu einer extremen Spannung unter den nicht angemeldeten Betrieben, die seither nur noch nachts produzieren. Und auch meine Recherche im Bereich der Schattenwirtschaft beginnt schwierig bis gefährlich zu werden.

Jetzt, wo Han durch das fortgeschrittene Stadium seiner Erkrankung kaum noch arbeiten kann, liegt die Last der Arbeit auf den Schultern der ganzen Familie. Nicht nur seine Frau betreibt jetzt die Werkstatt, auch ihr Sohn hat seine Schulausbildung abgebrochen, um sie an den Maschinen zu unterstützen. Der Schwiegervater hilft, so weit es seine Sehkraft noch zulässt, beim Auffädeln der Steine zu Ketten.

Die Familie Han ist aber nicht nur der Illegalität der Schwarzarbeit ausgesetzt. Die, die um Entschädigung kämpfen, dürfen keiner weiteren Arbeit mehr nachgehen. Ansonsten würden sie ihren Anspruch verlieren. Und somit sind die Opfer zweifach zum Schweigen verurteilt. Die Logik der Auslagerung von Arbeit kommt in den Familienklitschen der Opfer zu einem zynischen Höhepunkt. Sie impliziert sowohl die Illegalisierung und damit Einschüchterung und Demütigung wie schließlich die Mobilisierung zur Arbeit bis zum Tod.

Kohlewäscher und -wäscherin, Fushun

Nur wenige mit Kohle beladenen große LKWs bewegen sich einsamen urzeitlichen Getümen gleich Staub aufwirbelnd über das Gelände. Der Kohleabbau auf der vormals größten Tagebaumine Asiens in der nordöstlichen Stadt Fushun ist längst eingestellt und die Belegschaft abgewickelt worden. Der Schwerpunkt der Arbeiten hat sich von dem über Jahrzehnte in den Boden gefressenen Tal zu einem unweit der Mine gelegenen kleinen See verschoben. Hier reinigen jetzt WanderarbeiterInnen mit Sieb, Schüssel und Schaufel in der Hand buchstäblich Berge von Kohle mit Wasser von der sie verunreinigenden Erde. Die Mine war 2005 wegen inzwischen erschöpfter Kohlevorräte geschlossen worden. Aufgrund der gestiegenen Energiekosten ist die jetzt private Verwertung der ehemals liegen gebliebenen verunreinigten Kohlehalden wieder rentabel geworden.

ous family businesses and their illicit production in no way merely form a counterpart to the big world-market factories. Rather, as suppliers these small companies are an inherent part of the economics of global players. Through a chain of suppliers, the particularly dangerous production stages are often outsourced to the world of »quasi-self-employment« and its family businesses.

As much as, on the one hand, the shadow economy props up the system, it is also invariably linked to illegality and exclusion. A regional sports event is all it takes to prompt a series of raids by local authorities. That has led to extreme tension among illicit companies, who have since resorted to working only at night. And my research into the shadow economy, too, is beginning to get difficult and dangerous.

Now that Han can hardly work due to the advanced state of his disease, the burden is shouldered by the entire family. Not only does his wife now run the workshop, her son has dropped out of school to relieve her of some of the machine work. As far as his failing eyesight permits, the father-in-law helps with the threading of stones onto bracelets.

The Han family, however, is not only affected by the illegality of unreported employment. Those that fight for compensation are not permitted to have jobs. They would otherwise forfeit their right to compensatory damages. Hence, victims are condemned to silence twice. In these small-time workshops operated by the victims, the outsourcing of work reaches a cynical climax. Illegalization, intimidation and humiliation and, ultimately, work to the death.

Coal Washers, Fushun

Only a few big trucks loaded with coal move around the terrain like lonely prehistoric monsters. In 2005, coal mining in the once-largest Asian strip mine in the northeastern city of Fushun was shut down, and its workforce was dismissed. The focus of activities has since moved from a valley that decades of mining have cut into the ground to a small lake not far from the mine. Sieve, bowl, and shovel in hand, migrant workers here use water to clean loose soil and rocks from mountains of coal. Due to rising energy costs, private exploitation of the once discarded heaps of unclean coal has become profitable again.

An unlikely pair catches my eye. Looking tense and strained, they doggedly perform the ever-same movements of coal washing. It's Wen Feng (63) and He Juan (36), his son's ex-wife, who together pour over two tons

Mein Augenmerk fällt auf ein ungleiches Paar, das zäh wie verkniffen die immer gleichen Bewegungen des Kohlewaschens verrichtet. Es sind der Großvater Wen Feng (63) und He Juan (36), die Ex-Frau seines Sohnes, die hier zusammen täglich über zwei Tonnen gewaschene Kohle auf einen Haufen schütten. So kommen sie auf einen jeweiligen monatlichen Verdienst von 3000 Yuan (ca. 354 Euro). Es liegt am Großvater sich neben seiner Kräfte zehrenden Arbeit auch noch um seine Enkelin zu kümmern.

He kann ihre Tochter nicht mit nach Hause nehmen, das untersagt ihr jetziger zweiter Ehemann. Und so treffen sich Mutter und Kind nur, wenn Hes Tochter sie auf der Arbeit besuchen kommt.

Im Hintergrund der um den See versammelten Wäscher und Wäscherinnen zeichnet sich schon der Umriss der neuen Kohle-Waschanlage ab, die ab dem nächsten Frühjahr ihre Arbeit weitgehend ersetzen soll. Dort wird auch Wens Sohn Tian arbeiten, der sich neu verheiratet an seiner Tochter aus erster Ehe weitgehend desinteressiert zeigt. Damit wird Tian zum Teilnehmer an der Modernisierung, die die Arbeit des Vaters und vieler anderer KohlewäscherInnen wegrationalisieren wird. Es ist eine Knochenarbeit, die da der Rationalisierung zum Opfer fällt. Aber es sind auch gute Verdienstmöglichkeiten, die ihr folgen werden. Und so heißt Modernisierung ebenso, dass Tian in der neu errichteten Anlage dann nicht mehr über 2000 Yuan (ca. 236 Euro) pro Monat verdienen wird.

Großvater Wen wird sich nächstes Jahr nicht nur um eine neue Arbeit, sondern auch um eine neue Wohnung kümmern müssen. Unter der Siedlung, in der auch die von ihm gemietete Holzbaracke steht, ist ölhaltige Kohle gefunden worden. Ihr Abbau ist im Zeitalter gestiegener Energiepreise lukrativ geworden. Und so ist auch Wens Hütte längst mit dem chinesischen Schriftzeichen für »Abriss« markiert.

Zum Schutz von Personen wurden einzelne Namen geändert.

of washed coal onto a heap every day. This earns them a monthly wage of 3000 yuan (approx. 354 euros) each. Aside from his strength and energy-sapping work, Wen also needs to take care of his granddaughter. He's current, second husband prohibits He from taking her daughter home with her. Thus, the only time the two can meet is when the daughter visits her mother at work.

Visible in the background behind the coal washers gathered at the lake is the silhouette of a new coal-washing plant, which is slated to assume operations next spring and render their work obsolete. Wen's son Tian will get a job there. He has also remarried recently and mostly shows no interest in his daughter of his first marriage. And so, Tian will play a part in the modernization that is going to replace the work of his father and many other coal washers. To be sure, it is backbreaking work that will be superseded by rationalization. But good income opportunities will be lost, as well: modernization also means that Tian will not earn above 2000 yuan (approx. 236 euros) per month at the newly built plant.

Next year grandfather Wen will not only have to find a new job, but also a new apartment. Oily coal has been discovered underneath the shantytown where the wooden hut he rents stands. In an age of rising energy prices, extracting it is a lucrative business. For this reason, Wen's hut has already been marked with the Chinese character for »demolition.«

Some names have been changed to protect the identity of persons involved.

1. Auflage 2012
© 2012 Vice Versa Verlag, Berlin
Alle Rechte vorbehalten. All Rights reserved.

Vice Versa Verlag
Gabriela Wachter
Leuschnerdamm 5
10999 Berlin
www.viceversaverlag.de

Übersetzung Translation Matthias Goldmann
Gesamtgestaltung Design
Wolfgang Müller / Pina Lewandowsky
Gesamtherstellung Production
AZ Druck und Datentechnik, Berlin

ISBN 978-3-932809-70-5

Dank von ganzem Herzen an die, ohne deren aktive Mithilfe dieses Buch so nie hätte entstehen können:

We extend our heartfelt thanks to those whose active help and cooperation have made this book possible:

Labour Action China / Hongkong, Little Bird / Beijing, Shenzhen

Marc Prüst, Florian Büttner, Stefan Canham, Tim Deussen, Andrea Diefenbach, Jan Garup, Gregor v. Glinski, Felix Hoffmann, Christian Jungeblodt, Thomas Kellner, Celina Lunsford, Alex Majoli, Uwe H. Martin, Anke Nowottne, Andreas Reeg, Paola Riccardi, Steffen Rother, Erik Schiemann, Ruth Schimanowski, Heiner Schmitz, Eberhard Schorr, Gitta Seiler, Frank Sieren, Heinrich Völkl, Hannes Wanderer, Wolfgang Zurborn

Dank auch für die großzügige Projektförderung durch das Kulturwerk der VG Bild-Kunst.

We also extend our sincere thanks to Kulturwerk der VG Bild-Kunst for its generous sponsorship of this project.

Dr. Kristin Kupfer, Jahrgang 1974, Sinologin und Politikwissenschaftlerin. Sie arbeitete von 2007 bis 2011 als freie Journalistin in China. Seit März 2011 ist sie wissenschaftliche Mitarbeiterin an der Albert-Ludwigs-Universität Freiburg und forscht über Religion, Informationstechnologie und Proteste in China.

Dr. Kristin Kupfer, born 1974, is a sinologist and political scientist. From 2007 to 2011 she worked as an independent journalist in China. From March 2011, she has served as a research associate at the Albert Ludwig University of Freiburg, Germany, and focuses her research on religion, information technology and protests in China.